THE NEW

Boxer

by

BILLIE McFADDEN

First Edition

HOWELL
BOOK HOUSE
New York

Howell Book House
Macmillan Publishing Company
866 Third Avenue, New York, NY 10022

Collier Macmillan Canada, Inc.
1200 Eglinton Avenue East, Suite 200
Don Mills, Ontario M3C 3N1

Library of Congress Cataloging-in-Publication Data

McFadden, Billie.
   The new boxer / by Billie McFadden. — 1st ed.
     p.   cm.
   Summary: Examines the origin, history, development, showing, training, and breeding of boxer dogs.

    1. Boxers (Dogs)—Juvenile literature. [1. Boxers (Dogs)]
    I. Title.
SF429.B75M34   1989   636.7'3—dc19   88-32233
ISBN 0-87605-062-3

Macmillan books are available at special discounts for bulk purchases for sales promotions, premiums, fund-raising, or educational use. For details, contact:

        Special Sales Director
        Macmillan Publishing Company
        866 Third Avenue
        New York, NY 10022

10 9 8 7 6

Printed in the United States of America

Contents

Foreword

IN 1939, John P. Wagner wrote in *The Boxer:*

"Other breeds have pronounced specialized talents . . . hunting, herding, trailing, and so on . . . but for a combination of the outstanding virtues of many with the faults of a few, our Boxer is the most gifted of canines . . . For the man, woman or child who wants an all-round dog, he has no equal . . ."

The Boxer was first imported into the U.S.A. from Germany in the very early 1900s. In 1932, Ch. Check von Hunnenstein, an import, became the first Boxer to be awarded an American Kennel Club Best in Show. An excellent dog, he aroused real American interest in Boxers, and the breed has steadily gained notice and popularity since then.

The achievements of notable Boxer breeders over the years are well documented in this book by Billie McFadden. It will prove a valuable addition to existing information on the Boxer breed. It boasts an excellent collection of pictures and many carefully researched biographies of important producers. Sections on foreign individuals as well as Americans are included. Since the intercontinental exchange of dogs has become commonplace, some bloodlines have become universal.

The author, a longtime student of the canine world, was born and raised in England. She developed an early interest in dogs, as her mother was a Pomeranian breeder. A few years after she emigrated to the U.S.A. in 1959, Billie and her husband, Dave, purchased the first of their Boxers. As her interest in the breed grew, so did her participation in a number of dog clubs, and she became secretary of the New Jersey Boxer Club. There she started a newsletter focusing on health problems, which gained worldwide circulation.

As president of the Dog Owners Educational League, which was founded in 1976, Billie McFadden has diligently attempted to educate the public on all phases of dogs. By distributing valuable informative literature and conducting programs on responsible care, training, and breeding, her work has been comprehensive and very extensive. She is helping to prepare a health questionnaire and Code of Ethics for the American Boxer Club. For years the proceeds from the sale of Boxer memorabilia at her booth at the National Specialty have been donated to the University of Pennsylvania, University of Illinois, and Cornell University. She continues to publish a calendar which gives Boxer lovers an opportunity to share her collection of precious Boxer pictures.

Herself a breeder of champion Boxers, Billie McFadden is a true Boxer enthusiast. We are indeed most fortunate to have this product of her efforts to enjoy and add to our libraries.

Eleanor Linderholm Wood

Ch. Eldic's Landlord by Int. Ch. Eldic's Darius, owned and bred by Mr. and Mrs. Richard Haeberle, Jr. A sire of merit, he produced 15 Champions.

Acknowledgments

THIS BOOK would not have been written without assistance from numerous people. Otto Donner was especially helpful with information on early Boxers in Germany. Early photographs and personal memories were provided promptly and in abundance by Alice Downey, Jane Forsyth, Barbara Cosgrove and Dorothy Ortman.

I am especially grateful to Maxine Carter who sent information from Australia, to Ron and Norette Herd who extended themselves to provide information and assistance on the section on Canada, to Joe Heine who obtained the excellent photographs from Germany and Holland, to Rick Tomita who worked with Dr. Nagazawa to see that the Japanese section was accurate, Paul Scott of Norway and especially Ronald Lindroos of Sweden who were of the greatest assistance with the Scandinavian section, Johannes and Lea Pelser who were instrumental in obtaining the prompt and accurate information from the Federation of Boxers of South Africa and to Andrew Brace, Bill Malcolm, Kay White and Pat Withers of England.

My thanks go to Jeanie Crosby and Tron Jordheim for their research and explanations of schutzhund.

I am indebted to that wonderful researcher and Boxer devotee, Sturlene Arnold, who not only assisted my research and work, but gave me enthusiasm and encouragement along the way. Her scrapbooks of pedigrees of U.S., Canadian and English Boxers were an invaluable help.

As in any breed book, many important dogs and some people of note must go unmentioned. There are those who have protected rather than promoted this precious breed. All Boxer breeders are indebted to those who have advanced breed type while maintaining the character of the breed.

Long may he reign—that canine exemplar of love, devotion, and understanding—the fun-loving, tail-wagging clown who can behave with the dignity of a gentleman . . . when he has to. I acknowledge and thank my truest friends—Boxers.

Bullenbeisser (old German print)

Bull Dog 1802 – The Sportsman's Cabinet   *Will Judy Publishing Co.*

1

German Ancestors

Most Breed Historians believe the Boxer is descended from hardy, solid medieval German hunting dogs, the heavy Danziger Bullenbeisser (bull-biter), and the smaller Brabenter Bullenbeisser (both now extinct). These tough, tenacious dogs were used for hunting deer, bear and wild pigs in dense forests. They were bred by peasants and supplied to the aristocracy in large numbers as great losses were suffered in every hunting expedition. The dogs were described by one source as fawn or gray in color with black masks, and by another as tawny or speckled.

These dogs were descended from the *Saupacker* (sow chargers), a dog noted for capturing bears and bulls. They had a robust constitution, were massive with imposing teeth and erect ears.

When the cruel sports of bull-baiting, bear-baiting and baiting of other animals became popular, large dogs such as the Danziger Bullenbeisser were at a disadvantage, as they lacked the agility needed to avoid their adversary's horns or claws. Thus the smaller, quicker Brabenter was developed for fighting at close quarters. In time, the Brabenter was crossed with other breeds such as the Great Dane (German Boar Hound or *Deutsche Dogge*), the English Bulldog and refined to a smaller size by natural selection. (The Bulldog of this period bears little resemblance to the English Bulldog as we know it today.) In fact, we can still see modern Boxers with incorrect heads resembling those of the Bulldog or the Great Dane.

9

Dog fighting and bull baiting were outlawed by civilized people in the middle of the 19th century. The period that followed is one of mystery for Boxer historians. Although the Brabenter became extinct, the Germans retained a sound, solid dog of the Brabenter type with a good working ability. He was probably used as a guard dog and because of his background as a fearless Bulldog became useful to butchers and slaughterers.

An article from an 1891 German publication states,

> A unique character is a Boxel kept by a Berlin slaughterhouse, where he is worth his weight in gold. If one of the animals turns wild and runs amok, and none of the other dogs dare do anything, they call for "boxl". The latter sinks his teeth into the animal's nose and drives it into the stable, where it can be caught. If by chance this does not work, then, as a last resort he bites him in his vital parts! However wild the beast is, this always does the trick. Hardly a day goes by when he does not prove his worth, or one can observe his intelligence.

Boxl's fearless behavior certainly suggests terrier-like qualities, and Kay White, in her book *The Boxer*, states that the Bull Terrier and the Giant Schnauzer were incorporated into the modern Boxer breed. In fact, the Bull Terriers of that era looked very similar in body to the brindle Boxer of today.

In any case, all of these dogs had to be very agile, with powerful bodies and with short, deep-muzzled heads to allow them to breathe while holding their prey. It was found that the undershot or protruding lower jaw allowed them to hold the quarry for a greater length of time. An undershot lower jaw gives leverage that once made cannot be broken; pulling only makes it tighter. The intense power of the teeth and jaws enabled tenacious holds against all but the greatest efforts. Bulldogs, for example, have been known to hang on to the lip of the bull after their entrails had been torn out, and while they were in the last agonies of death. Sometimes the grip could only be broken by inserting a metal rod or sheathed hunting knife and twisting it. The same undershot bite and strong jaws are required in today's Boxers.

All ancestors of the Boxer had to be fearless, possess great courage, tenacity and intelligence. The head formation of all these dogs mentioned met with Cuvier's description "namely muzzle more or less shortened, skull high, frontal sinus enlarged, the condyle of the lower jaw extending above the level of the upper cheek tooth, and the cranium diminished in capacity."

Early History

In the 1880s and early 1890s, there was no Boxer—only the *Boxl* or *Boxel.* The adjectives used to describe these dogs were not very flattering. The usual terms applied to them were "field-wood," "meadow-boxel," "herding mutt," "knife-grinder"—all meaning mongrel or cur. In short, a common mixed breed.

In 1893 a union of dog-breeding clubs in Germany decided to enter all dogs, regardless of breed, in a general Stud Book following the system of the Kennel Club in England. Purebred fanciers worried that crossbreeds would be listed and registered. As an example, Otto Donner, in an article in the 1980 *Der Boxer Spiegel* (The Boxer Mirror) quotes the following:

> In the future every baggage carrier in Koblenz can have his herding mutt registered in the Stud Book. Paradisical times begin, the herding mutt's face radiates with joy, unsuspected delights await him. How strong he will feel, herding mutt's heaven!
>
> Yesterday the baggage carrier had a good day with earnings of six marks. "Boxel, now it's my turn, for three marks I can have you entered in the Stud Book." But should one have him registered at all? After the initial enthusiasm wore off, he realized it had almost cost him three marks, equal to six hours of work at 50 pfenning an hour. Why?
>
> Would Boxel be worth more, or improve, even though no one knows where Boxel comes from, who bred him, or when? Moreover, to broadcast the shame—and on top of that to pay! To pay three marks? Boxel himself didn't cost that much. The matter becomes more and more strange, more and more puzzling. To what end and why have him registered? He's not a stud dog, and the registration is only of value to a breeder. No, this doubtful pleasure isn't worth that much. Boxel isn't registered, the Stud Book is minus three marks; the baggage carrier is plus three marks.

In the same year an interesting series of articles appeared about housepets and watchdogs. Experts and lay people gave their opinions on the breeds which were best suited for this purpose. The Boxel was often cited, and arguments followed in the articles in this vein:

> Is the Boxel a housepet and watchdog? Of course, he is the best, the most spirited! His intelligence is indescribable, no purebred can match him!"
>
> This was countered by "Boxels! Those are supposed to be dogs? They are descended from Bulldogs. No, there were never any such dogs. Those are all just dog fairy tales."

The debates continued:

> Should we still write about the Boxel at all? Is this herding mutt even worth another round? Nelly had pups by Bobby. Two of the little beasts had cleft palates. One will be wire-haired, and the little yellow one will be decidedly long-haired. There's still a great lack of consistency, in spite of the fact that Bobby and Nelly seem tolerably similar.

The turning point came in 1894 when a breeder of both Bulldogs and Airedale Terriers, Friedrich Roberth, took a stand in defense of the ostracized Boxer. He was well-known in the dog world and, therefore, his words carried considerable weight. Roberth wrote a detailed article about the "Boxer"—the first to call it by that name. A translation of his article follows:

Now I own, terrible to say, a Boxer bitch that, in spite of the fact that she has a cleft palate, and a loose shoulder, is generally astonishing. She always impresses everyone. No one who sees the two breeds side by side could deny that Bulldogs and Boxers are completely different in both outward appearance and temperament.

Without wanting to offend the Bulldogs, I claim that the Boxer far surpasses the other in physical and mental merits. Until 23 years ago I kept only Boxers, and was always satisfied with them. But then I got rid of the whole lot, and during that time had two German Great Danes, a Fox Terrier, four Bulldogs, and a Poodle; previously I have owned a Leonberger, a Newfoundland, a Pointer, a smooth-haired Miniature Pinscher, a wire-haired Pinscher and a Bull Terrier. Naturally not all at the same time. Among all these breeds, none could replace for me the common German Boxer!

. . . Nevertheless the Boxer is a thankless dog for the breeder. The whelps are very different, and one can be happy when there are one or two good ones in the litter. In every litter there are pups with cleft palates and often loose shoulders.

. . . The many requests to buy them proves that their worth is recognized and valued by many people. Whoever owns a good Boxer will seldom give it up. The way I hear it, even the greatest of dog breeders, Mr. Thiermaler Strebel of Munich, owns a true Boxer, of which he delights in showing pictures. He gave up his other dogs, but supposedly still owns his Boxer and expounds upon the virtues of the dog. That probably says it all.

I also return repentantly to them. Would it not then be possible to form a club that undertakes the breeding of this dog? Perhaps there is some well-known person within the circle of dog fanciers who would take on the founding of such a club. Then members and devoted friends of this breed would soon be found.

In 1894, the Boxer arrived. In Germany, he would never again be called "herding mutt" or "knife grinder." A Boxer Club was officially formed in Munich in February of 1895, and conditions were set for registration in the "Boxer Club Stud Book." In Austria, however, it was a different story, and "those mongrels" were refused recognition for many more years.

A trial class of Boxers was allowed at the Third International show of the St. Bernard Club in Munich in 1895. Compared with 232 St. Bernards and 293 Dachshunds, the entry of four Boxers was a tiny one. The 1st place winner was Flocki, owned by Gg. Mühlbauer of Munich and honorable mention went to Prinz, owned by W. Weber of Stuttgart.

Flocki was described as being by Dr. Toeniessen's Tom, a Bulldog, ex Alt's Schecken (daughter of an imported French dark brindle bitch). Early photographs show that Tom did not resemble the Bulldog but was more similar to the early Boston Terrier. This is not surprising as the Bulldog is the predecessor of the Boston Terrier according to Josephine Z. Rine in her book *The Ideal Boston Terrier*.

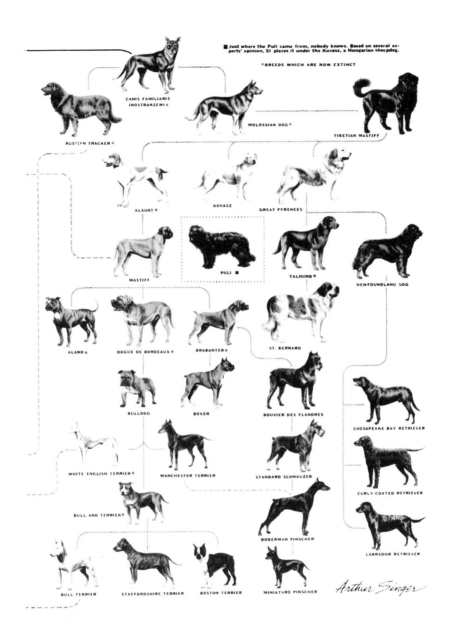

■ Just where the Puli came from, nobody knows. Based on several experts' opinion, SI places it under the Kuvasz, a Hungarian sheepdog.

*BREEDS WHICH ARE NOW EXTINCT

CANIS FAMILIARIS INOSTRANZEWI *

MOLOSSIAN DOG *

TIBETIAN MASTIFF

RUSSIAN TRACKER *

ALAUNT *

KUVASZ

GREAT PYRENEES

MASTIFF

PULI ■

TALHUND *

NEWFOUNDLAND DOG

ALANO *

DOGUE DE BORDEAUX *

BRABANTER *

ST. BERNARD

BULLDOG

BOXER

BOUVIER DES FLANDRES

CHESAPEAKE BAY RETRIEVER

WHITE ENGLISH TERRIER *

MANCHESTER TERRIER

STANDARD SCHNAUZER

CURLY-COATED RETRIEVER

BULL AND TERRIER *

DOBERMAN PINSCHER

LABRADOR RETRIEVER

BULL TERRIER

STAFFORDSHIRE TERRIER

BOSTON TERRIER

MINIATURE PINSCHER

Arthur Singer

Dog Genealogy Chart by Arthur Singer

Sports Illustrated

13

Later in 1895 A. Nerf, C. Mühlbauer, Friedrich Roberth, and J. Widman proposed to found the German Boxer Club. Because of Friedrich Roberth's knowledge of the breed, he was asked to prepare a breed standard and present it at the club's first meeting in January, 1896.

Years later, Otto Donner came across a copy of this first standard in its original form, which is presented here:

> The outward appearance should be of a compact, solid, sturdy, powerful and active dog that stands proudly and moves on straight healthy legs. Tail and ears are docked.
>
> The skull is round and high between the ears. A flat head or one having a furrow (broken) indicates too much Bulldog blood, and are frequently occurring faults. The nose cannot be split, namely because with a split nose the incisors of the upper jaw almost cross, and frequently the lower jaw is then deformed. The lower jaw juts out, curved over the upper jaw, but not that much to expose the teeth. The muzzle is moderately short and not too strongly flewed; folds and wrinkles on the head, as well as dewlap are faults.
>
> The hair is short, tight, firmly lying on the body, with a beautiful sheen— uniform of colour. Head and tail are carried proudly. Eyes are round and not too full, back short, forechest full yet not too wide. The entire dog must be completely symmetrical and sturdily built.

With the founding of the Boxer Club, historical interest in the Boxer was born, and fanciers became fascinated with Boxers of the past—the former "herding mutts" and "knife grinders." It was discovered that the "Bavarian Hiesel," alias Mathias Klostermann, a notorious robber of the 18th century, had owned a Boxer. The robber was executed on the wheel in Dilligen on the Donau in 1771. His Boxer is portrayed in every contemporary engraving and must have made a big impression on the people living at that time.

The first Boxer Show was held on March 29, 1896, with "50 representatives of these ideal big city dogs, which have only in the past few months found approval." The judge, E. Koenig, stated that the Boxer could have neither a too short, wrinkled Bulldog head, nor a too long muzzle with a light head. One dog had a cleft palate and one bitch displayed too much of the Bulldog type. Emphasis was placed on the correct, sturdy build.

The top dog of this period was Flock St. Salvator (a fawn), the fourteenth dog registered; the first standard was written with him in mind. Even so, Boxers varied so much that, at a later Munich show, 25 Boxers were shown in three different weight classes.

Many Boxer clubs were formed and there was much in-fighting. Fanciers differed strongly in their interpretations of the standard as well as matters of business management, shows, judges and Stud Books. The Munich Boxer Club and the German Boxer Club were principal rivals. In 1906 there was much argument about the black Boxer and a "Club for Black Boxers" was formed, but it was short-lived.

14

Bull Terrier by
George Townley
Stubbs 1812
*The Staffordshire
Bull Terrier Hand-
book – J.F. Gordon*

Muhlbauers Flocki
Der Boxer

Meta v. d. Passage
Der Boxer

Champion Rolf v. Vogelsberg
Der Boxer

Champion Blanka v. Angertor
Der Boxer

16

At the great Mannheim convention in 1911, all the Boxer clubs amalgamated and accepted the Munich Club's Standard and Stud Book as official. Dr. Schulein became head of the club and also Editor of the *Boxer Blatter,* the noted breed magazine which was founded in 1904 and is still published today.

Dr. Toenniessen's Bulldog Tom sired the white bitch, Ch. Blanka v. Angertor. She was the mother of Meta von der Passage (a parti-color), who appeared in every early pedigree of the Boxer breed. A great line of sires all trace directly back to her.

Meta was also the mother of Hugo von Pfalzgau, a leading sire who played a major role in the breed's development. Hugo sired the Ch. Kurt von Pfalzgau, father of Ch. Rolf von Vogelsberg, who was one of the great stud forces in the breed's history. In 1910 Rolf was acquired by Philip Stockmann, known as the "father of the modern Boxer."

Over the next decade, the Boxer developed rapidly and gained in popularity in Germany and elsewhere. In fact, some of the best Boxers were being bred in Holland. When World War I broke out in 1914, Boxers were recruited in Germany as pack dogs, messenger dogs, mail dogs and as scouts for snipers. The regional group of Munich donated the first ten Boxers, which were sent by car in 1914 to the Infantry Veterans Reserve Battalion in Strassburg. They were immediately put to work as guard dogs at prison camps and at munition depots. They were also used as mail dogs.

By 1917 German troops had over 60 fully trained Boxers from Bavaria alone. Obviously, only young dogs were recruited. While they acquitted themselves with distinction, many died in the service of man and his country.

One dog that survived the war was the great Ch. Rolf von Vogelsberg, a brindle dog regarded as one of the pillars of the breed. He returned from battle and, at the age of 11 years, again won the Sieger (Champion) title, establishing a record for all time. He was owned by the famous breeder, gifted artist, and sculptress, Friederun Stockmann and her husband, Philip. They founded their von Dom Kennels in 1910, when they acquired Rolf von Vogelsberg. For many years Philip was Chief Breed Warden for Boxers in Germany. He became Editor of the *Boxer Blatter* in 1914 and continued in that position for almost 30 years.

Both Philip and Friederun Stockmann have written books on the Boxer. Perhaps the most well-known is *My Life With Boxers* by Frau Stockmann, which has been translated into English, and is a fascinating book with unique sketches of Boxers in the outside margin on every page.

In 1919, the Ministry of the Reich, Department of Army Leadership, decided to recognize the Boxer as the fifth breed of working dogs and to admit Boxers to the state schools for dog training. Boxer owners were encouraged to train their dogs, and in 1921 at the age of eight and one-half years, Ch. Rolf v. Walhall became the first Boxer to pass the guard dog test combining beauty and working ability.

In 1925 the Boxer was one of the first breeds selected by the Germans for police work, a job that demands intelligence, fearlessness, agility and strength. Around this time, the Boxer also became a guide dog for the blind, for which he is still used.

Five dogs can be called principal ancestors of the modern Boxer: Flock St. Salvador, Meta von der Passage, Mirzl, Wotan and Bosco Immergrun. The "mother of the breed" Meta was sired by Piccolo von Angertor (a white), a brother to Mirzl (a red fawn) out of Ch. Blanka von Angertor (a white), the daughter of a white Bulldog. One of her sons was the great Ch. Gigerl, a brindle, who did much to further this color.

Flock and Meta produced Schani von der Passage, who became the mother of Ch. Rigo von Angertor. Rigo created a demand for fawns in the same way that Gigerl had for brindles. Parti-coloreds or checks diminished in numbers and are seldom seen today.

Sigurd von Dom was born in 1929, sired by Iwein von Dom ex Belinde Hassia. He won the Austrian Sieger (Champion) title in 1931 and followed with the German titles in the next two years. Before leaving Germany for the United States, Sigurd sired two famous dogs, Zorn von Dom, a black brindle dog, and Xerxes von Dom, a golden brindle dog, who in turn produced their own lines in their native Germany. Zorn was bred to a daughter of his sire, Sigurd, and produced the famous Lustig von Dom, a fawn with white markings. Xerxes produced the famous Dorian von Marienhof.

In 1935, Lustig won the Sieger in fawns and Dorian won the title in brindles.

2

American Pioneers

IN THE EARLY PART of this century, few attempts were made to establish the Boxer breed in the United States. Only two Boxers were shown at the Westminster show in 1898. In 1904 the first Boxer, Arnulf Graudenz, was registered in the *American Kennel Club's Stud Book*. This dog was registered as American-bred but actually was imported *in utero*. His dam was Rose v. Graudenz, imported in whelp by James E. Welch of Harvey, Illinois. However, Arnulf had little influence on the breed.

Mrs. Herbert Lehman, wife of the governor of New York, bought the 1912 German Brindle *Sieger* in Germany and brought him to the United States, where he was shown in the Miscellaneous Class. He was Sieger Dampf von Dom, ex Behna v. Muenchenberg, a brindle with white markings sired by Rolf von Vogelsberg. He completed his championship in April, 1915, but he did not receive much attention that year. Soon after becoming a champion, he met a tragic death in a fight with Flock v. Salvadore, an unregistered Boxer house pet of the Lehmans.

During the next 27 years only two more Boxers became American champions. Bluecher von Rosengarten (a fawn with black mask), who finished in 1926, was later owned by G. J. Jeuther, the first Boxer handler. Sieger Check von Hunnenstein (by Carsar v. Deutenkofen ex Dina V. Hunnenstein), whelped March 3, 1927, a brindle with white toes and a patch of white on his chest, was the first important Boxer champion.

Int. Ch. Check von Hunnenstein, imported in 1932 by Cirrol Kennels owned by Marcia and Joseph Fennessey.

Int. Ch. Sigurd von Dom, imported in 1934 by Barmere Kennels. He is shown with owner Mrs. Miriam Breed.

Check had won championship titles in Germany, Austria, and Czechoslovakia. Though considered small (65 lbs.) in Germany, he had balance, style and showmanship. He was imported at five years of age by William Hacker, the professional handler, for Cirrol Kennels, owned by the famous brother and sister Great Dane breeders, Marcia and Joseph Fennessey of Chappaqua, New York. The American dog show world was startled when a Boxer, Check, won his first Non-Sporting Group at Hartford, Connecticut, but that was only the beginning.

In May, 1932, Check, handled by George Andrade, was the first Boxer to win a Best in Show award at Profile K.C., Concord, New Hampshire, under Mrs. T. E. L. Kemp. He repeated this triumph in July under respected all-rounder judge Mr. Alva Rosenberg. Check is credited with stimulating the first real American interest in the breed.

Arthur Frederick Jones, writing in the *American Kennel Gazette* of November 1, 1932, wrote that "This Boxer's record is almost unbelievable. Check has flash and fire about him, due to his marvelous condition, that commands attention immediately."

From 1932 to 1934, Check was shown 36 times and was Best of Breed 35 times. He placed in the Group a total of 22 times and was first in the Non-Sporting Group twelve times. He won Best in Show four times.

Despite this impressive record Check had trouble finishing. As Arthur Frederick Jones wrote,

> Perhaps the most surprising part of the whole situation, to the layman, is the fact that despite his many triumphs, Check von Hunnenstein has been unable to win his championship. Lack of competition in Boxers has given him but five points in that manner. Practically all the championship points he has gathered have come from winning the Non-Sporting group. No other exhibit, so far, has offered him his needed "three pointer," yet he has many more than the required 15 points.

After completing his championship in 1932, Check was in demand as a stud. Unfortunately there was a scarcity of good bitches in the United States at that time. He left few litters behind him in Germany and did not sire a single American bred champion. However, some Check children such as his daughter, Saxonia's Andl, became outstanding producers. Nonetheless, Check put Boxers in the public's eye and set a high standard for Boxer fanciers.

By 1931 only 18 Boxers had been registered with the American Kennel Club. Late in that year, Mr. and Mrs. Henry Stoecker of Stoeckersburg Kennels imported two bitches, one of whom, Ulotte v.d. Lowenburg, arrived in whelp. From this German breeding, a litter of puppies was whelped on November 9, 1931. One of them, a brindle bitch with a black mask, Dodi v.d. Stoeckersburg, was the first Boxer bitch to become an American champion in 1933.

Barmere

Mrs. Miriam Young (to become Mrs. William C. Breed in 1938) was raised in a family of dog lovers. By the time she was 23 years old, she had owned four Brussels Griffon, three Boston Terriers, a Cocker Spaniel, a Wire Fox Terrier and Irish Terriers. In 1922, she was given a Boxer who later died of distemper. The vaccines we take for granted today did not exist then, and many dogs died of distemper and other diseases.

Mrs. Young's Boxer had obviously won a place in her heart, however, because she purchased Ch. Dodi v.d. Stoeckersburg in 1933. With this bitch, Miriam Breed established Barmere Kennels, combining the "mere" sound of Miriam with the "Bar" from her older daughter's name (now Mrs. Barbara Cosgrove). Dodi was bred to Check that year and the first Barmere Boxer litter was born at Cedarhurst, Long Island.

In 1934, Barmere acquired the five-year-old *Weltsieger* (World Champion) Sigurd v. Dom (a fawn), by Iwein v. Dom ex Belinde Hassia, bred by Frau Stockmann. Sigurd arrived in 1932 just two days before the prestigious Morris and Essex Show. He looked rather thin after his transatlantic trip, but was still shown by Mrs. Breed to Best of Breed.

Sigurd von Dom of Barmere was heavily advertised and campaigned all over the United States. He garnered 54 Bests of Breed, 43 Non-Sporting Groups and two Bests in Show. Mrs. Breed rendered a great service by showing Sigurd so widely, as it gave people, who may have only read about Boxers or seen pictures of them, the opportunity to see a superb living specimen. Sigurd sired 16 American champions and was the leading sire in 1936. He died at 12 years of age.

Sigurd's contribution to American Boxers cannot be overstated. Remember, he was the grandsire of the three other members of Boxers' "Big Four"—Dorian von Marienhof of Mazelaine, Lustig von Dom of Tugley Wood and Lustig's full brother, Utz von Dom of Mazelaine.

Mrs. Breed imported many other dogs and continued breeding and showing on a large scale in the East and later in California. She owned or bred over 50 champions, and many successful kennels were established with a Boxer purchased from Barmere Kennels.

Mazelaine

In Milwaukee, Mazie and John Wagner succumbed to the charm of the Boxer. Originally breeders of Great Danes, they purchased their first Boxer in 1933. She was their foundation bitch, Landa, obtained from Dr. Benjamin J. Birk of Milwaukee, Wisconsin. They founded their Mazelaine Kennels, coined from Mrs. Wagner's first name, Mazie. Their first imported Boxer was Dirndl v. Stolzenhof—the only Boxer imported with a German Police Certificate.

During a trip to Germany in 1934, the Wagners purchased a fawn

Int. Ch. Lustig von Dom of Tulgey Wood was owned and imported (1937) by Edwin Freund. This Group and Best in Show winner sired 27 American Champions and 17 title holders from other countries.

Int. Ch. Dorian von Marienhof, imported in 1937 for Mazelaine Kennels, was the first Boxer to win the Working Group at Westminster. The year was 1937. He also sired 37 Champions.

male, Argus v. Konigssee, who played no small part in their breeding program. In 1936, they visited Germany again and bought a Sigurd grandson, a large brindle male, Dorian von Marienhof, by International Ch. Xerxes v. Dom ex Saxonia's Andl (a daughter of Ch. Check v. Hunnenstein), whelped April 15, 1933.

Dorian proved to be a wise choice for the Wagners. He won many Bests of Breed, and, in fact, was never beaten for the breed. The AKC had moved Boxers into the Working Group by 1935, and Dorian failed to win the Working Group on only five occasions. He was the first Boxer to win the Group at Westminster; the year was 1937. It would be another ten years before another Boxer was named Best in Show, and that would be a Dorian grandson, Ch. Warlord of Mazelaine.

Dorian sired 39 champions. Twenty-seven were produced from eight bitches, and eleven from eleven other bitches. The modern Boxer owes much to this great foundation dog. Unfortunately, Dorian died of a heart attack in 1941 at the age of only eight years.

Mr. John P. Wagner later imported Ch. Utz von Dom, by the great Sigurd son, Zorn v. Dom, ex Esta v.d. Wuerm, whelped December 8, 1933. Utz was bred by Frau Stockmann. A great show dog, he was the second Boxer to win the Working Group at Westminster, where he was handled by Len Brumby. Utz sired 35 champions including Overture, Gavotte, Konzert, Volante, Suzette, Warbride and the famous Warlord, all of Mazelaine. Utz died in his sleep in April, 1945, at the age of nine years.

In 1939, Mr. Wagner wrote his book *The Boxer*. Although out-of-print, this work continues to reign as the "Boxer Bible." Anyone seriously interested in the breed should not be without it. Indeed, as Francis A. Bigler writes in the preface, "Drink it deeply *and wisely*."

The Wagner advertisements of this period used the slogan "The Winning Strain is Mazelaine," and so it seemed. Both a successful breeder and a popular judge, John Wagner gave powerful direction to the breed. Mazelaine Kennels bred or owned 123 champions—a great legacy.

Tulgey Wood

A former Bulldog breeder, Erwin O. Fruend of Tulgey Wood Kennels, founded in the 1930s in Illinois, purchased his first Boxer from Mazelaine Kennels. This was Tweedle Dee of Tulgey Wood, a son of Dorian. He then imported Dorian's old rival, Lustig von Dom, from the Stockmanns. He was sired by Zorn v. Dom (a son of Sigurd) ex Esta v.d. Wuerm and whelped on December 28, 1933. Lustig was a German and Czechoslovakian Sieger in 1935 and was a candidate for the CACIB title (Certificate of Aptitude Championship International Beauty awarded by the Federation Cynologique Internationale).

Lustig finished his championship in one week—March 27th and 28th at Mississippi Valley K.C., St. Louis, B.O.B. and first in Working Group; March 30th and 31st, at Tri-City K.C., Illinois, B.O.B., first Working Group and B.I.S., followed by April 3rd and 4th at Chicago International K.C., B.O.B.—a sensational record. Dorian and Lustig were never competed with each other, as both were exhibited by the same professional handler, Jimmie Sullivan.

Lustig sired 24 American champions and 17 imported dogs who gained their titles in this country. His total of 41 champions exceeds Dorian's total of 39. He also sired one Canadian champion. Lustig died in 1945 at the age of 11½ years.

More than 40 Boxers from the Tulgey Wood Kennels obtained their championships. After 1941, Mr. Fruend stopped showing dogs but continued breeding. He died in November, 1947, and Tulgey Wood Kennels was purchased by his kennel manager, Bob Rogers. Later, it had to be moved to Lemont, Illinois, to make way for the Argonne National Laboratories. Lustig's grave was also moved, and his gravestone bore the inscription "I am the splendid Lustig." Later Bob Rogers sold Tulgey Wood to John Wagner.

Bladan

Dr. Dan Gordon, author of *The Boxer* (another fine out-of-print book), imported Ch. Klaus von der Uhlanshohe for his Bladan Kennels in Detroit, founded in 1936. With other imports, including the Dutch Champion Ivo v. Haus Germania, purchased at 3½ years from Peter Zimmerman of Holland, he embarked on an extensive breeding and exhibiting program. One imported dog, Ch. Brokas v. Germanenstolz of Bladan, produced Ch. Sir Galahad of Bladan, C.D.X., who became a Sire of Merit by producing 11 champions. (A Sire of Merit is an award given by the American Boxer Club to any Boxer siring seven or more champions. Sir Galahad sired Ch. Bladan's U-Chetnik, another Sire of Merit (9 champions).

Fostoria

Mr. Walter C. Foster, owner of Fostoria Kennels of Westbury, New York, was another Bulldog breeder. He turned to Boxers and became a professional handler of all breeds. He owned the first American-bred Boxer to win a Group I, Ch. Baldur of Fostoria. Mr. Foster was later to be the owner/handler of Ch. Merry Monarch.

Other notable kennels of this period were: Sumbula Kennels of Connecticut (Harold and Lillian Palmedo); Slugger Hill Kennels of Dallas, Texas (Jim and Pokey Culp); Dorick Kennels of Westbury, New York (Mr. and Mrs. Richard Kettles); Bravenhartz Kennels of Pennsylvania (Mr.

Frank Bigler, prolific writer on the Boxer in early dog magazines); Kernia Boxers, Pennsylvania (Mr. Robert Kerns); Stuttgarter Kennels in Woodbridge, New Jersey (Mr. Valentine Martin); Meritaire Kennels, Pennsylvania (Mr. and Mrs. Henry Lark); Wolf Trap Kennels (Mr. and Mrs. Jouett Shouse); and High Spot Kennels, North Hollywood, California (Mr. and Mrs. Paul Ladin).

Prior to 1937 imported Boxers dominated the champions list. In 1936, there was only one American-bred champion—Ch. Banner of Barmere, sired by Sigurd ex Ch. Dodi v. Stoeckersburg. In 1937 29 Boxers finished their championships, and five were American bred—four sired by Dorian and one by Sigurd.

In 1938 Philip Stockmann judged Boxers at the Westminster show. He drew an entry of 116, and all his placements went to imported dogs with the exception of his Winners Bitch—Nocturne of Mazelaine, sired by Dorian ex Ch. Dagmar of Mazelaine. Nocturne became a Dam of Merit (seven champions). (Dam of Merit is an award given by the American Boxer Club to any bitch producing four or more champions.)

During Philip Stockmann's visit, he took part in lengthy discussions about the Standard with Enno Meyer, an interpreter from the American Kennel Club, and three judges familiar with the German language. As a result of these deliberations, the German Standard was adopted with the exception of the color requirements. The Americans disqualified all white and check Boxers. Germany was later to follow suit, but at that time white or check Boxers could still be registered. Prior to the disqualification rule in the U.S.A., only one check Boxer completed its championship.

In October, 1939, War was declared in Europe, and obviously any further importations were impossible. Breeding was curtailed in Germany. While entries at American shows plummeted during the War years, the registration of Boxers continued to climb.

The Boxer reached fourth place in popularity, with much indiscriminate breeding to meet the demands of the pet market. Too much popularity can be a curse for any breed. Bitches are bred by puppy mills and others eager to cash in on the latest fad. Unfortunately, this multiplies faults both physical and temperamental. Nonetheless, many dedicated breeders clung to high standards. The breed endured, and Boxers of high quality prevailed.

In 1942, Mrs. Breed judged the Westminster K.C. show, drawing an entry of 90 Boxers, which was large at that time. She picked her Winners Bitch and Best of Winners, Volante of Mazelaine (later a champion and dam of Mazelaine Kapellmeister—Sire of Merit (34 champions) from the 6-9 months class and Winners Dog, Mahderf's El Chico (a Dorian son, later a champion and Sire of Merit (16 champions) from the 9-12 months class. One could say that Mrs. Breed had both an eye for a dog and a lot of courage.

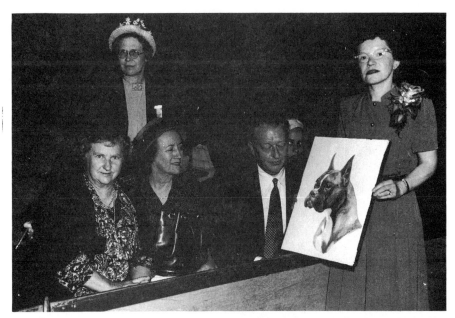

Frau Stockmann (left) seated next to Mazie and John Wagner in 1949. Standing at back: Alice Rosenthal, Editor of the defunct *Dog News*, and right, Judge Evelyn Goff.

At three months, "Bang Away" won a match show judged by Frau Stockmann. He is shown with Russell Zimmerman.

Larry Downey with Boxers he brought back from Germany. They are (from left): Zack von Dom, Sonni von Dom and Reichseiger Karlo v.d. Wolfsschlucht. The latter co-owned with Mr. and Mrs. John Wagner.

Ch. Spark Plug, sired by Ch. Zack von Dom, owned and bred by Larry Downey, sired 11 Champions. He won the American Boxer Club Specialty under Mr. John Wagner and the Working Group at Westminster in 1954.

The magazine *Boxer Briefs* made its debut in 1944 edited by Bob Rogers, kennel manager for Tulgey Wood Kennels. After Rogers' death in 1950, *Boxer Briefs* continued for several years produced by John and Natalie Grinstead, but finally folded. Needless to say *Boxer Briefs* are a collector's item these days.

The Post-War Comeback

The years of 1946 to 1956 were truly golden years for Boxers, when they dominated both the Group and the Best in Show rings.

In 1946, Enno Meyer wrote one of the most educational books on the Boxer, *Judging the Boxer,* which, although out-of-print, is a widely read and coveted book even today. His Furore Kennels produced many champions, and he was in demand as a judge.

Dog News, 1948, states "Barmere Kennels donated another Boxer to a paraplegic out-patient at the Birmingham Hospital at Van Nuys. There was always a waiting list for Boxers at the hospital as the breed appears to top all others in popularity with the boys who want dogs."

Larry Downey returned from the service and brought three Boxers from Germany. They were the German Sieger Karlo von der Wolfsschlucht, a seven-year-old brindle male, available only because his owners could not feed him; Zack von Dom, aged 11 months, and a two-year-old bitch, Sonne von Dom. His favorite was always Zack, who went through the War with him and slept at the foot of his army cot.

Karlo was co-owned by John Wagner. He finished his championship in three shows and produced five champions. He died peacefully in his sleep a few months after Larry and Alice Downey were married in 1949. Larry could not allow co-ownership of his beloved Zack and showed him to his championship himself. Zack became a Sire of Merit producing 31 champions including Ch. Zacksappeal owned by Mrs. Frances Abercrombie and, of course, Ch. Spark Plug, another Sire of Merit (11 champions). Ch. Spark Plug won the 1954 American Boxer Club Specialty under John Wagner and followed the next day by winning the Working Group at the Westminster K.C. show.

Ch. Warlord of Mazelaine (a fawn), whelped October 1, 1942, sired by Utz ex Ch. Symphony of Mazelaine, bred by John Wagner and owned by Mr. and Mrs. Richard Kettles of New York, was the first Boxer to be awarded Best in Show at the Westminster K.C. in 1947. He was handled by Walter Foster and is considered to have had a perfect head. Warlord was Utz' best producing son and, as Sire of Merit, produced 16 American champions. Warlord died April 2, 1953.

Warlord's record was soon surpassed by Ch. Mazelaine's Zazarak Brandy, sired by Ch. Merry Monarch (a Dorian and Utz grandson) ex Ch. Warbaby of Mazelaine. He went Best in Show at Westminster in 1949 while collecting 60 other Bests in Show—a record at that time. Brandy is a Sire of Merit, producing 19 champions, including the well-known Ch. Mazelaine's Zenith, the bitch, Ch. Mazelaine's Hot Toddy, and Ch. Mazelaine's Shot O' Brandy.

Warlord was also the sire of the 1950 Reichsieger (Winner of the Annual Specialty Show, therefore named Champion of the year) Mazelaine's Czardas, whom Frau Stockmann took back with her to Germany as a puppy after judging in the United States. Mazelaine was surely the leading American kennel of the day, and there is little doubt of the enormous contribution made to the breed by John and Mazie Wagner.

Sirrah Crest

In 1938, Sirrah Crest Kennels was established by Dr. and Mrs. Rafael C. Harris of Santa Ana, California, by the purchase of the future Ch. Marshall v. Bismark, a golden brindle male sired by Ch. High Spot Major ex Ch. High Spot Dotti Major (Paul Ladin, breeder). The kennel name Sirrah is Harris spelled backwards.

In 1950, Dr. and Mrs. Harris, after more than a decade of breeding, dispersed their kennels of 70 Boxers, keeping only three young bitches, Ch. Yoomph of Sirrah Crest and the young Bang Away, who would soon make Boxer history.

Two years later, Dr. and Mrs. Harris visited the Wagners and purchased two puppies from them. One was an eight-week-old golden brindle male who appeared on practically every Sirrah Crest pedigree as Ch. Duke Cronian. The other puppy was four-month-old Ouida of Mazelaine. One year later, Mr. and Mrs. Harris purchased another Mazelaine puppy, Kantatrix of Mazelaine, who was followed yet another year later by Ch. Endymion of Mazelaine. With this foundation, they embarked on an extensive breeding program based on Mazelaine stock. The culmination of their efforts was the famous Ch. Bang Away of Sirrah Crest.

The immortal Ch. Bang Away of Sirrah Crest, sired by Ch. Ursa Major of Sirrah Crest ex Verily Verily of Sirrah Crest, was whelped on February 17, 1949, one of a litter of three puppies. He made his debut before the renowned German breeder, Frau Stockmann, who awarded him Best Puppy In Match and called him "Little Lustig." He was shown at the American Boxer Club show in 1950 and went Best of Winners from the 9-12 months class handled by Nate Levine. Best of Breed went to Ch. Yoomph of Sirrah Crest, also owned by Dr. and Mrs. Harris and handled by Nate Levine. Bang Away was next shown under Mr. John Wagner in Chicago and went Best of Winners, Best of Breed, and Group I. Bang Away was on his way, and he never looked back.

Bang Away finished his championship at his fourth show. In 1951 he became the third Boxer to win Best in Show at Westminster K.C. Shown extensively across the country, on the West Coast, he was handled by

Ch. Mazelaine's Zazarac Brandy had 60 Bests in Show and was the second Boxer to win Best in Show at Westminster, this in 1949.

Ch. Bang Away of Sirrah Crest, owned and bred by Dr. and Mrs. R. C. Harris. He was handled by J. Nate Levine and won 121 Bests in Show and sired 81 Champions during his long, distinguished career.

Russel Zimmerman until he retired and then by Harry Sangster. Harry's brother, George Sangster, wrote that Bang Away was "like a piece of machinery. You'd just wind him up when you got to the show and forget about him."

Bang Away amassed 121 Best in Show awards in 27 states. Articles about him appeared in many different publications including *Life*, *True* and *Colliers*, as well as countless dog magazines, and he had a tremendous impact on the public. He was bred to over 200 bitches and produced 81 champions in the United States alone.

Bang Away's progeny include seven top producers, including Sires of Merit Ch. Barrage of Quality Hill (45 champions) owned by Jouett Shouse; Ch. Marquam Hill's Comanche (23 champions) owned by Dr. and Mrs. Robert Burke; Ch. Jered's Sovereign (14 champions) owned by Joe Gregory and C. Long (later by Mary and Donald Smith); Ch. Lewgin Lane's Whizz Bang (10 champions) owned by Hazel Cowie; International Ch. Helixview Noble Knight (10 champions) owned and bred by Trella White; plus Dams of Merit Jered's Sky Siren (five champions) owned by Mr. and Mrs. O. Berges; and Ch. Marwal's Satisfactual (four champions) owned by Jenette Hecox.

Dr. and Mrs. Harris campaigned Bang Away from coast to coast for six years and made the great showman the center of the public's attention. He was retired in 1956 and given a famous testimonial dinner where he wore a collar studded with rhinestones and was crowned "King of Dog Shows" by George Foley. Although he had never sat on a chair before, he remained seated for the entire long and exciting evening.

Bang Away died suddenly of a heart attack in September of 1957. Upon his death Mrs. Phoebe Harris wrote:

> Owning him was indeed, a pleasure and satisfaction but, you know, we never could feel as possessive of him as of other dogs we owned. It always seemed as if the many hundreds of his admirers—his public—owned a part of him too. I am sure that is the way Bang Away felt, too, because he did love people so much.

Dr. R. C. Harris died in November of 1983, but his widow, Phoebe, lives with her daughter, Penny, in Missouri. Although much sought after as a judge, she accepts only a few assignments. In 1985, she made a trip to Munich with other Boxer fanciers to see the Atibox show, and in 1986 she judged in England.

While Bang Away dominated the 1950s, other breeders found success with their Boxers. Jay Stead bred Ch. Captain Lookout of Thorhall who sired 31 champions including Ch. Marjack's Golden Windjammer. Windjammer was campaigned extensively by the Wagners and became a Sire of Merit with 18 champions.

Other Notable Dogs and Fanciers

Professional handlers showing Boxers exclusively piloted many of the

32

Ch. Barrage of Quality Hill, owned by Jouette Shouse, was Best American-bred in Show at Westminster 1955 under Albert C. Van Court. He was sired by Bang Away and became a Sire of Merit with 45 Champions.

Ch. Marquam Hill's Comanche, sired by Bang Away and owned by Mr. and Mrs. Robert Burke, was the sire of 23 Champions.

33

country's top dogs during the next decade. Among them were Larry Downey and Phil Marsh, now deceased; Jane Forsyth and Joe Gregory—all became judges.

Sire of Merit Ch. Spark Plug (11 champions), sired by Ch. Zack v. Dom, owned by Larry Downey and bred by Stephen Lovett, won the Working Group at Westminster in 1954. Larry then showed Ch. Barrage of Quality Hill to Best American Bred in Show at Westminster in 1955 and Best of Breed at the American Boxer Club Specialty. Barrage's littermate, Baroque of Quality Hill, and Bang Away's son, Ch. Marquam Hill's Commanche, plus Ch. Treceder's Painted Lady and Ch. Salgray's Fashion Plate were all Westminster Working Group winners.

In 1957 *Boxer Review* magazine, edited by Kris Dahl, made its debut and still flourishes as the top monthly magazine for the breed in the United States today and has many subscribers overseas.

Brayshaw Kennels, established by Charlotte Brayshaw in the early 1940s, produced 22 champions including the Sire of Merit Ch. Brayshaw's Masquerader who sired 15 champions. Miss Brayshaw died in 1984, and a special Memorial Award is given every year at the American Boxer Club Annual Dinner to the Bitch making the most wins in the Bred By Exhibitor classes. This award is given jointly by Mr. and Mrs. Bruce A. Korson and Mr. and Mrs. Victor Clemente.

Canyonair Kennels of California was established by the late Mr. and Mrs. Paul Newhall Davis in the late 1940s. They produced 18 champions including the Dams of Merit Canyonair Diamond Lil, C.D., and Ch. Canyonair's Honey Chile, and Sires of Merit Ch. Canyonair Hickory Dick, C.D., producer of 20 champions, and Ch. Canyonair Man of Fire, producer of seven champions. Man of Fire was later purchased by Mr. and Mrs. Ted Wurmser of New York and was a multiple Best in Show winner.

Mr. and Mrs. Ted Wurmser also bred and showed the lovely Ch. Terudon's Kiss Me Kate, sired by Ch. Barrage of Quality Hill ex Canyonair's Katrinkia II, another popular winning bitch with a well-remembered headpiece.

Grayarlin Kennels were established by Jane Kamp (now Mrs. Robert Forsyth) of Southbury, Connecticut, with the purchase by her mother of an El Chico sister whom they bred to Champion Utz von Dom of Mazelaine. Jane showed a bitch of this breeding in Junior Showmanship. Later she sold Ch. Sally of Grayarlin to Mr. and Mrs. Daniel Hamilburg, starting them on their road to success in Boxers. Jane was to become one of the finest and best-known all-breed professional handlers.

Richard and Eleanor Haeberle owned Boxers from 1946. They founded their Eldic Kennels in 1952 and finished the first dog of their own breeding from their fourth litter in 1956. Their Ch. Everready of Woodcrest was bred to Bang Away.

The kennel produced over 70 litters in 20 years, but their claim to fame

Mrs. Peg Davis, founder of Canyonair Kennels which produced 18 Champions. She is shown with Ch. Canyonair Hickory Dick, CD, in his later years.

was the Int. Ch. Eldic's Darius, a fawn, sired by Ch. Barrage of Quality Hill ex Eldic's Beaux Brite (daughter of Ch. Everready of Woodcrest). He became a Sire of Merit, producing 13 champions.

Darius was the first champion sired by Ch. Barrage of Quality Hill. He in turn produced Ch. Eldic's Landlord ex Eldic's Dark Dream, also a Sire of Merit producing 15 champions. Landlord, a rich dark brindle, probably did much to promote the brindle color.

Landlord was retired at three years of age after winning Best of Breed at Westminster K.C. show in 1967. He had an outstanding record in the East. Her kennel is no longer active, but Mrs. Haeberle continues to be a popular judge of Boxers.

In the early 1950s, Dr. and Mrs. Lloyd Flint founded their Flintwood Kennels in Massachusetts and finished 30 champions. Among the most famous are Sires of Merit Ch. Flintwood's Bag N' Baggage (seven champions), Ch. Flintwood's Linebacker (eight champions) and Ch. Flintwood's Rabble Rouser (nine champions). Rabble Rouser was later sold to Mrs. Cheever Porter and garnered many Bests in Show handled by Jane Forsyth. He was later acquired by Mrs. Forsyth. Dr. Flint followed a very careful line breeding program on which he lectures today. He became a judge in 1974 and lives in Myrtle Beach, South Carolina.

In 1947, Mrs. Velma Hiser established her Vel-Hi Kennels in Iowa and finished 11 champions under the Vel-Hi banner. She is still active in the breed and is also an approved judge.

Mr. and Mrs. Donald Starkweather began breeding in the middle 1950s and finished 13 champions under the Rainey Lane Kennel name. Among the most famous was Ch. Elixir of Raineylane, sired by Ch. Mazelaine's Kapellmeister. Elixir was a Sire of Merit with 18 champion get to his credit. One of his famous offspring was Ch. Jered's Spellbinder, who sired 51 champions (Bang Away was the only dog to top this record). Spellbinder was owned by Mr. and Mrs. Edward J. Garich, Jr. Both Mr. and Mrs. Starkweather are judges and reside in Florida.

When Arnault Seidler died in 1958, Mr. and Mrs. Donald Smith purchased the outstanding winner Ch. Dempsey's Copper Gentlemen, sired by Ch. Jered's Spellbinder ex Fontana's Crimson Mist. He became a Sire of Merit, producing 11 champions. Joe Gregory handled this dog and the popular winning bitch Ch. Rancho Chiquito's Yanna, also sired by Spellbinder ex Rancho Chiquito's Dancer.

Mr. and Mrs. Garich finished 11 champions under the Jered name, including Dams of Merit Jered's Sky Siren (five champions), Ch. Jered's Sweet Stuff and Sire of Merit Ch. Jeder's Sovereign (14 champions), later acquired by Mary and Donald Smith.

On the West Coast a popular winner was Ch. Evo-Wen's Impressario, owned by George and Hazel Cowie. He was sired by Ch. Evo-Wen's Big Story ex Evo-Wen's Mecque Mecque. His bloodlines were a combination

Int. Ch. Eldic's Darius, sired by Ch. Barrage of Quality Hill. He was owned and bred by Mr. and Mrs. Richard Haeberle, Jr., and sired 13 Champions.

Ch. Baroque of Quality Hill, bred by Mr. and Mrs. M. E. Greiner and owned by Mr. and Mrs. John P. Wagner, was a littermate of Ch. Barrage of Quality Hill and, like her brother, a Westminster Working Group winner.

of two top Boxer sires—Ch. Bang Away of Sirrah Crest and Ch. Jered's Spellbinder. "Imp," as he was called, garnered 10 Bests in Show, 16 Groups and won a Boxer Specialty, all in 18 months, handled by Harry Sangster. He travelled East and won the breed at Westminster handled by Larry Downey while he was still under three years of age.

The Treceder Kennels was founded in 1945 by Hollyce Steward. Upon her death in 1972, Bobbee Owens (sister of Hollyce) continued the kennels in partnership with Mrs. Ann Harr. Bobbee Owens has since died, but Mrs. Harr still continues Treceder with partners Dr. Mark L. Harrison and Terri M. Harrison. There are 45 champions with the Treceder prefix, including Sires of Merit Ch. Treceder's Selection (16 champions), Ch. Treceder's Sequel (son of Selection) who produced 23 champions, and Ch. Treceder's Shine Boy, sire of 20 champions. One cannot forget Ch. Treceder's Painted Lady, a brindle bitch who produced two champions by Ch. Salgray's Fashion Plate. Painted Lady, or "Ladybug," as she was called, was owned by Donald and Mary Smith and won many Bests in Show.

Other kennels that should be mentioned before leaving this period are: Bea and George Stacy's Cherokee Oaks Kennel, California; Bill and Marge Rankin's Huck Hill Kennels, Connecticut; Dorothy Watson's Wyndyway's Kennels, New Jersey; Sandra and Chester Juredine's Jhinjheir Kennels, Ohio; Phyllis M. King's Canzonet Kennels, California; William and Nellie Anderson's Nutwood Kennels, New York; Garwood and Dorothy Anderon's Willow Ridge Kennels, Nebraska; Aimee and Robert Acklen's Ackland Kennels, Texas; and many more too numerous to mention who helped make contributions to the breed.

John P. Wagner died in July 1974 in his 80th year and his widow, Mazie, passed away in 1979. The Boxer breed was fortunate to have these truly dedicated and knowledgeable people among its fanciers. The words written many years earlier by Mrs. Harris of Sirrah Crest stand true today: "Mazelaine is the fountain-head of Boxer breeding."

3

Leading Kennels in the U.S.A.

ARRIBA Boxers, *Middleton, Massachusetts*

In 1964, Theodore S. Fickes, D.V.M., established Arriba Boxers with a plain bitch who was never shown—Nahum's Arriba. She produced one flashy bitch and one flashy dog, both of whom became champions. Arriba's daughter, Ch. Arriba's Amulet, sired by Ch. Mazelaine's Early Times (the last dog to stand at stud under the Mazelaine Kennel name), produced three champions by Ch. Capriana's Renegade, Ch. Arriba's Calypso, Ch. Arriba's Carioca and Ch. Arriba's Castanet. These dogs all became producers of champions and began a long, unbroken chain of champions and producers, all tracing back to "Riba."

The most famous by far was Ch. Arriba's Prima Donna, who won 23 all breed Bests in Show, including Westminster and Chicago International. This record may never be broken considering her short career (15 months as a Special) and the size of the shows in which she won Best in Show or won and placed in the Groups. This was accomplished when there were only about half the number of shows there are at present and before the Working Group was divided. At that time the Working Group often comprised nearly half the total entry of many shows.

As recently as the early 1980s, Prima Donna was the only Boxer of either sex to maintain a position in the top ten working dogs of all time in the Kennel Review System. She was sired by Ch. Flintwood's Live Ammo ex Arriba's Alicia and was co-owned by Dr. and Mrs. P. J. Pagano with Dr. Fickes for most of her Specials career.

While Prima Donna made the Arriba name well known with her triumphs in the show ring, her sisters, aunts, and cousins achieved equal success in the whelping box. A total of 52 champions have been bred by or finished under the Arriba banner.

Although best known for producing lovely prepotent bitches, Arriba has also had two American Boxer Club Sires of Merit—Ch. Arriba's Knight Revue (15 champions) and Ch. Arriba's Crescendo (10 champions). Knight Revue is the sire of Me-Don's Special Revue, Sire of Merit, and Ch. Arriba's Lady Revue, Dam of Merit. Ch. Arriba's Crescendo sired Arriba's Ultimate, Dam of Merit, and Ch. Wilderson's Demos, Sire of Merit.

Currently Dr. Fickes' Ch. Arriba's Footloose and Ch. Arriba's Associate of Karjean, co-owned by Carol Nesbitt of Ohio, show every promise of becoming Sires of Merit.

Arriba bitches have been the foundation of several leading kennels. Dams of Merit include Ch. Arriba's Zechin, Ch. Arriba's Lady Revue, and Arriba's Ultimate. Ultimate is a daughter of Ch. Arriba's Jubilee, who produced three other champions, Zechin, Zingara and Arriba's Up and Coming.

Ted Fickes is very proud of his many American Boxer Club Specialty wins including Best of Breed in 1969, Best of Opposite Sex more than once, Winners Dog and Winners Bitch many times. In 1987 Arriba's Cherkei Oh Boy went Reserve Winners Dog from the 6-9 months puppy class.

Dr. Fickes maintains a kennel of 15 Boxers, not counting puppies, and has also bred and shown Smooth Fox Terriers for many years.

As a veterinarian and Boxer breeder, he is in great demand for ear cropping, which has become his specialty, and he is considered an expert on the subject.

BITWYN Boxers, *Andover, Massachusetts*

In 1969, Dr. and Mrs. J. S. Bitler founded this kennel in New Jersey with the purchase of a Boxer bitch, Ronel's Tiffany of Bitwyn, sired by Ch. Eldic's Landlord ex Abruzzi's Heloise.

Subsequently Tiffany was bred to Ch. Quisto's Cornerstone, a grandson of Ch. Scher-Khoun's Shadrack and Landlord. She produced two champion sons, Ch. Bitwyn's Minuteman and Ch. Bitwyn's Midnight Rider. A litter sister, a large flashy fawn, Bitwyn's Shawsheen, co-owned by Carmen Skinner and Win Bitler, was bred to Ch. Nemrac's Ali-Bey and produced Ch. Nemrac's Away We Go and Ch. Nemrac's Montego Bay.

From this litter, Sam and Win Bitler kept a plain brindle bitch, Bitwyn's New England Summer, who was bred to Ch. Vel-Kel's Big Ben,

Sire of Merit Ch. Arriba's Crescendo, sire of 10 Champions, bred by L. and C. Reardon and owned by Theodore S. Fickes, D.V.M. Shown handled by John T. Connolly.

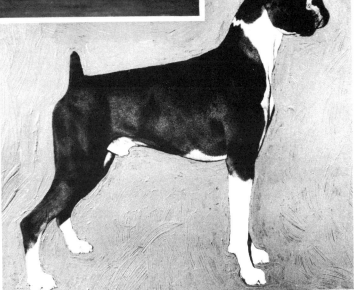

Sire of Merit Ch. Arriba's Knight Revue, sire of 15 Champions, bred and owned by Theodore S. Fickes, D.V.M.

41

producing a flashy brindle bitch who became Ch. Bitwyn's Star of Kings Pt. She was bred to Ch. Merrilane's April Fashion.

The two flashy males from this breeding both finished. Ch. Bitwyn's Orion of Chal-Vic., C.D., was co-owned by Carol Farrington and Sam Bitler. Ch. Bitwyn's North Star was purchased at 15 months by Janet Cushman, after her daughter, Allison, showed him in Junior Showmanship and earned his first point in conformation. The winning of that conformation point spurred Allison, then 12½ years of age, to compete in breed rather than Junior Showmanship.

Ch. Bitwyn's Star of Kings Pt., co-owned by Robert Norton and Sam Bitler, was bred to Ch. Moreleen's Al-le-lu-ia. This produced two champion bitches, Ch. Baroque's Dorable Dulcimer and Ch. Bitwyn's Black Magic, making Ch. Bitwyn's Star of Kings Pt. a Dam of Merit.

Ch. Bitwyn's North Star was used sparingly at stud. When bred to Ch. Bitwyn's Liberty Bell, a tall fawn male was whelped who became Ch. Bitwyn's Battle of Jericho, owned by Carole and Harry Walker. Jericho, handled to his championship by Allison Cushman, has already sired three champions. One of his progeny is Ch. Bitwyn's Aurora of Silkwood, owned by Jeff and Karen Ontell. Aurora was one of the top 10 winning Boxer bitches of 1984.

Bitwyn's Sheila of Wayward, C.D., was bred to North Star and produced American and Canadian Ch. Wayward's Opera Gloves, C.D., T.T. Opera Gloves was also handled by Allison Cushman and finished with a Group IV. Her owner, Eva Deane, earned her C.D. in the United States and Canada. Opera Gloves also obtained a high score in Temperament Testing.

Ch. Bitwyn's Beau Brummel was bred by Maureen McNulty and Win Bitler and owned by Arline Ellis. Beau was also shown by Allison, taking first in every Open class except one and winning many Bests of Breed and a Group I before Allison gave up handling to study at Boston University. Beau, since handled by Karen Ontell, has gone on to win more Bests of Breed and Group placements.

Ch. Bitwyn's Orion of Chal-Vic, C.D., finished at the Long Island Boxer Club Specialty and took Best of Breed at the Middlesex Boxer Club Specialty under Dr. Lloyd Flint with co-owner Carol Farrington handling.

At seven and one-half years of age Orion went Best of Opposite Sex at the Rhode Island B.C. Specialty under Mr. Victor Clemente.

Orion has sired five champions and many other pointed youngsters. Bitwyn's Stars and Stripes was bred to Orion and produced a flashy fawn bitch, Ch. Bitwyn's Star of Orion. She was bred to Ch. Bitwyn's Royal Flush and produced three champions, Ch. Starfire's Flame of Bitwyn, Ch. Starfire's Brandy Alexander, and Ch. Starfire's Galaxy of Chal-Vic, all handled by Allison Cushman.

Bitwyn's Runaway Sue was bred to Orion and produced Ch. Sir

The famous Best in Show winner Ch. Arriba's Prima Donna, shown winning under Judge Joseph E. Gregory, handler Robert S. Forsyth. Her Bests include Westminster 1970. Bred by V. Baribeault, she was owned by Dr. and Mrs. Pagano and Dr. Fickes.

Champion Arriba's Jambalaya with litter sister Ch. Arriba's Jubilee, sired by Ch. Flintwood's Linebacker ex Ch. Arriba's Carioca. They were bred and owned by Theodore S. Fickes, D.V.M.

43

Linden of Chal-Vic, C.D. Ch. Flying Apache Uprising was bred to Orion and whelped three champions, Ch. Brier Court's Flying Tigeress, Ch. Bitwyn's Flying Apache Chief, and Ch. Flying Apache's Little Bandit.

Bitwin Boxers was truly a family affair with Win as breeder, Allison the handler, and Sam Bitler the co-ordinator, kennel man, groomer, timekeeper and foreman. The total number of champions bred or owned by the Bitlers, and champions that were produced from both a Bitwyn sire and dam now stands at 23 through five generations. Sam and Win currently own four Boxers.

BOXELLA Kennels, *Cincinnati, Ohio*

During his service with the U.S. Army in World War II, Joe Heine travelled to Augsburg, Germany, where he bought a lovely Boxer bitch, Bella v. Steingarten, daughter of three times Reichsieger Karlo v.d. Wolfsschlucht (later purchased by Larry Downey) ex Siegerin Cilli v.d. Burg Hohenzollern, a daughter of Reichsieger Ajax v.d. Holderburg, owned by Herr Schubert of Augsburg. Ajax and Karlo were considered the two finest Boxers in Germany at that time. Joe Heine wanted to buy Ajax as well, but his owner refused to part with him. Many Boxers were being killed in the war, and Herr Schubert was determined to save Ajax. Nonetheless, Joe Heine remained greatly impressed by Ajax and Karlo and wanted to breed Boxers like them with Bella as his foundation bitch.

Joe's sister, Hermine, came up with the kennel prefix of "Boxella." Bella's call name was "Boxi" and she added the "ella' from her registered name. The name "Boxella" has been registered with the American Kennel Club ever since.

Over the years, Boxella has always kept the best bitches and outcrossed to many sires to create a genetic pool of the structural qualities that the Boxer standard demands. Joe Heine considers that much of Boxella's present success goes back to his early champions, namely the "Roaring R" litter. Rio Rita of Cross Acres, a Ch. Jered's Sovereign daughter, was bred to Ch. Dempsey's Copper Gentleman producing the "R" litter—Ch. Boxella's Rodger, Ch. Boxella's Ricardo, Ch. Boxella's Roxella and another fine male who was never shown.

The Central Indiana Boxer Club Specialty, judged by Robert Waters, proved to be a Boxella family outing. Rodger won Best of Opposite Sex, and his littermates, Ricardo and Roxella, each won five point majors.

Ch. Boxella's Nonita, sired by Spellbinder, was bred to Ricardo and produced Ch. Boxella's Wand O'Magic and Ch. Boxella's Wyatt Earp. Wyatt Earp sired Ch. Malabar's Anthony Earp, who became a top winning Boxer in Canada. Unfortunately, he died of cancer at an early age.

Ch. Boxella's Wand O'Magic was bred to Ch. Wedge Hollow's Hasty Harry and produced three champions—Ch. Boxella's Lustig, a Best in Show winner, Ch. Boxella's Locket and Ch. Boxella's Aquarius.

Ch. Bitwyn's Beau Brummel, a Group winner sired by Ch. Starfire's Brandy Alexander ex Bitwyn's Trinket of Maceire, is owned by Dr. and Mrs. J.S. Bitler and handled by daughter Allison.

Ch. Boxella's O'Samson, sire of six American Champions and Scandinavian Ch. Wedge Hollow's Sam's Son, a Best in Show winner. Breeder/Owner: Joseph Heine, Boxella Kennels, Reg.

Group winner Ch. Boxella's O'Samson produced Ch. Boxella's Mar-Ray's Jeanette ex Ray and Mary Freer's Ch. Mar-Ray's Jeanine.

Joe Heine considers Ch. Boxella's Hotrod to be one of his most outstanding champions, along with his litter sister, Ch. Boxella's Heide. Ch. Boxella's Marc Anthony, Ch. Boxella's Leonardo Da Vinchi and more recently Ch. Boxella's Brigitte are other favorites of Joe's. Ch. Boxella's Blitzkrieg Warlord, sired by import Xan v. Hasseler-Hof ex Boxella's Peggy Ann is the most recent Boxella champion.

In 1982 Joe Heine went to Holland and on to the *Jahrsieger* Show (Annual Championship show) held in Bremen, Germany. Again impressed with the high quality and close adherence to the standard of the European Boxers, Boxella Kennels started to import some really excellent males. The first was *Jugendsieger* (Young Champion) Zethos v. Adeltrots, bred by Jan de Vries of Holland, then Aktuell v. Okeler Forst, bred by Ralf Brinkman of Germany and lastly Xan v. Hasseler-Hof, bred by F. J. Grumer of Germany. Aktuell and Xan were sired by German Siegers Xanthos and Uhtz v. Bereler Ries.

Joe Heine became an American Kennel Club approved judge of Boxers in 1950. He has judged throughout the U.S.A. (including the American Boxer Club Specialty), Canada, Finland, Sweden and Australia. Being an artist and sculptor, with an early interest in horses, Joe Heine has developed an eye for balance and structure which he feels has helped him as both a breeder and a judge.

Boxella Kennels now has about 15 Boxers and has finished 35 champions to date.

BOX M Boxers, *Kailua, Hawaii,* and Other Hawaiian Kennels

In 1948, while living in California, Lois Matthews acquired her first Boxer. He was an Utz grandson ex a Sirrah Crest bitch. Then Lois and her husband moved to Hawaii in 1955. She has whelped many litters, and the house and kennel currently hold nine Boxers, six of whom are champions. Lois Matthews has judged the American Boxer Club Futurity in 1970 and many other Futurities in the United States. She has also judged in Australia, England, and twice in Japan but, by her own choice, is not an approved A.K.C. judge. A well-known writer and established breeder, Lois Matthews prefers to talk about Hawaii.

In 1912, Hawaii established a quarantine of 120 days for all carnivores entering the state. The basic quarantine fee is $466 for dogs and $412 for cats. Moreover, any veterinary attention, special services, medication for heartworm (which is essential) is extra. Visiting is allowed daily, except holidays, and "sponsors" may be obtained if owners are not present. The quarantine station, which is on the island of Oahu, handles about 3800 dogs annually, many of them belonging to military families.

Ch. Box M. Adonis of Seawest with handler Sue Gates. The top winning Boxer in Hawaii for 1986, he is owned by Gail Lindsey.

Sire of Merit Ch. Dormac's Gunslinger fathered 10 champions. He was bred and owned by Ramon and Dorothy McNulty.

This naturally creates a major problem for anyone dedicated to breeding and showing purebred dogs in Hawaii. However, Hawaii's Boxer fanciers are as determined as their dogs, and anyone who has ever watched a Boxer figure out how to undo his gate latch knows how determined that is.

The Boxer Club of Hawaii has held over 700 successful events. There are two all-breed clubs on Oahu and one on the island of Hawaii, each of which gives two shows a year. Including Specialties, all of this adds up to about eight opportunities for championship points annually—less than many mainland exhibitors can find in a month.

More than 50 Boxers have completed championships in Hawaii since the first Specialty in 1946. Five Boxers have won Best-in-Show over other breeds, Ch. Wilhemina Sue, Ch. Jondem's Makiki (twice), Elharlen's Gambling Man, Ch. Box M Royal Hawaiian, and Ch. Box M Tropic Storm. Only Wilhemina Sue and Royal Hawaiian were island bred.

The biggest problem caused by quarantine is maintaining and upgrading the quality of the Boxers when the sires to whom one would like to breed are on the mainland. In the future, artificial insemination with shipped semen may be the answer, but to date all attempts to breed Hawaiian Boxers by this method have failed. In the meantime, breeding kennels import the best Boxers they can, and several outstanding mainland kennels are represented.

Donna Sugihara, Pup-P-Luv Boxers, in Hilo, has a brindle male, Ch. Salgray's Samurai; Lois and George Trist, Kini's Boxers, have a brindle male, Ch. Huffand's Rite Nice, and Lois Matthews of Box M Boxers has imported several mainland lines. She also owns Ch. Merrilane's Holiday Fashion, who is kept on the mainland.

An outstanding producer in Hawaii was Ch. Box M Royal Hawaiian (five champions), sired by Ch. My-R's Imperial, who visited Hawaii on a six-month "loan."

Donna and Rick Keefer, of Seawest Boxers, own Ch. Box M Irving de Keefer, the leading living sire with three champion offspring to date. Bo and Gail Lindsey of Koawood Boxers have a male, Ch. Box M Adonis, who was the top winning Boxer in Hawaii in 1986.

Ch. Salgray's Argos of Memoryland, passing through quarantine on his way to Guntop Kennels in Sydney, Australia, sired a litter with an Irving daughter, Seawest Pretty in Pink. Two males from this litter offer high hopes for the future.

DORMAC Boxers, *St. Joseph, Missouri*

In 1949 Ramon and Dorothy McNulty purchased their first Boxer as a pet. Two years later they purchased their foundation bitch, Lee-Har's Sweetie Pie, sired by Heinrich of Bel Air ex Zelda of K Mitch, a line-bred great-granddaughter of Lustig. Sweetie was bred to Lee-Har's Thisisit, a son of Ch. Jered's Spellbinder, and produced their first champion. Ch. Dormac's Parade Socks finished in 1954 and was a group winner.

A repeat breeding produced a brindle dog—Ch. Dormac's Quite Unique, and a brindle bitch—Ch. Dormac's Royal Rhapsody. Royal Rhapsody became a multi-group winner, Specialty Best in Show and All-Breed B.I.S. winner.

Royal Rhapsody was bred to Ch. Captain Lookout of Thorhall and produced the brindle bitch, Ch. Dormac's Delightful Rhapsody. Royal Rhapsody was later bred to Ch. Patcha's Buccaneer and produced the brindle dog, Ch. Dormac's Keynote.

Ch. Dormac's Delightful Rhapsody produced two champions, but her most noteworthy offspring was Dormac's Risque sired by Ch. Salgray's Ovation. Risque was never shown due to a leg injury but was bred to four different males and produced a champion by each of them, making her a Dam of Merit. The most notable of her offspring was Ch. Dormac's Gunslinger, by Ch. Salgray's Ambush. Although not campaigned extensively and used sparingly at stud, he produced ten champions, making him a Sire of Merit.

Risque was bred to Ch. Salgray's Double Play and produced an outstanding male, Salgray's Zipcode of Dormac, who was Reserve Winners Dog at the 1971 American Boxer Club Specialty Show at the tender age of six months. Unfortunately Zipcode succumbed to an insect bite before reaching a year of age but left several champion get. Zipcode's littermate, Ch. Salgray's Zetta of Dormac, was bred to Ch. Salgray's Ambush and produced Ch. Salgray's Royal Flush, a Sire of Merit.

Zetta's next breeding was to Ch. Salgray's Bojangles and produced Salgray's Promise to Dormac, who was owned by Mr. and Mrs. McNulty. Promise was bred to Gunslinger, producing three champions. Ch. Dormac's Quite a Rhapsody was purchased by Mr. and Mrs. Rufus Burleson, and, when she finished her championship, she was sold to James Denney who bred her to Ch. Marburl's Joshua producing Ch. Marburl's Maverick, a Sire of Merit, who was also a multi-group and Best in Show winner.

Ramon and Dorothy McNulty bred on a very limited basis, since both were full-time handlers. Nonetheless, Dormac Kennels produced 18 champions and several more pointed youngsters. When the McNultys became A.K.C. approved judges, in 1982, they had to sell their boarding kennel but remained in St. Joseph. Currently there are three Boxers in the household, and they plan to continue breeding on a limited scale.

GLENNROE Boxers, *Danville, California*

Like many novices, Zona S. Grupe acquired her first Boxer on a breeding contract. Bea Goodman introduced her to the breed and co-

Dam of Merit Ch. Glennroe Opensesame, bred by Zona and Glenn Grupe. She was purchased as a foundation bitch by Gene and Jennifer Tellier, Telstar Boxers.

Ch. Glennroe Rum Runner, sired by Ch. Telstar's Front Runner ex Glennroe Elated Echo O'Dolor. Breeder: Dolores Schell. Owner/handler: Zona Grupe, Danville, CA.

owned Beagood Fantasy, sired by Ch. Los Arboles King Kong, a Bang Away son, ex Beagood Fan Dancer, a Bang Away daughter.

With very limited showing, Fantasy quickly acquired several wins, including a Best of Breed from the classes, but was never finished. Zona Grupe remembers the pain of losing Fantasy's first litter, but, in 1963, she bred her again to Ch. Cloudland Citation. This breeding produced Ch. Glennroe Christina, the first of 23 Glennroe champions.

Glennroe breeds on a small scale, since all the dogs are house dogs. Usually there are only two or three Boxers at home for showing and breeding. Zona Grupe is adamant that the key to the Glennroe success has been a strong line of champion bitches. The only male kept and used in her breeding program was Ch. Glennroe Eldorado, sired by Ch. Canzonet's Music Man ex Ch. Glennroe Christina. Eldorado sired four champions including two Dams of Merit—Ch. Glennroe Ingenue ex Glennroe Dulzura and Ch. Glennroe Alexandria ex Glennroe Our Golden Gadabout, C.D.

Zona Grupe is extremely proud of Ch. Glennroe Gimlet, the first recipient of the Charlotte Brayshaw Award for the most wins in the Bred by Exhibitor bitch classes. Zona enjoys showing her own dogs and feels that she would have missed some of her fondest memories if she had not done so.

Beyond the rewards of breeding and exhibiting dogs, Zona Grupe feels that helping a novice get started is also very rewarding. She is particularly pleased with the success of the Telstar line which began with an excellent foundation bitch, Ch. Glennroe Opensesame. When Gene and Jennifer Tellier came to look at eight-week-old "Chelsea," they had only a mild interest in showing and in fact were torn between a Boxer or a Golden Retriever. Fortunately, they purchased Chelsea, who easily finished her championship and went on to become a Dam of Merit. Gene and Jennifer have bred 13 champions including a Sire of Merit, Ch. Telstar's Highflyer, sire of the 1983 American Boxer Club Best of Breed Winner, Ch. Richaire's Domino. Like Zona Grupe, Jennifer Tellier is also an enthusiastic owner/handler.

1986 was an exciting year for Glennroe Boxers. They finished four dogs—Ch. Glennroe Cognac of Crown Hill, Ch. Glennroe Gin Fizz, Ch. Glennroe Chardonnay and Ch. Glennroe Rum Runner, a successful winner and sire in California.

HERNDON'S Boxers, *Jacksonville, Oregon*

In 1951, Freddie and James Herndon purchased a fawn Boxer bitch for their son, Jimmy, who was then five years of age. The Boxer, Stormy, lived to be 13 years old and was Jimmy's constant companion.

In 1965, Mr. and Mrs. Herndon bought their first show bitch, Bilger's

Lady of Leisure, sired by Salgray's Country Boy ex Bilger's Dixie Belle. Wendy gained her championship and was bred to Ch. Salgray's Flying High. This breeding produced Ch. Herndon's Desert Flyer, who became a Dam of Merit and American Boxer Club Dam of the Year in 1977. Ch. Bilger's Lady of Leisure was then bred to Ch. Holly Lane's Winter Forecast, who produced Herndon's Black Magic. These three became Herndon's Boxers foundation bitches.

Desert Flyer was bred to Ch. Holly Lane's Winter Forecast producing Ch. Herndon's Peerless Panda, who finished at the American Boxer Club Regional Show in 1977 and became a Sire of Merit (seven champions). Panda sired Ch. Herndon's Pure Magic ex Herndon's Black Magic, and Pure Magic also became a Sire of Merit (seven champions).

Herndon's Black Magic also was a top producer. She was the dam of Ch. Herndon's Pure Magic, Ch. Herndon's Magic Moment and Ch. Herndon's Peerless Perfection, all of whom were sired by Panda.

Mrs. Herndon is very proud of the fact that Ch. Herndon's Pure Magic produced two tri-champions by Lady Calisen Kayy, C.D., namely American, Canadian and Mexican Ch. Jensen's Pure Magic O'Herndon and American, Canadian and Mexican Ch. Jensens Chenin K. Blanc.

Pure Magic was also bred to Kar-Neil's Karma Kelly and produced the "Kelly Girls"—Ch. Vierra's Magic Star, Ch. Barisle's Happy Holiday II and Ch. Kar-Neil's Magic Gift—making Karma Kelly a Dam of Merit.

There are still five Boxers living at home with Freddie and James Herndon, who still breed and show on a limited basis. Mrs. Herndon co-owns the most recent Herndon champion—Ch. Herndon's Hershey Barre of GW, who lives with co-owner Pat Boyd in Long Grove, Illinois.

HOLLY LANE Boxers, *Topeka, Kansas*

Dr. and Mrs. E. A. McClintock were given a flashy fawn spayed Boxer, Jinx, as a gift when they purchased a house. Jinx became a devoted companion and had her own blanket near Eileen's desk in Dr. McClintock's office.

When Jinx died, Dr. McClintock decided he would like to own a champion Boxer, a thought that had never occurred to Eileen. Luckily, they lived near Mr. and Mrs. Garich who owned Ch. Jered's Spellbinder, and they were able to buy an eight-week-old fawn bitch, Sarazan's Love Story, sired by a Spellbinder son.

Love Story was bred to Sire of Merit Ch. Flintwood's Sundowner and produced the first Holly Lane champion, Ch. Holly Lane's Cookie. Cookie was bred to Sire of Merit Ch. Brayshaw's Masquerader producing the famous Wind litter in May, 1966. The male, Ch. Holly Lane's Wildwind, became a Sire of Merit with nine champions to his credit. His three sisters all finished. They were Ch. Holly Lane's Wind Siren, Ch. Holly Lane's Wind Snow, and Ch. Holly Lane's Windstorm, who herself produced 11

Dam of Merit Ch. Herndon's Desert Flyer, shown winning at the American Boxer Club 1970 Specialty under judge Mrs. R. C. Harris, with handler Dick Baum.

Ch. Holly Lane's Cookie, first homebred Champion for Holly Lane Boxers, is shown finishing her Championship under Theodore Wurmser, handler Eugene Haupt.

champions. Of these 11 champions, eight were from two litters sired by Ch. Scher-Khoun's Meshac. Ch. Holly Lane's Inherit the Wind, Sire of Merit with 11 champions, was owner-handled by Eileen McClintock to Best in Show.

Ch. Holly Lane's Prairie Chief, whelped October 2, 1979, was sired by Inherit the Wind ex Holly Lane's Taskaloosa and is Eileen McClintock's oldest dog.

Dr. McClintock died in 1980, but Holly Lane continues to produce champion Boxers, with a total of 44 to date. The latest is Ch. Holly Lane's Eagle Hendenbrand, who finished from the Bred-by-Exhibitor class with three Bests of Breed and Group placements to his credit.

Mrs. McClintock enjoys the exhilaration of the competition but hopes to find more time for the joy of breeding. Currently, there are 15 Boxers (not counting a puppy or two) at Holly Lane Kennels.

HUFFAND Boxers, *Miamisburg, Ohio and Gibraltar, Michigan*

In 1971, Carole Connolly and Linda Huffman formed a partnership called Huffand Boxers. Their first purchase was a six-week-old bitch, Huffand's All Spice. Linda showed her to her championship in 1972. Due to an untimely death at an early age, Spice left no offspring.

In 1974 Carole Connolly bred her bitch, Arriba's Ultimate, to Linda Huffman's dog, Ch. Arriba's High Hopes. This breeding produced the prolific Ch. Huffand's Charade.

In 1976 Charade was bred to her sire, High Hopes, and produced the winning "High" litter. This litter consisted of four flashy champions—Ch. Huffand's Highland Fling, Ch. Huffand's High Society, Ch. Huffand's High Test and Ch. Huffand's High Time.

In 1979 Charade was bred to Ch. Benjomin of Five T's, producing Ch. Huffand's Irish Rebel and Ch. Huffand's Irish Spring.

Arriba's Ultimate and Ch. Arriba's High Hopes, purchased from Dr. Ted Fickes (Flintwood lines), and Ch. Benjomin of Five T's are the founders of Huffand Boxers.

Since 1975, Huffand has produced and finished 25 champions, and these champions have produced 55 more champions.

In 1978 Huffand received the American Boxer Club's award for the kennel breeding the most champions and also the award for the kennel finishing the most champions. Arriba's High Hopes became a Dam of Merit with five champions, and Ch. Huffand's Charade became a Dam of Merit with six champions. Huffand also produced three Sires of Merit, Ch. Huffand's Irish Rebel (seven champions); Ch. Huffand's Nice Enough (15 champions) and Ch. Wincaster's Tigger of Huffand (nine champions).

Linda Huffman is a successful professional Boxer handler, finishing many dogs for other breeders.

Ch. Holly Lane's Inherit The Wind, Sire of Merit with 11 Champions. Shown with breeder/owner, Eileen McClintock.

Ch. Holly Lane's Eagle Helden-brand, sired by Ch. Holly Lane's Prairie Chief, finished from the Bred-By-Exhibitor class. He was bred by Eileen McClintock and Elvinia Heldebrand. Shown with owner Eileen McClintock winning under Charles Mulock.

Sire of Merit Ch. Happy Ours Fortune de Jacquet produced 25 Champions. He was sired by Ch. Merrilane's April Holiday ex Jacquet's Painted Lady. Breeder/owner: Richard Tomita.

American, Japanese, Canadian & Bermudian Ch. Jacquet's Urko (left) shown with handler Marylou Wilderson and Group-winning bitch Ch. Jacquet's Garnier shown with Bernie Schwerdtfeger. Judge is Eleanor Haeberle of Eldic Kennels fame.

JACQUET Boxers, *Paramus, New Jersey*

In 1972, Jacquet Boxers was founded by Richard Tomita, who had grown up with Boxers, and his partner, Bill Scolnik. Bill has a great interest in antique clocks and watches, and their first Boxer was named Jacquet Droz after an 18th century French clockmaker. Their second Boxer was Ronel's Jacquet Satie, sired by Ch. Eldic's Landlord ex Abruzzi's Heloise, who became their foundation bitch. She was subsequently bred to Ch. Rocky of Shawnee Trail. The litter produced an exciting brindle dog, Ch. Jacquet's Ronel Micah, who became "Boxer Review's" Top Boxer in the East. Unfortunately he was killed in a tragic car accident and sired only three litters. A puppy from the first litter, Ch. Jacquet's Mirah of Micah, played an important part in Jacquet's success.

Mirah of Micah produced the Best of Winners at the American Boxer Club's 1979 Specialty Show. His second breeding was to a Ch. Eldic's Landlord Daughter, who produced the dam of Ch. Jacquet's Candy Dancer. Candy Dancer was bred to Ch. Happy Ours Fortune de Jacquet and produced American, Japanese, Bermudian and Canadian Ch. Jacquet's Urko, one of Jacquet's best stud dogs. His third breeding to a bitch owned by Florence and Ed Wilderson produced Dam of Merit Jacquet's Perigal, who in turn produced Ch. Jacquet's Brass Idol.

A repeat breeding of Satie to Rocky produced Ch. Jacquet's Zephan, who proved to be the true foundation dog for Jacquet. Zephan was a very gentle dog with an outstanding temperament who shared Rick's home.

Around this time, Tom and Barbara O'Neil were closing their Barday Kennel and gave Ch. Barday's Chatterbox to Rick Tomita. Her friendly disposition made her a natural partner for Zephan, and her strong line breeding brought Jacquet excellent heads and bites.

Rick Tomita and Bill Scolnik are quick to point to several breeders who were extremely helpful when they began—Richard and Mavis Thornberg, Ed and Florence Wilderson, Ron and Eleanor Erickson, Eleanor Haeberle, Liane Dimitroff and Gerry Broadt. With this circle of friends, a few foundation Boxers, and sound advice ("Sell your best puppies, and don't show against them"), Jacquet Boxers began its ascent in the Boxer world.

Jacquet has bred over 75 champions in the United States and over 117 worldwide. Each year since 1982, Jacquet has won the coveted American Boxer Club award for the kennel breeding the most champions. Each year since 1981, Jacquet has won the equally prestigious award for the kennel making the most champions.

Jacquet has produced three Sires of Merit, Ch. Jacquet's Zephan (seven champions), Ch. Happy Ours Fortune de Jacquet (25 champions) and Ch. Jacquet Brass Idol (nine champions). Jacquet has had two Dams of Merit, Ch. Jacquet's Jolie and Jacquet's Perigal. Jacquet has produced

Dam of Merit Ch. Jacquet's Jolie at 10½ years. The matriarch of the house dogs at Richard Tomlita's and William Scolnik's Jacquet Kennels.

American, Canadian and Mexican Ch. Marburl's Joshua, Sire of Merit, producer of 23 Champions, shown with handler E. B. Johnson with Mike Millan at right. Breeders/owners: Rufus and Mary Frances Burleson, Dallas, Texas.

many international champions including American, Japanese, Canadian, and Bermudian Ch. Jacquet's Urko and American, Japanese, Canadian, and Bermudian Ch. Agassiz.

The top winning Boxer in Brazil is Ch. Jacquet's Gaspard ad Summus, and the top winning Boxer in India is Ch. Jacquet's Canara Coast Casey. In addition, Rick Tomita and Bill Scolnik are proud of the several obedience titles earned by Jacquet Boxers.

In 1977, when Rick saw Ch. Merrilane's April Fashion (Punki), he decided to bring him into the Jacquet line. Many champions have been produced from this outcross.

In 1979, Jacquet's Brass Idol was Winners Dog at the American Boxer Club Specialty Show and to add to the thrill, Jacquet's Shana of Talisman was Winners Bitch. Both later became champions.

About the same time, Jacquet's Painted Lady, a Zephan daughter, was taken to the West Coast and bred to another superb Merrilane dog, Ch. Merrilane's April Holiday (Punki's litter brother). This produced Jacquet's pre-eminent sire to date, Ch. Happy Ours Fortune de Jacquet (Caleb). Caleb's progeny have included American, Japanese, Canadian, and Bermudian Ch. Jacquet's Urko (top winning dog in Japan with 17 Best in Show awards); Ch. Jacquet's Garnier (#5 Boxer bitch 1983); Ch. Jacquet's Fleur-de-Lys (Best in Show and Specialty winner and one of the top ten Boxers in 1986); Ch. Kojak Von San Remo (#1 Boxer dog in 1983 and multiple Best in Show and Specialty winner); Ch. Arrow's Sky High (multiple Best in Show winner); and Jacquet's Fleur-de-Noel (Winners Bitch at the 1987 American Boxer Club National Specialty over a record entry).

Jacquet Boxers are usually seen on the East Coast but not exclusively. The telephone rings at all hours with news of American wins, and letters bring news of international wins. Rick Tomita has created a "Jacquet family" which celebrates every Jacquet win. Rick and Bill have also aided Boxer Rescue, particularly on the East Coast and in England.

Jacquet Boxers have been featured in calendars, books, including Carol Lea Benjamin's best-selling *Mother Knows Best*, T.V. and print commercials, jewelry, fashion magazines, and catalogues.

Six generations of Boxers live at Jacquet house and kennels, which are a hive of activity. Behind Rick Tomita's personality and salesmanship are the patience and astuteness of his less visible partner, Bill Scolnik. It takes a team to forge the kind of success Jacquet Boxers has achieved.

MARBURL Boxers, *Dallas, Texas*

In 1957 Mary Frances and Rufus Burleson bought their first Boxer, a fawn male named Fritz. Their next Boxer was a Bang Away grandson, Hans Graf Schnultze, who proved to be a disappointing show dog. Study and observation helped the Burlesons realize they needed help if they were to succeed in showing dogs.

Their mentors were Bob and Aimee Acklen, who took the time and patience to explain the fundamentals. Their third Boxer puppy was a brindle male, Acklands Marco Polo. The Texas Circuit soon had a new novice handler and entry as the pup travelled far and wide. The excitement, travel, and ribbons were thrilling. The next logical step was a well-bred brindle bitch to start a new dynasty.

The Acklens agreed to sell them a flashy bitch if their Ch. Candy Princess had a litter by Ch. Salgray's Fashion Plate. The breeding was supervised at a discreet distance by Larry Downey and took place in the ladies room at the Texas K.C. show. The only puppy bitch became Marburl Boxers's first champion, American and Mexican Ch. Ackland's Fashion Belle. She started her show career by going Best Puppy in Atlanta under Dr. R. C. Harris. The thrill of her wins from British Columbia to Mexico City set the stage for many generations of Marburl Boxers to come.

Early breedings to Capriana (John and Patsy Connolly) and Holly Lane Boxers (Dr. and Mrs. McClintock) were building blocks to fix type and improve the line. The elegance of Salgray, the soundness of Ackland, and the movement of Holly Lane helped form the early Marburl Boxer.

The most important early stud selection was Moreleen Goneau's young Ch. Moreleen's Al-le-lu-ia, sired by Ch. Salgray's Ambush ex Merwin Hill's Flare Up. Marburl's Fireball was bred to him and produced two outstanding dogs—American, Canadian, and Mexican Ch. Marburl's Joshua, Sire of Merit, and his litter brother, American and Canadian Ch. Marburl's Jason.

Joshua was introduced to the fancy by E. B. (Johnny) Johnson, who handled him far and wide. Joshua won Best of Breed at the 1976 American Regional Specialty held in Denver and also at the 1977 Regional in San Francisco. He won 27 Boxer Specialties, took more than 150 Bests of Breed, and two all-breed Bests in Show. He produced 23 champions, many of whom were producers of champions.

One of Joshua's most fortunate breedings was to Wesley and Ann Tomhaven's Ch. Wesan's Dark Apache Miss. A puppy bitch named Penny from that litter went to live with the Burlesons. She became Ch. Marburl's Rahab of Wesan, who won the American Boxer Club Specialty Shows in 1979 and 1980. She won Best in Show on six occasions and garnered over 100 Bests of Breed and Boxer Specialties. Penny's daughter, Ch. Marburl's Scarlet Cord, became a Dam of Merit.

The blood of Fashion Hint became infused into the Marburl line when the Burlesons purchased Ch. Jo-Jac's Magic Moment, bred by Mr. and Mrs. Jack Loughlin. She became a Dam of Merit, and her offspring combined well with Joshua. Other infusions came from Indian Bend (Kent and Nancy Durfee), Niklof (Paul and Shirley Folkins) and Baldr (Robert Conrad).

Ch. Marburl's Rahab of Wesan, all breed Best in Show winner and Best of Breed at the 1979 and 1980 American Boxer Club Specialty shows. Breeders: Wesley and Ann Tomhave. Owners: Rufus and Mary Frances Burleson, Houston, Texas.

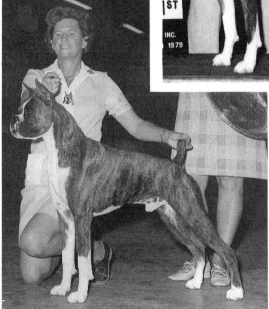

Sire of Merit Ch. Merrilane's Holiday Fashion, producer of 10 Champions, was bred by Eleanor Linderholm and owned by Lois Matthews.

The Marburl banner is carried now by a Joshua son, Ch. Marburl's Maverick, ex Ch. Dormac's Quite A Rhapsody. Sire of three champions, his offspring continue to bring spark to kennels across the country. In all, Marburl Boxers have won over 20 Annual Awards from the American Boxer Club. Rufus Burleson is now an approved A.K.C. judge and has officiated in Canada and Mexico and at the American Boxer Club Specialty show in 1985.

Rufus and Mary Frances Burleson believe the years of fun, showing, breeding, and pedigree planning, were made possible by the help of many friends and associates. Johnny and Joyce Johnson, Marshall Comerer, Jr., and Houston and Toddie Clark have been the professional handlers who made ambitious plans work. An army of friends in the American Boxer Club and at Specialty Clubs around the country have made it all worthwhile for the Burlesons. Mary Frances and Rufus treasure the friendships made along the way and a legion of memories, some happy and some sad but all part of building a successful kennel. They look forward to the challenge of the future.

MERRILANE Boxers, Reg. and WOODCREST Kennels, Reg.,
La Selva Beach, California

One of the most successful Boxer breeders of the present day is Eleanor Linderholm Wood, owner of Merrilane Boxers.

Known to her friends as "Ellie," her devotion to the breed developed in her early teens. A friend of her mother's had a Boxer bitch from Fred Hamm's Mahderf Kennel, who needed summer care when the family travelled. Ellie became a summer dog sitter, and this opportunity sparked her interest and career in Boxers. The second summer, the bitch was joined by a male puppy, who was later donated to the Seeing Eye in Morristown, New Jersey. He reportedly was the first Boxer and one of the earliest males trained to guide the blind.

In the autumn of the same year, Ellie's parents purchased a Boxer bitch for her, Mahderf's Lucky Chance. When she was bred, the resulting litter's ears were cropped by Al and Mary Cousins (Rexob Boxers) then of Yonkers, New York. Al and Mary were about to become kennel managers at Mazelaine, and they persuaded Jack and Mazie Wagner to invite their new friend to work for them. Ellie jumped at the opportunity and worked at Mazelaine for two summers absorbing all phases of Boxer lore.

During these two summers, Ellie met Carl and Alice Wood. They were quick to solicit her help in training their newly acquired Mazelaine puppy, and she showed their first Woodcrest Boxer for them, Robin Hood of Mazelaine, and also finished their first champion, Ysolde of Mazelaine. From this beginning, Carl and Alice Wood developed their highly respected Woodcrest line of Boxers, which boasts of 26 homebred champions.

Dam of Merit Ch. Exhuberant of Woodcrest, by Ch. Philanderer of Woodcrest ex Eldic's Onederful, shown winning Best of Breed at Middlesex Boxer Club 1963 handled by Alice Wood. Judge (left) is Joseph E. Gregory; Scott Rutherford (Rococo Boxers) presents the trophy.

Sire of Merit Ch. Philanderer of Woodcrest, by Ch. Eldic's Darius ex Katydid of Woodcrest. Bred by and owned by Woodcrest Kennels, Reg.

63

Carl and Alice Wood are both well known for their many years of dedication to the breed and their contributions to the dog fancy at large and especially to the American Boxer Club. Both have been (and Carl still is) approved A.K.C. judges.

It had always been Ellie's ambition to become a veterinarian. She took up pre-med studies at Cornell University in an effort to obtain a solid background for veterinary medicine. However, when World War II ended, the returning veterans were offered the first chances for openings in the Veterinary College. Women applicants were barely considered.

During the summers between her terms at Cornell, Ellie joined the Henry Larks, working and handling Boxers for them at their extensive Meritaire Kennels in Pennsylvania. When she left Cornell, unable to get into veterinary school, Ellie returned to Meritaire on a full-time basis. From this point on, she developed her own self-taught veterinary skills, as the Larks were most generous in providing equipment and supplies.

Ellie worked closely with well-known professional ear croppers at Meritaire and improved her own cropping skills. She also learned much about the business management of a large kennel and a great deal more about handling. Since the Larks were very seriously committed to breeding excellent Boxers, Ellie was able to put into practice what she had learned at Mazelaine about breeding principles. At the same time, she gained experience raising and caring for quality individuals of the breed. While she was in the Larks' employ, Ellie had the fun of showing Ch. Yller of Mazelaine to her many Best in Show awards.

In 1947, Eleanor married and only dabbled in Boxers. After having daughters Ann in 1948 and Gail in 1950, she handled a fair amount from 1951 to 1954. She also worked as head assistant to a Silver Spring, Maryland, veterinarian. Together they cropped ears for a number of Boxer breeders in the area. Ellie's experience in the veterinary field continued to grow.

Following her divorce in 1954, Ellie returned to Mazelaine, working for a time at the Texas Kennel, and then in the Chicago area. Later, Ellie moved to Nevada, where she could concentrate on raising her daughters. Of course, there were Boxers with her, and she was drafted by Carson City to head the newly created, one-person Department of Dog Control. This proved to be a controversial job, as the residents had mixed feelings about the much needed new animal control ordinance.

A friend in Carson City bred a lovely Boxer bitch to Frances Lowman's Impressario son, Ch. Space Man of Jofra, and Ellie bought a fawn puppy who became Ch. Merrilane's Silver Dollar. He finished in 17 months and along the way went Best of Breed three times from the classes over Specials. Silver Dollar won 11 Bests of Breed, including the East Bay Specialty Show, before Ellie retired him from competition. Ellie had begun handling again and could not keep him out against clients' dogs.

In 1968, Eleanor married Victor Linderholm in Carson City, Nevada. They moved to California, where Ellie started the Boxer kennel of her dreams and became a full-time professional handler. She finished a great many champions and gained an imposing array of top awards for her clients. In two and a half years, she also finished eight homebred Merrilane champions. Silver Dollar's daughter, Merrilane Mad Passion, C.D., became the kennel's foundation bitch producing ten American champions, placing her in position as the second top producing bitch in the history of the breed.

Between July, 1971, and July, 1987, 55 homebred Merrilane champions gained their American titles and many more championships in other countries. Merrilane champions have been sold to Japan, Taiwan, Indonesia, Brazil, Spain, Norway, and South Africa.

Ellie is proud that Merrilane bloodlines have strongly influenced the success of a number of kennels in this country, the most notable being Jacquet Boxers, owned by Richard Tomita and William Scolnik.

Victor Linderholm died in 1977 and Alice Wood passed away in 1980. Eleanor Linderholm and Carl Wood were married in 1981. Since Carl is an American Kennel Club approved judge, Ellie is no longer eligible to handle dogs professionally. She has retired to breeding and showing her own dogs and continues to enjoy motor homing to shows all over the country with Carl and their Boxers. Their dedicated efforts for the benefit of the breed are reflected in their separate capacities with the American Boxer Club. Carl was recently elected to the position of Honorary Vice President, and together they both have helped restructure the proposed revisions to the Boxer standard. Carl has also worked on the By-Laws Committee and serves as Historian to the American Boxer Club.

MY-R Boxers, *Rockford, Illinois*

In 1942, Lorraine Meyer was given a Boxer puppy, an Easter gift which has never been equalled. Lorraine and her late husband, Ken, loved their new pet, Elsa v. Zorn, and wanted to learn more about the breed.

Lorraine and Ken soon discovered that the puppy had all the loving attributes of a Boxer but was a poor physical specimen of the breed.

Entered in obedience, the puppy earned her C.D.X. but was never very enthusiastic about training. After telling her what to do and how to do it, they learned that Boxers are best when *asked* to do things for their owners. Lorraine advocates "working *with* the dog and *not* in competition with the will of the dog. They certainly love to please, but resent regimentation and may well become stubborn." This philosophy helped her earn three C.D.X.'s and two U.D.'s with her Boxers.

Eighteen champions bear the My-R prefix, with two others bred at

Ch. My-R's Rain Maker, CD, bred by Lorraine Meyer and owned by Dr. Donald Dye.

Ch. My-R's Marquette, by Ch. Salgray's Fashion Plate ex Ch. Salgray's Cricket, bred by Lorraine Meyer and H. Mandell and owned by Frank and Helen Kobielak.

My-R on a co-ownership. Of the remaining three champions at My-R, two were bred by a My-R sire.

In 1960, the third My-R litter produced three champions from a Ch. Marjack's Golden Windjammer daughter, My-R's Tessar, C.D., bred to her grandfather, Ch. Captain Lookout of Thorhall. One puppy, My-R's Magic Spell, was Best Puppy in Futurity at the 1961 American Boxer Club Specialty. After finishing her championship, My-R's Magic Spell was bred to Ch. Salgray's Fashion Plate and produced Ch. My-R's Brag About, who became the Best Puppy in the 1965 American Boxer Club Specialty.

Ch. My-R's Brag About, C.D., was bred to Ch. Salgray's Fashion Plate and produced Ch. My-R's Sensation, who finished her championship at the 1970 American Boxer Club's Regional Specialty.

A litter brother of Ch. My-R's Magic Spell, Ch. My-R's Wizard produced Verand's Cloud Dawn. She was bred to Ch. Salgray's Fashion Plate producing five champions for My-R, plus two others. One of these five was Ch. My-R's Rain Maker, who was Winners Dog at the American Boxer Club Regional Specialty in 1969.

Lorraine now lives with a trio of bitches, Ch. Keil's Krystal, a Futurity winner, Ch. Carlon's Classy Cookie, and a Dynasty daughter.

Besides her many years of service as Secretary of the American Boxer Club, Mrs. Meyer still teaches obedience and is an approved American Kennel Club obedience judge.

Lorraine Meyer's only comment when asked to speak about the success of My-R's Boxers was, "If our Boxers had done nothing but been the loving companions that they are, the effort would have been well spent."

OMEGA Boxers, *Oakton, Virginia*

In 1973, Colonel and Mrs. James Jackson hit the jackpot with their first show bitch, Weber's Hustling Black Garter (Libby), a Fashion Hint granddaughter. She went Winners Bitch and Best of Winners at the 1974 American Boxer Club Specialty. When she finished her championship, she was bred to Ch. Scher-Khoun's Shadrack, her double uncle, and produced one plain male. This male became Ch. Omega's Rockfire, Sire of Merit (11 champions).

Libby was later bred to Ch. Salgray's Market Wise and produced Ch. Omega's Electra, a class winner at the 1978 American Boxer Club Specialty.

In 1975, the Jacksons acquired Canadian Ch. Aracrest's Velvet Sensation. She was bred to Ch. Omega's Rockfire and produced Ch. Aracrest's Talisman (Rocky), Sire of Merit (18 champions).

Ch. Aracrest's Talisman was bred to his litter sister, Omega's Lovefire, who produced Omega's Windfire, Dam of Merit and recipient of the 1984

Ch. Omega's Rockfire, Sire of Merit, producer of 11 Champions, shown with handler Robert Forsyth. He was bred and owned by Colonel and Mrs. James Jackson.

Ch. Aracrest's Talisman, by Ch. Omega's Rockfire, became a Sire of Merit producing 18 Champions. Shown handled by Jane Forsyth. Breeders/Owners: Lu Jackson and Nora McGriskin.

American Boxer Club award for dam producing the most champions. Windfire whelped Ch. Omega's Nightstar, a multi Best in Show bitch, American and Canadian Ch. Omega's Sophia, Ch. Omega's Maja, Reserve Winners Bitch at the 1984 American Boxer Club Specialty, and Ch. Omega's Opium, class winner at the 1984 American Boxer Club Specialty.

Ch. Omega's Maja was bred to her grandfather, Ch. Aracrest's Talisman, and produced Ch. Omega's Tycoon and Ch. Omega's New Yorker. Ch. Omega's Opium was also bred to her grandfather, Ch. Aracrest's Talisman, and produced Ch. Omega's Elle.

Canadian Ch. Aracrest's Velvet Sensation was next bred to American and Canadian Ch. Scottlea's Billy Be Damned producing Ch. Omega's Starfire, Reserve Winners Bitch at the American Boxer Club Specialty, Ch. Omega's Black Magic, and Canadian Ch. Omega's Hurrah.

In 1981 and 1982 Omega Boxers co-bred and co-owned with Quebo's Boxers. Ch. Aracrest's Talisman was bred to Vidana D Capigua producing Ch. Quebo's Miss Saturday Night, the 1982 Best of Breed winner at the American Boxer Club Specialty, and Canadian Ch. Quebo's Mr. Boxer. A repeat of this breeding in 1982 produced American and Canadian Ch. Quebo's Enrique Mingo, a Best in Show winner, and Ch. Quebo's Al Fin.

To date Omega Boxers has bred or co-bred 17 American champions, two American Boxer Club Sires of Merit, one American Boxer Club Dam of Merit and six Canadian champions.

SALGRAY Boxers, *Mansfield, Massachusetts*

In 1952, Mr. and Mrs. Daniel Hamilburg purchased their first Boxer as a gift for their three children. She was Sally of Grayarlin, bred by Jane Kamp and her partner, George Pusey.

Jane Kamp remembers that the Hamilburgs were loathe to part with their beloved Sally long enough for her to travel to shows. However, Jane talked them into it and showed Sally to her championship, which she completed at one of the famous Morris and Essex Shows. Another male Boxer, also purchased as a pet from Jane Kamp, Sabot of Grayarlin, became a champion at the same show.

In January 1955, Jane Kamp tried to talk Mr. and Mrs. Hamilburg into buying Barrage of Quality Hill, but they felt they were not ready to commit themselves to the extensive campaign that a dog like Barrage deserved. Jane feels they always regretted this decision. However, Barrage did sire the Hamilburg's first Best in Show winner.

The kennel name was coined from their first dog, SALly of GRAYarlin, and Salgray firmly holds its place in the history of the breed.

Dan and Phyllis Hamilburg purchased a third Boxer, who became Ch. Slipper of Grayarlin. When they saw what three Boxers were doing to their lawns, they started to build the famous Salgray Kennels.

Ch. Slipper of Grayarlin was bred to Ch. Barrage of Quality Hill and produced Ch. Salgray's Battle Chief in 1956, who was their first Best in Show dog. Chief won several Bests in Show and many, many Groups.

In 1959, Salgray Boxers purchased a four-month-old brindle bitch from Dr. Robert Burke. This puppy grew up to be the American and Canadian Best in Show winner Ch. Marquam Hill's Flamingo, shown mainly by Bob Forsyth. She became the dam of seven champions.

"Mingo" was bred to Ch. Salgray's Battle Chief, son of Slipper, and produced the history-making "F litter" of four bitches and two males. The males were both multiple Best in Show winners—Ch. Salgray's Fashion Plate, Sire of Merit (63 champions) and Ch. Salgray's Flying High, Sire of Merit (27 champions). Ch. Salgray's Flaming Ember, also a Best in Show winner, became a Dam of Merit. Ch. Salgray's Fanfare was sold to Mr. and Mrs. Judson Streicher after she was awarded Best Puppy at the American Boxer Club Futurity Stakes and became a Best in Show winner. The remaining two bitches were Ch. Salgray's Frolic and Ch. Salgray's Flame Crest.

The Hamilburgs then decided to try careful inbreeding. They bred Flying Ember to litter brother Flying High and produced Best in Show winner and Dam of Merit Ch. Salgray's Auntie Mame and Best in Show winner Ch. Salgray's Ambush, Sire of Merit (34 champions).

Flying High was also bred to Ch. Salgray's Roulette and produced Sire of Merit Ch. Salgray's Ovation (23 champions), another multiple Best in Show winner.

Salgray champions are too numerous to mention, but they include these greats: Ch. Salgray's Double Talk, Ch. Salgray's Double Play, Ch. Salgray's Jitterbug, Ch. Salgray's Balladeer (Sire of Merit), Ch. Salgray's Bojangles (Sire of Merit), Ch. Salgray's Chances Are (sold to Japan), Ch. Salgray's Expresso (Sire of Merit), Ch. Salgray's Good Grief (Sire of Merit), Ch. Salgray's Market Wise (Sire of Merit), Ch. Salgray's Minute Man (syndicated to Australia), Ch. Salgray's Royal Flush (Sire of Merit), Ch. Salgray's Valentino, Ch. Salgray's V.I.P., and more recently Ch. Salgray's Argos of Memorylane (sold to Australia). Mention should also be made of Dam of Merit Autumn Years. There have been a multitude of winning Boxers and producers from Salgray both in the United States and worldwide.

Salgray Boxers were professionally handled by Jane and Bob Forsyth and the late Larry Downey. Stan Flowers has successfully shown them in recent years.

Salgray has won every American Boxer Club award many times over. As early as 1955, Salgray won the American Boxer Club's annual award for the most American-bred class wins. In 1958, Salgray made the most champions and tied for "Dam of the Year." In 1959, Battle Chief was named "Boxer of the Year." In 1962 and 1963, Salgray made the most

American and Canadian Ch. Marquam Hill's Flamingo, bred by Dr. Robert Burke, a Dam of Merit, and dam of the famous "F" litter. Owned by Mr. and Mrs. Daniel Hamilburg (Salgray Kennels) she was shown by Stanley Flowers.

champions, the most homebred champions, and the most Best in Show wins. They had *both* Sire *and* Dam of the Year for 1963. 1964 and 1965 saw top awards given to the dogs of the "F" litter: Best of Breed at the 1964 and 1965 American Boxer Club National Specialties, Best of Breed at Westminster both years with a Group I in 1964, the Best Puppy and Best Futurity Puppy, plus other annual awards for the most Best in Show wins, the greatest number of Group 1 and the most Specialty wins. In 1965 Ch. Salgray's Fashion Plate was the "Top Boxer Dog" and Ch. Marquam Hill's Flamingo was "Top Boxer Bitch" according to the Phillips System. Salgray had seven Best in Show winners, six of whom were homebreds.

Daniel and Phyllis Hamilburg have garnered every honor in Boxers and are justly proud of their achievements despite the heartaches along the way. They always say, "It was not always easy, but it was always more like fun than work."

Lest you think it was all luck, Sally of Grayarlin's first litter had only one puppy—a white! Her second litter had eight puppies, but only one had the flash a Boxer needs to shine in the ring. He was shown and finished but died at a young age.

Phyllis Hamilburg's first love was the whelping and raising of puppies, and she was not as interested in showing as her husband. However, she has always had an "eye" for a good puppy or dog.

The Hamilburgs have sold their large house and kennels in Brookline, Massachusetts, and moved to a smaller place in Plymouth. With their help and advice, daughter Jane Guy and her husband keep the Salgray banner flying.

TuRo Kennels, *Houston, Texas*

TuRo Boxer Kennels was established in 1964 by Sandy Roberts and Pat Turner in Oklahoma City. Their goal was to purchase two good foundation bitches and start showing.

For two years they traveled to Canada and across the United States studying the breed. Then, they decided on a plan of action.

Canadian Ch. Hansparke's Fashion Fair (Tootsie), ex Canadian Ch. Hansparke's Pride of Step Aside, was imported from the Hansparke Kennels in Canada owned by Mr. and Mrs. Gerald Hanson. Two years later, they bought another bitch, Hansparke's Dominique. Both bitches were sired by Int. Ch. Millan's Fashion Hint and became the foundation of TuRo Kennels.

After Fashion Fair completed her American championship, the partners returned to Canada to examine the dogs and bitches in Tootsie's pedigree. This resulted in Fashion Fair being bred to her sire, Fashion Hint. This breeding of a totally outcrossed bitch back to her sire produced what the partners feel has been an extremely powerful producing force. A male from this litter, Ch. TuRo's Native Dancer, a double Fashion Hint

72

Sire of Merit Ch. Salgray's Ambush (34 Champions) shown with handler Larry Downey. Owners: Mr. and Mrs. Daniel Hamilburg.

Sire of Merit Ch. Salgray's Expresso with handler Stanley Flowers. Owners/breeders: Mr. and Mrs. Daniel Hamilburg.

73

son, became a Sire of Merit with 18 champions. Fashion Fair subsequently became a Dam of Merit and won the American Boxer Club award for Top Producing Bitch in 1976.

Ch. TuRo's Vanity Fair, owned by Bessie McElhone, and American and Canadian Ch. TuRo's Nut Kracker followed Native Dancer as champions, and Vanity Fair produced the only litter of six champion bitches in the history of the breed to date. She became a Dam of Merit with her first litter and winner of the American Boxer Club award for Top Producing Bitch in the United States for 1978.

Ch. Hansparke's Fashion Fair became the dam of five champions when Ch. TuRo's Dacquiri Ice and Ch. TuRo's Deseree finished.

Ch. TuRo's Vanity Fair produced the 1978 American Boxer Club's Winners Bitch and Best of Winners, along with several Dams of Merit and Best of Breed winners. Ch. TuRo's Whisper of Five T's, owned by Dr. Robert Burke, was one of these bitches and the dam of three champions in her first litter. One of these was Ch. Marquam Hill's Traper of TuRo, currently the top living sire and the American Boxer Club award winner for top producing sire in 1986 and 1987.

Ch. TuRo's Angel Fire of D.J. became TuRo's first multiple Best in Show bitch and the foundation bitch for D. J. Kennels, owned by Dick and Jenna Dunn. She was sired by Ch. TuRo's Native Dancer as was Ch. Niklof's Empress of TuRo's, the top winning Boxer bitch in the East for 1980 and 1981. Empress was also the Best of Breed winner at the 1981 American Boxer Club Specialty Show and returned to win the Veteran Bitch class at the American Boxer Club 1987 Specialty.

Ch. TuRo's Monogram, sired by Native Dancer, finished in five shows with two Bests of Breed from the Puppy class.

Hansparke's Dominique was imported from Canada only two days before her sire, Fashion Hint, died. She produced four champions for TuRo—Ch. TuRo's Trumpet, Ch. TuRo's Truffian, Ch. TuRo's Magic Spell and one Canadian champion. Trumpet stayed at TuRo's Kennels, but Truffian became the foundation bitch for Carlon Kennels, owned by Bob and Carol Long.

In 1979, Elizabeth Esacove joined the partnership at TuRo and brought two important Boxers to the Kennels. They were Ch. TuRo's Touche, sired by Ch. Benjamin of Five T's ex Ch. Holly Lane's Baubles, and Ch. Mephisto's Warlock of TuRo, sired by Int. Ch. Mephisto's Vendetta ex Canadian Ch. Mephisto's Scarlet Lady.

Touche was bred to Ch. TuRo's Trumpet and produced Ch. TuRo's Tidal Wave, Ch. TuRo's Tribute, and Ch. TuRo's Triumph. When Touche was bred to Ch. Marquam Hill's Traper of Turo, the breeding produced Ch. Turo's Emblem, Ch. Turo's Empire, and Ch. Turo's Escapade, maker her a Dam of Merit.

74

Sire of Merit Ch. Salgray's Market Wise, shown with Jane Forsyth. Bred and owned by Mr. and Mrs. Daniel Hamilburg.

Canadian Ch. Hansparke's Fashion Fair, by Int. Ch. Millan's Fashion Hint ex Can. Ch. Hansparke's Pride of Step Aside, formed part of the foundation for TuRo Kennels. She is shown with handler Corky Vroom.

Top Producing Sire in 1986 and 1987 Ch. Marquam Hill's Traper of TuRo, owned by TuRo Kennels.

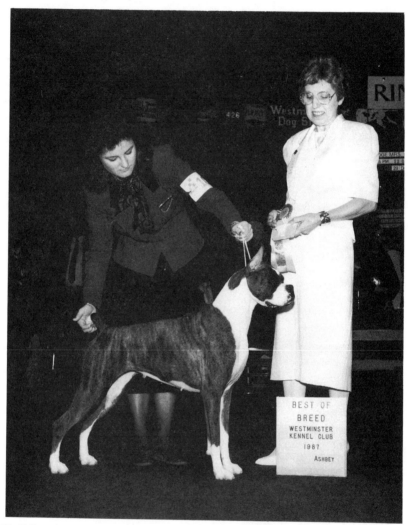

Ch. TuRo's Cachet, owned by Leonard and Susan Magowitz, is the top-winning Boxer bitch of all time. Her record includes 33 Bests in Show, 40 Specialty Bests including the American Boxer Club, 137 Group 1sts including Westminster 1986 and 1987 and 375 Best of Breed wins. She was the #1 Boxer 1983-86 and #1 Working Dog 1986. Breeders: TuRo Kennels. Shown winning Best of Breed at Westminster 1987 under Mrs. Barbara Gaines, enroute to Group 1, handler Kim Pastella.

Ch. Mephisto's Warlock of TuRo produced a multiple Best of Breed winner on the West Coast, Ch. TuRo's Mirage, owned by Ed Goldfield.

Ch. TuRo's Native Dancer continued to play an important role in TuRo's breeding program. His daughter, TuRo's Katrina of Cross Bar, produced four champions. The first breeding produced Ch. TuRo's Caress, Ch. TuRo's Cachet, and Ch. TuRo's Courtisan. A repeat breeding produced Ch. TuRo's Accolade, Ch. TuRo's Applause, and Ch. TuRo's Allure.

Ch. TuRo's Caress, the top bitch in TuRo kennels, was bred to Ch. TuRo's Tidal Wave and produced Ch. TuRo's Mediator and Ch. TuRo's Monoplay. She has been bred again, producing more exciting puppies.

Ch. TuRo's Cachet, owned by Leonard and Susan Magowitz, is the top winning Boxer bitch and Working Group bitch of all times to date. She has now become their foundation bitch.

Today at TuRo Kennels there are two bitches, Ch. Carlon's Sassy Kate of TuRo and Ch. TuRo's Caress. The stud force includes Ch. TuRo's Escapade, sire of six champions from his first two litters, Ch. TuRo's Empire, who sired Ch. TuRo's Executive and is on his way with more promising pups, Ch. TuRo's Tidal Wave, sire of the No. 3 Boxer Ch. TuRo's Dakota of Shar-Rea, Ch. Marquam Hill's Monarch of TuRo, and, of course, Ch. Marquam Hill's Traper of Turo, No. 1 Sire for 1986 and 1987.

TuRo Kennels considers that selective line breeding and occasional inbreeding of dogs and bitches can be the most powerful combination for the future. The secret to outcrossing is knowing when and where.

In 1983 Pat Turner left the partnership due to ill health and other interests.

Today at TuRo Kennels, Sandy Roberts and Elizabeth Esacove are watching history repeat itself. Fashion Fair, bred to her father, produced a line of champions, so they feel that Cachet, bred to her sire, Traper, will make tomorrow more exciting than ever.

Fireball of Emefar, imported into Australia by Mrs. Gerardy.

Felmoor Rainey Lane's Raffles, imported by Mrs. Barden, strongly influenced the style of Boxers in the State of Victoria.

Hollee's Po-Tan, imported from the United States, figures heavily in the pedigrees of modern Australian Boxers.

4

The Boxer
in Other Countries

THE BOXER'S popularity did not spread beyond Europe and the United States until after World War II. Today, however, Boxers are found in many lands. Breeders the world over have tried to produce the best type of Boxer in an effort to unify the breed regardless of what strain is incorporated. Nonetheless, there are still distinct differences of opinion and even rivalries between breeders/owners of Dutch, German, English, or American Boxers. Fashion plays no small part, and often the popularity of a few dogs can cause a country to develop its own type.

Australia

In 1948, the first Boxers from the Tirkane Kennels in England reached Australia. They were imported by Mr. F. Wheatlands of Tinara Kennels, Victoria. Shortly thereafter, Mrs. Rena M. Gerardy, owner of Park Royal Kennels in New South Wales, imported more English Boxers. Around the same time, Mr. H. E. Taylor of Brackley Kennels in Victoria also imported Boxers from England. These three breeders set the scene for Boxers in Australia, and between them they imported a considerable number of dogs, establishing themselves as the foundation breeders of Boxers in Australia. As the breed gained popularity, other kennels came upon the scene.

For Australians, England was the most accessible source of supply. As

American & Canadian Ch. Tradonalee's Trade Win. Currently Top Sire in Australia with winning progeny in all States—24 Champions to date. Owned by the Munro Syndicate, South Australia.

Australian Ch. Intrends Wind Storm, by American & Canadian Ch. Tradonalee's Trade Win ex Australian Ch. Intrends Wind Song.

Boxers were still a relatively new breed in England, dogs available for export were not always the cream of the crop. Imported Boxers of real quality stood out clearly and drew many admirers. The most outstanding dog of that era was Ch. Panfield Zest, a stylish dog, a prolific winner, and sire of many champions.

The first American import was a Bang Away grandson, Fireball of Emefar, imported by Mrs. Gerardy. He was followed by Felmoor Rainey Lane's Raffles, imported by Mrs. Barden. Fireball of Emefar added much needed style to the Boxers of New South Wales. "Raffles" had the same influence in the state of Victoria. Eventually a division grew between those who preferred the American type and those who preferred the English type. Each camp tried to breed better Boxers than their rivals, and each seemed determined to breed a completely different type from the other.

Fortunately, dedicated breeders used the best of the imports to produce the finest dogs they could regardless of origin. For example, Boxers from the famous Wardrobes Kennels in England started to arrive in Australia and seemed to combine well with American imports.

Outstanding American-bred dogs or stock from American imports included Fireball of Emefar, Rainey Lane's Raffles, Hollee's Po-Tan (son of Ch. Dion of Rainey Lanes), Boxella's Yankee Doodle, Beaucrest's Chief Cochise, Rainey Lane's Grand Slam, Rainey Lane's Shomun, American Ch. Salgray's Minute Man, Canadian and American Ch. Tradonalee's Trade Win, Vimar's Magic Goes On, Jacquet's Bayside of the Wind, Jacquet's Phoenix Playgirl and American Ch. Salgray's Argo of Memory-lane. Most of these fine imports were never shown in Australia, even for exhibition, because cropped ears are forbidden.

The main English kennels to export to Australia have been Tirkane, Panfield, Gremlin, Marbleton, Cherryburton, Wardrobes, Seefeld, Skelder and Winuwuk.

There are seven Boxer clubs in Australia at the present time, each one representing the interests of members in that state. New South Wales has two clubs, and there is one club in each of the states of Victoria, South Australia, Queensland, Western Australia and Tasmania. Each of these Boxer clubs is subject to the rules of their controlling bodies.

The controlling bodies are the Australian National Kennel Council, Canine Association of Western Australia, Canine Control Council, Queensland, Canberra Kennel Association (Inc.) A.C.T., Kennel Control Council of Victoria, Kennel Control Council of Tasmania, Royal Agricultural Society Kennel Control of New South Wales, South Australian Canine Association Inc., and Northern Australian Canine Association. Each of these bodies handles registrations and each has its own rules. A National Boxer Club is currently being founded.

There are seven Groups in Australia, and Boxers regularly win the Utility Group and occasionally go Best in Show, usually at the larger shows around the country.

The royal shows are the most spectacular dog events, and a win at such a show is of considerable importance to Australian breeders. The Royal Agricultural and Horticultural Society shows are conducted under the patronage of the Royal Family. Everything from goldfish to cabbages to Rolls Royce cars are exhibited. Each section usually has a higher entry in its respective category than any other show. Judges for each section are specialists in their fields and the awards are the most sought after in the country. It is often stated that a Royal Show win is more important in Australia than a Specialty Show because it receives much more exposure to the general public and to the dog world generally.

Becoming a bench champion in Australia is not easy. A winner is awarded five points, plus one point for each exhibit of the same sex and breed competing in all ordinary classes at a Championship Show. Best Exhibit in Group and Best in Show awards carry more points, but the total points won at any one show cannot be more than 25. When a dog attains a minimum of 100 points comprised of at least four Challenge Certificates under four different judges, the owner may apply for a Champion Certificate. Champions then compete in the Open Class.

The most dominant sire of winners in Australia during the late 1980s is American and Canadian Ch. Tradonalee's Trade Win, imported from Canada. His progeny have accounted for major wins in almost every state in Australia.

As one of the very few rabies-free countries in the world, Australia has very strict quarantine laws. A dog imported from England (provided it was born in England) is quarantined for only two months. A dog arriving from the United States must complete nine months of quarantine.

Until 1983 the Australia Boxer clubs each went their own way, holding their own shows under their controlling bodies' rules and regulations. In that year the Boxer clubs got together and held four championship shows with six Specialist judges in the space of three weeks. This unique event was held in three states, drawing spectators from the United States and England. The enthusiasm and success of this "happening" resulted in the first National Boxer Specialty held in the latter half of 1988.

Outstanding Australian Kennels

GUNTOP Boxers, *Bankstown, New South Wales*

In 1971, Liz and Miles Gunter purchased their first Boxer, a brindle bitch, Groningen Lady Afia, who was descended from old Australian bloodlines tracing back to the beginnings of the breed in that country. She was not an exceptional specimen, but Mr. and Mrs. Gunter entered her in a dog show and she won first prize. One might say that was the beginning of Guntop Boxers.

American Ch. Mazra's Miss Spitfire, sired by American Ch. Warlord of Cherokee Oaks ex American Ch. Diamond Lil of Rio Vista. Owned in Australia by Liz and Miles Gunter.

Australian Ch. Lalaguli Woowookurung, bred by Mrs. C. A. Rangeley. Owned by Liz and Miles Gunter.

In 1972, the Gunters bought a flashy fawn male puppy with the unusual name of Lalaguli Woowookurung. He was from the first litter sired by English Ch. Cherryburton Playboy ex Ch. Lalaguli Meekyluka. His breeder was Mrs. Chris Rangley of Sydney, who never owned a large number of Boxers but produced a succession of champions, of whom Meekyluka was the first. The Gunters also acquired "Meeky," who became their house pet until she died in 1980 at the age of 12 years.

Lalaguli is an Australian Aboriginal word meaning "Spirit of the Billabong" (lake) or water nymph. Mrs. Rangeley gave all her Boxers Aboriginal names and Woomookurung means "plentiful," as he indeed proved.

In time "Kurung" grew into one of the top show dogs in Australia. He won ten all-breed Best in Show awards and became a champion twenty times over. He was Best in Show winner at the Boxer Club of New South Wales and won five Challenge Certificates at the prestigious Royal Shows. Altogether he won 108 Challenge Certificates and 87 Bests of Breed.

Kurung sired 12 champions. Several carried the Guntop prefix, including their first champion, Ch. Guntop Scotch on the Rox, owned by Mr. Joe Gerada (Sarose Boxers) of Melbourne.

Among his other progeny were the big winners Ch. Zweckromney Zarana, Ch. Zweckromney Cavalier, and Ch. Zweckromney Amber Glow, all owned by Guntop Boxers. He also produced Ch. Rosemullion Regal, a prolific winner with two royal challenge certificates and ten all-breed Best in Show wins, and Ch. Debronel Superstar and Ch. Coghurst Liza, two top winning bitches. Kurung left many other winning get in numerous kennels, and his place as an important stud dog in the history of the Boxer in Australia seems assured. He died suddenly in 1983.

In March, 1976, the first American champion was brought to Australia. She was American Ch. Mazra's Miss Spitfire, by Ch. Warlord of Cherokee Oaks ex Ch. Diamond Lil of Rio Vista, bred by Colonel Carl E. Welchner in California. She accompanied her American owners, Mr. and Mrs. Raymond E. Moore, III, formerly of Hawaii, and arrived in whelp to Ch. Box M Punchline Precedent, owned by Lois Matthews. From the ensuing litter, born in quarantine in Brisbane, Mr. and Mrs. Gunter acquired their first American-bred Boxer, Kasmor's Miss America.

Later, Mr. and Mrs. Moore bred Miss Spitfire to a brindle dog they had also brought with them to Australia, a Ch. Popham's Firebrand son. Guntop Boxers acquired a bitch from this litter, who in time became Ch. Kasmor's American Maid. Two others from the same litter, Kasmor's Mr. President and Kasmor's Cincinnati Kid, also became champions.

In 1987, the well-known American Ch. Salgray's Minute Man arrived in Australia. He made a tremendous impact, and Guntop Boxers was among the first to use him and continued to do so until his death in 1984. He produced the sensational littermates Ch. Guntop Rocketman and Ch.

Australian Ch. Guntop Minutemaid, bred and owned by Liz and Miles Gunter.

American Ch. Salgray's Argo of Memorylane, bred by Vera Bartol. Owned in Australia by Liz and Miles Gunter.

Guntop Minute Maid. Minute Man also sired the fawn male, Ch. Guntop I Like Ike and the brindle bitch, Ch. Guntop Up to the Minute. At the time of his death, Guntop had six bitches sired by Minute Man, the basis of their future breeding program.

Rocketman has been used extensively at stud by many breeders who appreciate his type, beauty, and the strength of his American bloodlines. He has produced several champions in Australia and New Zealand, where he has been used by Mrs. Maureen Boyd of the well-known Quo Vadis Boxers.

At Guntop, Rocketman produced Ch. Guntop Battle Star and the winning brindle bitch, Ch. Guntop Once Upon a Time, who is from the Minute Man daughter, Ch. Guntop Up to the Minute.

In 1987, Guntop Boxers imported Ch. Salgray's Argo of Memorylane, sired by Ch. Salgray's Valentino. His first Australian puppies make Mr. and Mrs. Gunter very confident that Argo will be very useful to the Boxer breed in Australia.

Both Liz and Miles Gunter have been active in the Boxer Club of New South Wales. Liz was Secretary for nearly ten years, and Miles was Treasurer for almost as long. Both are licensed judges for Groups 6 (Utility) and 7 (Non-Sporting).

INTRENDS Kennels, *Ormond, Victoria*

Intrends Kennels is owned by Mrs. Judy Horton, who, in 1965, purchased a young dog who became Australian Ch. Jaywick Copperplate. Besides being a Best in Show winner, he also sired three champions, one of whom became an Intrends foundation bitch, Ch. Arakoola Autumn Haze. Another foundation bitch was Autumn Haze's half-sister, Kiss 'N' Tell ex Ch. Topline Thomasina. These bitches were not prolific producers, but each left her mark by whelp that contributed to the breed in Australia.

Judy Horton has bred or owned 18 champions, one of the most notable being Australian Ch. Atones Mujuba, a specialty Best in Show winner. She was the dam of Intrends Pot O Gold, dam of six champions—an Australian record.

Other champions of note from this kennel are Ch. Intrends Be Dazzled, Ch. Intrends Winds O Change, Ch. Intrends Wind Song, Ch. Intrends Great Gatsby, Ch. Intrends Star Spangled, Ch. Intrends Wind Storm, and Ch. Intrends Niten Day. These dogs were all specialty, Best in Show or royal winners. Star Spangled and Wind Storm are daughters of American and Canadian Ch. Tradonalee's Trade Win, who was imported into Australia in 1983 by Judy Horton and seven other dedicated Boxer breeders. Unfortunately, his stud life was limited by an illness that left him sterile. Judy Horton, one of the lucky ones, had three bitches by him to continue his line. Trade Win had a considerable influence on the breed for

Australian Ch. Intrends Star Spangled has won Specialty shows under Don Bradley and Lorraine Meyer (U.S.), Teoh Eng Hong (Singapore), Maureen Boyd (New Zealand), Andrew Brace (U.K.), and Robert Verhulst (Canada). Owner/Breeder: Judy Horton (shown).

Australian Ch. Phoenix Jason Argonaut, owned and bred by Maxine and Terry Carter. Australia's top winning Boxer in 1980/81 and sire of 27 Champions. Shown with Maxine Carter.

the short time he was available with his progeny winning the majority of specialty shows over the past four years. Star Spangled has won five specialty Challenge Certificates and two Reserves. Wind Storm has won one specialty and two Reserves. Wind Storm's progeny is already winning. A daughter, Intrends Auntie Mame, has already become a champion, winning many specialty classes along the way.

A city ordinance makes it impossible for Judy Horton to keep many Boxers on her property, so in 1970, she decided to keep only her very best bitches. Since then, all show quality males are sold to show homes. Bitches being campaigned are kept at home, and the others are placed out, either on breeder's terms or co-ownerships. This has enabled Mrs. Horton to establish a line based on the strength of her bitches. She uses the finest stud dogs available, breeding type to type, offsetting faults, and strengthening virtues, thereby forming a strong genotype.

Obviously, Mrs. Horton's strategy has been very effective. Over the past 14 years, Intrends stock has continued to win at all the major specialty shows throughout the eastern states of Australia, even though no more than three litters are bred each year.

Judy Horton is a popular judge and is licensed to judge Terriers, Working, Utility and Non-Sporting Groups. Judging assignments and business commitments keep her from showing her dogs as much as she would like, but she still concentrates on breeding. Many of the top Intrends dogs and bitches are now in co-ownership, enabling other breeders to own and show top class stock.

PHOENIX Boxers, *Kilkenny, South Australia*

Maxine and Terry Carter established Phoenix Boxers over 28 years ago. In that time they have bred and/or owned 53 champions. Their stud dogs have sired numerous other champions for proud owners all over Australia and overseas.

This kennel has a high reputation for breeding top quality Boxers. Their stock was originally bred from the best of English and American lines. In recent years, however, the Phoenix line has been more heavily influenced by American Boxers.

The kennel has always aimed for the correct balance of substance and elegance, and this has proved to be a winning recipe. Phoenix Boxers have been successful throughout Australia and their stock has been the foundation of many other winning kennels. They have also been exported to the United States, New Zealand and Malaysia.

At the close of 1986, Maxine and Terry Carter decided to curtail their breeding and showing activities. The demands of business and health took priority. Maxine Carter is still handling for owners of Phoenix Boxers and occasionally accepts judging assignments. They have reduced their kennel

Australian Ch. Phoenix Mister P, by American & Canadian Ch. Tradonalee's Trade Win ex Australian Ch. Phoenix Chat 'R' Box. Consistent winner in South Australia. Owned by M. Avison, South Australia. Shown with the breeder: Terry Carter.

Australian Ch. Sjecoin Raggety Ann, bred by Mrs. R. J. Olifent-Brace and owned by Terry Collicut (shown). She is the winner of 5 "Royals," 8 Bests in Show and Best Exhibit in Group at Sydney 1986.

from 25 Boxers to the current list of three oldies, one young bitch and four imports. Keeping just eight Boxers is like a holiday after more than 20 years with a minimum of 25.

ROSEMULLION Boxers, *North Turramurra, New South Wales*

In 1967, Les and Cleone Baker and their family emigrated to Australia from England. The first few weeks in their new land were very strange and strained for them. They had owned dogs in England, and a rescued Boxer puppy brought a familiar note to their lives. With four people living in a two-bedroom apartment, raising a puppy can't have been easy, but this was how the Bakers became involved in dogs again.

In 1975, when their house was built in an area suitable for kennels, they bought a Boxer bitch, Sabari Sari Minta. She produced two litters, but none of the pups were noteworthy specimens. Her third litter was sired by Liz and Miles Gunter's Australian Ch. Lalaguli Woowookurung. This breeding produced Rosemullion Regal, who rapidly gained his Australian championship. He competed and won Challenge Certificates at the Melbourne Royal Show in 1981, the Toowoomba Royal Show in 1982, and the Sydney Royal Show in 1982. In 1981, he was top scoring dog in Challenge points both in Queensland and in New South Wales.

Since then, Rosemullion and Guntop Kennels have worked very closely. The Bakers have purchased a number of champions with Liz and Miles Gunter's encouragement and help.

Les and Cleone Baker are especially proud of their daughter, Jacqueline, who has become an excellent handler. She handles all Rosemullion dogs and a number of dogs for other people. Jacqueline has also trained and encouraged other youngsters with considerable success.

Jacqueline started handling in the show ring at the age of eight, enduring all the criticism that was thrown at her. In 1986, she won the 11-18 year-old Handlers Class at the Royal Easter Show in Sydney, having placed for the four previous years. Her greatest thrill came at the 1983 Boxer Club of New South Wales, judged by Mrs. Fraser of Canada, when she handled all the Guntop dogs entered, one in each class, and won many awards.

Websters Veterinary Laboratories, the largest in Australia, once chose Rosemullion as an example of a well-run and well-managed kennel. At Websters' request, Les and Cleone Baker addressed a seminar on kennel management, hygiene and the prevention of parvovirus which was attended by over 200 breeders from the state of New South Wales.

SJECOIN Boxers, *Melbourne, Victoria*

In 1975, Sjecoin Boxers was registered in Victoria, Australia, by Mrs. Rosina Olifent-Brace. Mrs. Brace had emigrated from New Zealand where she had owned and bred Boxers and Boston Terriers under the Anisor prefix since 1959. She has owned or bred more than 75 champions, including 35 at Sjecoin in Australia.

Commencing with New Zealand dogs bred from English Gremlin and Wardrobes bloodlines, Rosina gradually introduced American lines. Today, Sjecoin pedigrees carry the names of many American-bred dogs and their descendants.

Sjecoin Boxers have enviable show records. Ch. Sjecoin Winter Forecast, the present top Boxer winner, has been awarded 15 Bests in Show, 30 Group I's, and eight royal show Challenge Certificates. He has accumulated more than 2000 challenge points. A bitch, Ch. Sjecoin Fashion Parade has also achieved a noteworthy record with nine Bests in Show, 25 Group I's and six royal show challenge certificates. Much recognition must also go to the great producing bitch, Australian Ch. Sjecoin My T Sweet, herself a consistent Group winner and dam of six champions. My T Sweet was a daughter of Rainey Lane's Grand Slam and her influence on the breed in Australia has been notable.

Rosina Olifent-Bruce is a Boxer and Boston Terrier judge. She has officiated at shows in New Zealand, Australia, Europe and the United States. She states there is no greater reward than judging the Boxer breed.

TONUP Kennels, *Prestons, New South Wales*

In 1968, Miss Elaine Davies was given a Boxer bitch, Willander Firecracker, to replace a dog who turned out to be a cryptorchid. The breeder assured Miss Davies that the bitch would make an excellent brood bitch as she was line-bred on the American dog, Rainey Lane's Raffles. This proved to be correct. When Firecracker was bred to Ch. Wardrobes Morning Canter, she produced two champions, one of whom was the top winning dog, Ch. Tonup Roman Candle. She had two more litters and produced another four champions.

Two years later, Miss Davies formed a partnership with Lu Cope under the TONUP banner. Three years after that, they took a third partner, Robyn Jones. In 1978, Miss Davies became a partner in Chelveston Kennels with Merv Chapman and Delma Nelson. She now breeds under both prefixes.

In 1971, Roman Candle died of cancer at the age of three and a half years. Fortunately, Miss Davies had kept his full brother, Tonup Canterbry Gallop. When the brother died, the partners decided to import a stud dog from England and bought Gremlin Sunarise, who was line bred to Rainey Lane's Sirocco with a line to Ch. Treceder's Sequel.

Later, the partners imported Rainey Lane's Grand Slam and Rainey Lane's Shomun from the United States and Gremlin Mere Delight, Marikarlos Abbra Dabra of Gremlin, Gremlin Mere Frivolity, and Gremlin Great Gale from England.

The two American dogs could not be shown because of their cropped ears, but they were excellent stud dogs. Grand Slam produced 21 champions, three of whom were Best in Show winners. Shomun has produced five champions so far.

Gremlin Sunarise produced 26 champions including Ch. Tonup Quality Street, Australia's top winning male, who took his last Best in Show at seven and a half years of age. Sunarise also sired Ch. Tobana August Queen, one of the top winners in the breed.

Ch. Gremlin Great Gale, a son of English Ch. Gremlin's Summer Storm, produced 21 champions before his early death of a brain tumor at four and a half years. He was the sire of Ch. Tonup Glory Be, Australia's greatest winning bitch, who took her last Best in Show at eight and a half years of age.

Ch. Marikarlos Abbra Dabra of Gremlin produced ten champions in Australia. The other two imported bitches, Gremlin Mere Delight and Ch. Gremlin Mere Frivolity, produced two champions each and their daughters and granddaughters are still at the kennels.

Miss Davies believes the three most outstanding dogs bred by Tonup Boxers were Ch. Tonup Roman Candle, Ch. Tonup Quality Street, and Ch. Tonup Glory Be. During his three and a half years, Ch. Tonup Roman Candle won almost 2,000 challenge points, 19 all-breed Bests in Show, and nine specialty Bests in Show. He was unplaced only once in his career. He sired ten champions from 15 breedings, and five of his progeny were Best in Show winners. Ch. Tonup Quality Street won 17 all-breed Bests in Show, 11 specialty Bests in Show, and more than 3,000 challenge points. He sired 22 champions, four of whom were Best in Show winners. He died in 1986 at 11½ years of age. Ch. Tonup Glory Be was sired by Ch. Gremlin Grand Slam ex a daughter of Rainey Lane's Grand Slam. She won four all-breed Bests in Show and nine specialty Bests in Show. One B.I.S. was awarded by Mr. Tom Perret of the United States at 15 months, and her last Challenge Certificate was given by Mr. Joseph Heine at eight and a half years. She had a heart condition due to parvovirus at eight weeks of age and was bred only once. However, her daughter, Ch. Tonup Gracious Me, is proving to be a fine producer.

Tonup is a small kennel and only breeds two or three litters per year. Miss Davies believes that Boxers require a family environment to develop the correct temperament. Nonetheless, there have been 50 Tonup champions and eight Chelveston champions, 16 of whom are Best in Show winners.

Other successful Australian kennels are Keldaren Kennels owned by Ron and Rhonda Rudd of Port Pirie, South Australia, Kee Tin Syndicate with partners Liz Lee, Rex Summers and Teena Hume of Launceston, Tasmania, Penlord Kennels owned by David Pinel of Penna, Tasmania,

Ch. Tonup Dam Yankee—first Ch. son of Rainey-Lane's Grand Slam. Breeders: Tonup Kennels.

Ch. Tonup Bobby Bellringer—7th Ch. son of Ch. Tonup Dam Yankee. Breeders/Owners: Tonup Kennels.

Taswest Kennels owned by Michelle Roberts, Canning Vale, Western Australia, Bokson Kennels owned by Brian and Sue McKie of Canning Vale, Western Australia, Sandshuri Kennels owned by Helen and David Weil, Glass House Mountain, Queensland, Beawinna Kennels owned by Terry Collicutt, Toowoomba, Queensland, Thrasrite Kennels owned by David and Juanita Strachan, Murrumbateman, New South Wales, and Bamberg Kennels owned by Keith and Christina Luff, MacGregor, A.C.T.

Brazil

The first Brazilian Boxer, Ch. Duque V. do Alto do Corcovado, was registered in São Paulo in 1944. In 1945, Mr. Americo do Canto Liberator imported American Ch. Pepper of Goldsburg. He had Von Dom bloodlines and was extensively used at stud in the early Brazilian breeding programs.

In 1947, American Ch. Garnet of Dorick was imported by Mr. Francisco Diedrich. This dog was a descendent of Xerxes v. Dom and Dorian v. Marienhof and produced many Brazilian champions. One of these was the great Ch. Jeep de Iquassú, owned by Mrs. Magdalena Aranha. He sired 36 champions and was a great winner in the show ring.

In 1960, one of the most important influences on Brazilian Boxers arrived from the United States. This was Ch. Eldic's Creme de Cocoa, imported by Mr. Mario Cilento. This beautiful Boxer produced many champions and became the foundation of many of today's top lines. Other prolific American imports of the sixties include American Ch. Brayshaw's Black Eagle, sire of more than 20 champions, and American Ch. Ginger's Aristofanes, another top producer.

In 1969, a new era began in Brazil when Evelina and Jayme Martinelli imported American Ch. Salgray's Stuffed Shirt and Salgray's Miss Minx. Also in that year, the young breeder, José Carlos Gasparini, imported English Ch. Ashgate Reubens, sired by English Ch. Seefeld's Picasso.

Up to this time, Boxers in Brazil varied enormously in quality, and some very poor specimens were seen in the show ring. However, importations from Salgray and other prominent kennels improved the consistency and over-all quality of Brazilian Boxers. American contributors to Brazilian success included Arriba, Jacquet, Merrilane, Notelrac, Paragon, Pinebrook, Salgray, Treceder and Tudosal. With careful breeding, educational programs, exchanging of experiences and information, and much hard work on the part of a few dedicated breeders, Boxers achieved popularity through the high quality of the dogs being bred and exhibited. Now the Boxer ranks No. 1 in popularity in Brazil, and the future of the breed looks promising.

There are presently five Boxer specialty clubs in Brazil located in the states of Rio Grande do Sul, Santa Catarina, Paraná, São Paulo and Rio de Janeiro. Brazil does not have a national Boxer club.

94

Brazilian Ch. Jacquet's Gaspard Ad Summus shown going Best Male in Show under Judge Robert S. Forsyth. Owners: Ad Summus Boxers, Rio de Janeiro.

Ch. Ad Summus Harmony Quo Vadis, by Ch. Jacquet's Gaspard Ad Summus. Breeder: Ruth Vieira. Owners: Ad Summus Boxers.

Principal Brazilian Kennels

AD SUMMUS Boxers, *Rio de Janeiro*

In 1980, João Carneiro and Carlos Cordovil founded this kennel with the purchase of a brindle male, Quo Vadis Herculanus, who quickly became a Brazilian champion. Their next purchase was a brindle bitch, Quo Vadis Justina, who swiftly finished her championship.

In partnership with Quo Vadis Kennels, some new blood was introduced from the United States with the purchase of a fawn bitch, Jacquet's Harmony of Quo Vadis, sired by Ch. Happy Ours Fortune de Jacquet ex Jacquet's Harmony for Adler. Harmony rapidly attained her Brazilian championship.

Another import was Jacquet's Gaspard Ad Summus, who became Grand Champion in just one year of limited showing. Gaspard is a multiple all-breed Best in Show winner and is currently the No. 1 male Boxer in Brazil. He has sired two outstanding fawn champion bitches. One of these, Ch. Ad Summus Harmony Quo Vadis, finished at 15 months and has won many Bests of Breed and Groups. She currently ranks third in the Brazilian Working Group.

HEXASTAR Kennels, *São Paulo*

Agnes Buchwald acquired her first Boxer in 1972. He was not a show dog but a great family pet. Desiring a show quality Boxer, Agnes Buchwald visited Jayme and Evelina Martinelli of Pent Kennels, also located in São Paulo, and the two families became firm friends.

In 1972 the Buchwalds purchased their foundation bitch, Ch. Funny Girl of Pent Kennels, and an imported American male, Brazilian Ch. Pinebrook's Trade Mark. With these two good specimens, the Buchwalds began breeding and competing in earnest.

They imported fifteen Boxers from such outstanding American kennels as Arriba, Ruhlend, Tudosal, Omega, Merrilane, and Pinebrook.

Ch. Pinebrook's Trade Mark, sired by Ch. Pinebrook's Radiation, produced over 50 champions, among them the top winning Ch. Quo Vadis Augustus Caesar, owned by Dr. and Mrs. Vieira, and American and Brazilian Ch. Hexastar's Royal Mark.

Ch. Burke of Cair Paravel became a top winner and top sire producing the first Brazilian-bred Boxer to become an American champion, American, Brazilian and Uruguayan Ch. Hexastar's In Legacy of Ruhlend, who is still living and producing in Uruguay for owner Mr. Julio Rueda.

Ch. Tudosal's Butterfly, sired by American Ch. Tudosal's Pazzaz, died tragically at a young age leaving a plain fawn puppy who became Ch. Hexastar's Fly Again in five straight shows.

American and Brazilian Ch. Merrilane's Kiss of Fire became a Best in Show and specialty winner in Brazil and produced four champions in two

Ch. Candlelight Aye of Hexastar, owned by Hexastar Kennels.

American & Brazilian Grand Ch. Barday's Country Squire, shown at three years. Owners: Jayme & Evelina Martinelli, Pent Kennels, Sao Paulo.

Ch. Quo Vadis Julius Caesar, by American Ch. Paragon's Night Ryder ex Ch. Claudio's Sunset of Fire, bred by Quo Vadis Kennels. Owner: Henrique Magno Ferreira, Campo Grande.

litters. One of these was American and Brazilian Ch. Hexastar's Legend of Xanadu, a top winning dog and a good producer.

American and Brazilian Ch. Arriba's Command Performance, sired by Ch. Arriba's Knight Revue ex Ch. Salgray's Beau Cherie, was undoubtedly one of the best American imports and became one of the greatest sires producing over 50 champions. He sired three Brazilian-bred American champions: Hexastar's Native Dancer of Ruhlend, Hexastar's Ted's Stamp of Ruhlend and Hexastar's American Graffiti. In 1983 Ch. Hexastar's Native Dancer of Ruhlend became the No. 1 Boxer, No. 1 Working Dog, No. 1 Brazilian-bred Dog and No. 5 All Breed in the national ranking. Ch. Hexastar's Ted's Stamp of Ruhlend left winning offspring in Brazil and in the United States before his sudden early death.

Arriba's Command Performance sired Ch. Hexastar's Be A Pepper, the dam of two champions, one of whom is the young Ch. Candlelight's Aye of Hexastar, already winning Bests of Breed and group placements.

The Buchwalds have campaigned many of their dogs with well-known professional handlers in the United States and in other countries of South America. Their stud dogs have produced over 200 Brazilian champions and over 30 home bred champions. They have imported and bred Best in Show winners and innumerable Group and specialty winners of both sexes.

In 1983 Int. Ch. Hexastar's Native Dancer of Ruhlend became the biggest winning dog for Hexastar Kennels to that date. However, in 1985, his half-brother, Int. Ch. Hexastar's American Graffiti became No. 1 Boxer, having won the prestigious São Paulo State Boxer Club Specialty three times, once under the highly respected American judge and breeder, Mrs. Phoebe Harris.

Mrs. Buchwald and her sons, Dr. Jean Milan Buchwald and Dr. Daniel Alan Buchwald (both veterinarians), continue to breed top quality Boxers and are proud of their accomplishments over the past 15 years. They are even more proud of being able to introduce and assist new kennels. These include Tannenberg, formed in 1978 by Dra. Marcia and Dr. Helio Rosa Baldy, who own Brazilian Ch. Candlelight Aye of Hexastar, and the Candlelight Kennels, formed in 1982 by Dra. Inácia and Dr. Roald Moreno.

Mrs. Agnes Buchwald is also a judge and officiated at the 1985 American Boxer Club Specialty Show. She is the former President of the São Paulo State Boxer Club and presently Vice President of the Brazilian Kennel Club, as well as President of all Brazilian Specialty Clubs.

PENT Kennels, *São Paulo*

In 1968, Jayme and Evelina Martinelli imported American Ch. Salgray's Stuffed Shirt (Willie) from the United States. He was sired by Ch. Salgray's Balladeer ex Ch. Salgray's Frolic. Willie was shown 11 times and

American & Brazilian Ch. Aracrest's Rockin' Annie, owned by Pent Kennels, Sao Paulo. She is shown with her handler, Chuck Steele. Breeder: Nora McGrisken, Canada.

Brazilian Ch. Jacquet's Richard of Quo Vadis, by American Ch. Happy Ours Fortune de Jacquet, shown going Best Male in Show. Owners: Ruth and Valneide Vieira, Quo Vadis Kennels, Rio de Janeiro.

won Best in Show 11 times. He produced many champions for Pent Kennels and other breeders. Many of his progeny became Best in Show winners and top producers themselves. A modern type with good movement, excellent head and expression, he changed the profile of Brazilian Boxers. While he was only the first of the many importations by Pent Kennels, he began their reputation for producing top quality Boxers.

In 1969, the Martinellis imported a fawn bitch, Salgray's Miss Minx, sired by Ch. Salgray's Ambush ex Salgray's Diamond Lil. Her excellent pedigree and good qualities made her a top producing dam. Bred to Salgray's Stuffed Shirt, her first litter of six produced six champions, and her second litter of three produced three champions.

In 1970 Pent Kennels imported American Ch. Salgray's Beau Gem, sired by Ch. Salgray's Fashion Plate ex Ch. Salgray's Auntie Mame. She became a Best in Show winner but produced only one litter by American Ch. Salgray's Bojangles. Of the three puppies, two became champions.

In 1973, the Martinellis bred American Ch. Aracrest's Rockin' Annie to Ch. Salgray's Stuffed Shirt. This litter produced Ch. It's A Pleasure of Pent Kennels, who in turn produced the famous Ch. Baldo di Verona, owned by Mrs. Alda M. Micheloni. Baldo became top Boxer in Brazil in 1985.

In 1974, the Martinellis imported American Ch. Barday's Country Squire, sired by American Ch. Salgray's Ambush ex American Ch. Barday's Chatterbox. Squire won many all-breed Bests in Show and specialties.

Country Squire and Stuffed Shirt made a great impact on the Boxer breed in Brazil and their names appear in many of today's pedigrees. Among the many champions sired by Squire are Ch. Gabriel de Maiorca, owned by Mr. and Mrs. Bento Bellani, and Ch. Funny Girl of Pent Kennels, the foundation bitch of Hexastar Kennels.

In 1975, Mr. and Mrs. Martinelli visited the United States and acquired a fawn dog, Salgray's Minstrel Man, sired by Ch. Salgray's Ambush ex Ch. Salgray's Jitterbug. Minstrel Man was a full brother to American Chs. Salgray's Minute Man and Salgray's Market Wise. He quickly became a Brazilian champion, siring many champions.

Pent Kennels also purchased American Ch. Merrilane's Frolic of Passion, sired by Int. Ch. Scher-Khoun's Shadrack ex Ch. Merrilane's Mad Passion. Frolic became a Grand National Winner (a title given to dogs that win B.I.S. awards in three different Brazilian states under three different judges). Her first litter, sired by American Ch. Benjamin of Five T's, produced the top winner, Ch. Benjie's Point of Honour of Pent Kennels. Her second litter was sired by another Merrilane import, Ch. Merrilane's Fiesta Fortune, and produced two more champions. Another breeding to American Ch. Cava Lane's Pippin, owned by Mr. José Américo Borba de Oliviera, produced the outstanding winner, Ch. Vagabond King of Pent Kennels.

In 1978, American Ch. Tudosal's Pazzaz, bred and owned by Mrs. Betty Claire Frohock, was sent to Pent Kennels to attain his Brazilian championship and to stand at stud. When he returned to the United States as a Brazilian champion, he left many champion progeny in Brazil.

In 1980, Ellie Linderholm sent three Boxers to Pent Kennels, Ch. Merrilane's Call Me Madam, Ch. Merrilane's Fiesta Fortune, and Merrilane's Saint and Sinner (later sold to Uruguay). Madam was bred to Ch. Thorwood's Bucksaw, owned by Hexastar Kennels, and produced a lovely fawn bitch, Ch. Ziglia of Pent Kennels.

Ch. Merrilane's Fiesta Fortune attracted the favorable attention of both judges and breeders, and he sired Chs. Ximente and Xenia of Pent Kennels.

In 1986 Pent Kennels purchased an 11-month-old fawn bitch, TuRo's Tradition, sired by Ch. Marquam Hill's Traper of TuRo, and Ch. TuRo's Gamine of Hyde Park (also sired by Traper). Gamine has been shown only once since her arrival in Brazil, and on that occasion she won Best of Breed at the prestigious São Paulo State Boxer Club Specialty Show.

Jayme Martinelli is President of the São Paulo State Kennel Club and judges all breeds. He has judged in most South American countries and was a member of both the Board of Judges and the Board of Directors of the Brazilian Kennel Club.

Evelina Martinelli is the Vice President of the São Paulo State Boxer Club and is licensed to judge Boxers, Sporting, Toy and Non-Sporting Groups.

QUO VADIS Kennels, *Rio de Janeiro*

In 1972, Ruth Cavalheiro Vieira established this kennel with the purchase of a brindle bitch, Sá Brito's Liza, a granddaughter of Ch. Treceder's Invader. She became an International Champion and was bred to Ch. Pinebrook's Trade Mark. This breeding produced the famous Int. Ch. Quo Vadis Augustus Caesar. A Multiple Best in Show winner, Caesar produced an excellent line of champions including the outstanding bitch, Ch. Claudio's Sunset of Fire. She was bred to American and Brazilian Ch. Paragon's Nyte Rider, sired by Ch. Benjomin of Five T's.

This breeding produced Brazil's most famous Boxer litter—three males and three bitches, all of whom became champions either in Brazil or in other countries. They were named Julius Caesar, Juliana, Justinianus, Jacinthus, Justina and Jacina. By far the most well known was Julius Caesar, named after his grandfather, Augustus Caesar. Quo Vadis Kennels considered him their most brilliant star. He was recognized by many well-known judges from Brazil and overseas, including Heather Logan, Michael Millan and Bruce Korson. In 1983, he attained No. 1 ranking in Brazil.

Canadian Ch. Boxella's Wyatt Earp, bred by Joe Heine and owned by Bill Scarpa.

Ch. Joculu's Charming Fashion, owned by Norah McGriskin, was the foundation matron of Ms. McGriskin's Aracrest Kennels.

102

Mrs. Vieira currently has the No. 1 Boxer bitch in Brazil, Caesar's granddaughter, Ch. Bright of Talahassee, a multiple Best in Show winner.

A very modest person, Ruth Vieira has great breeding plans for the future, which she hopes will result in more winners and, more importantly, in good quality Brazilian Boxers.

Canada

Because of the geographical proximity of Canada to the United States, it is hard to trace pure Canadian Boxers, as they are closely interwoven with American lines. While Canadians occasionally import English and German dogs, they usually prefer Canadian and American lines. Each country boasts high quality Boxers, and breeders use the best stud dogs available in either country to complement their bitches. Exhibitors from Canada and the United States compete in each other's countries, not only in the conformation ring but also in obedience.

The first Boxer was registered in the 1934-1935 Canadian Kennel Club Stud Book under the breed name "Boxer Spaniel." In 1946 the first Canadian Boxer Club was formed by 12 people and called the Western Boxer Club. It is no longer in existence. In 1947 the Boxer Club of Canada was organized, and today it holds one Specialty show a year and two "boosters" (supported entries at all-breed shows). Their annual awards are numerous and coveted.

In 1985, 299 litters of Boxers were registered with the Canadian Kennel Club, with 867 dogs registered, making the Boxer 17th in popularity.

In 1986, 324 litters of Boxers were registered, showing an increase of over eight percent, with 1309 dogs registered, an enormous increase. Again the Boxer placed 17th in popularity.

By the end of June 1987 registration had already reached 606 dogs with 173 litters registered. It would seem that the popularity of the Boxer in Canada is increasing, which is a tribute to dedicated breeders north of the border.

The greatest number of Boxer breeders are located in the Toronto area, although there are some famous kennels situated in other parts of Canada.

One of the first Boxer breeders of significance was Mr. S. W. Scarpa of Malabar Kennels, Pointe Fortune, Quebec. In the mid-1940s he purchased a son of Ch. Dorian v. Marienhof from Mazelaine, who became the Canadian Ch. Allison Adonis, and Dorinda of Fostoria (sired by American Ch. Klaus v.d. Uhlandshohe of Bladan ex American Ch. Prima of Fostoria), who also became a Canadian champion. Adonis and Dorinda produced three Malabar champions, including Ch. Allison Carrol.

Allison Carrol was bred to Ch. But Good of Lilac Hedge and produced Ch. Allison Premier, who finished in 1947.

Mr. Scarpa used Mazelaine lines tracing back to Sigurd and Dorian. Records show that Mr. Scarpa used the finest stud dogs available, as we can see by the fact that there are 33 Malabar champions recorded.

Perhaps the best remembered are Ch. Malabar's Janus, who finished in 1955 and sired four Malabar champions, Ch. Malabar's Anthony Earp, a top winning dog in Canada, and Ch. Commander Roger, who finished in 1973 and sired five Malabar champions.

Mr. Scarpa was killed in an automobile accident, and his kennel manager, Luc Boileau, closed the kennels. Despite his untimely death, there is no doubt that Mr. Scarpa played an important role in early Canadian Boxer history.

Another pioneer of Boxers in Canada was Miss Jean Grant of the famous Blossomlea kennels. She was born in Scotland around the turn of the century.

Blossomlea Kennels was founded with a plain brindle Lustig daughter, Ozark Jerris, whom Miss Grant bred to Robin of Three Britches, a son of Warlord.

Several generations of careful breeding and planning finally produced Ch. Painted Besom of Blossomlea, the first Canadian Boxer to win a Best in Show. Besom was bred to the immortal American Ch. Bang Away of Sirrah Crest, whom Miss Grant considered to be the supreme Boxer. This breeding produced Ch. Chat Away of Blossomlea, who in turn was bred to American Ch. Jered's Spellbinder, producing Ch. Fireside Chat of Blossomlea. Fireside Chat was then bred to American Ch. Salgray's Flying High, producing Ch. Bobby Pin of Blossomlea. Bobby Pin became the dam of Ch. Salgray's Double Talk.

There is hardly a kennel in Canada whose pedigrees do not reflect Jean Grant's foresight and judgment. Even though she had no formal knowledge of genetics, she realized the importance of correct line breeding and insuring that the best bitches were bred to the most suitable studs. Although she was a single person without great financial resources, she always seemed to find enough money or, if need be, make some kind of arrangement, to go to the top studs in the United States.

Jean Grant pursued her adopted vocation as Boxer breeder with a tremendous amount of energy and determination , and she not only gave Canadian Boxers a proper foundation but also acted as a guide and mentor to the few people she considered able to carry on her work. She died at the age of 94 in September, 1983.

Outstanding Canadian Kennels

ARACREST Kennels, *Pickering, Ontario*

In 1969, Nora McGriskin founded Aracrest Boxers with the purchase

American & Canadian Ch. Aracrest's Velvet Sensation, by Int. Ch. Millan's Fashion Hint ex Ch. Joculu's Charming Fashion. A most successful campaigner, she won the Grand Futurity at the American Boxer Club Specialty in 1973.

of a six-month-old brindle bitch, sired by Int. Ch. Millan's Fashion Hint.

At that time, Ms. McGriskin had no intention of showing the bitch, but as she began to grow and develop Nora decided to seek some professional advice as to her show potential. She was encouraged to show the bitch and to start training her.

The advice proved to be sound, and the brindle bitch grew up to be Ch. Jocolu's Charming Fashion, the foundation of Aracrest Kennels, and a Dam of Merit.

In 1970, "Charm" won Winners Bitch at Westminster K.C., and plans were made to breed her to Int. Ch. Scher-Khoun's Shadrack (a Fashion Hint son). The resulting litter included American and Canadian Ch. Aracrest's Jered, American and Canadian Ch. Aracrest's Kaylib, American and Canadian Ch. Aracrest's Trinket, and Canadian Ch. Aracrest's Brocade.

Jered is the youngest Boxer on record to win an American championship. He gained his Canadian title with two Bests in Show from the Open class. A multiple breed, group, and Best in Show winner, Jered was retired at three years of age after winning the American Boxer Club Specialty in 1973. He became a Sire of Merit with 22 champions.

Jered's littermate, American and Canadian Ch. Aracrest's Kaylib, owned by Joyce Johnson of Grangerland, Texas, is also a Sire of Merit (15 champions).

Trinket was bred to her grandfather, Int. Ch. Millan's Fashion Hint, producing American and Canadian Ch. Aracrest's Fashion Impact. Brocade was bred to her littermate, Kaylib, and produced two American champions, Aracrest's Rockin' Annie and Aracrest's Cotton Jenny.

Charm's second litter was sired by her father, Int. Ch. Millan's Fashion Hint, and produced American Ch. Aracrest's Courier and littermate Canadian Ch. Velvet Sensation.

Velvet Sensation's son, Ch. Aracrest's Talisman, another Sire of Merit, has produced 18 American champions to date with other promising youngsters being shown. Talisman sired the 1982 Best of Breed winner at the American Boxer Club Specialty, American Ch. Quebo's Miss Saturday Night.

Canadian Ch. Aracrest's Rhinegold, a Velvet daughter, sired by American and Canadian Ch. Scotlea's Billy Be Damned, is also a good producer. She is the dam of American Ch. Aracrest's Irish Cream, American Ch. Salgray's K.O., Canadian Ch. Aracrest's Ad Hoc and South African Ch. Aracrest's Ipsofacto.

Nora McGriskin is well known as a successful professional handler of both Boxers and Doberman Pinschers. In 1983, she judged the 12 to 18 month classes of the Futurity Stakes at the American Boxer Club Specialty. She was only the second Canadian ever to judge this show.

American & Canadian Ch. Malabar's Crackerjack, bred and owned by O. S. Scarpa and Luc Boileau, shown scoring a Working Group first under breed authority Stanley Whitmore.

Ch. Hot Spell of Blossomlea, a top-producing sire in the late 1950s, bred by Jean Grant and owned by Stanley and Eve Whitmore. He is shown here in an owner-handled Group first under judge Lloyd Brackett.

American & Canadian Ch. Aracrest's Kaylib, bred and owned by Norah McGriskin.

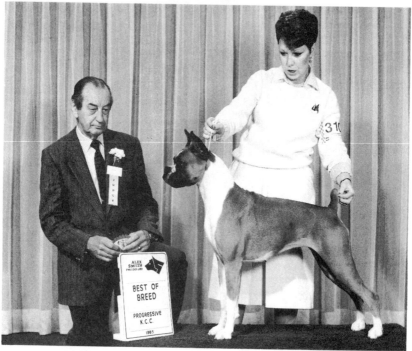

Canadian Ch. Hershey's In Vogue, owned and handled by Norah McGriskin to this Canadian Best of Breed win.

DONESSLE Boxers, *Oakville, Ontario*

When Frank Rouse was still in medical school, he and his new bride, Betty, saw a Boxer and decided that was the dog for them. However, they didn't buy one until their son's seventh birthday. Then they acquired a brindle bitch from Pat and Gerry Hanson of Hansparke's Kennels. Her name was Dynamite Dot, and she was a daughter of Int. Ch. Millan's Fashion Hint. Dr. and Mrs. Rouse agreed to breed her, and in time Dot was bred to her half brother, Int. Ch. Scher-Khoun's Shadrack. Frank and Betty Rouse kept a flashy brindle bitch puppy, who became Ch. Donessle's Miss Fancy. This first Donessle champion began a long line of top producers.

Under the careful guidance of Shirley and Ben De Boer, Miss Fancy was bred twice to American and Canadian Ch. Grayroy's Minstrel Boy. She produced four American champions, making her a Dam of Merit in America as well as Canada. One of her sons, American Ch. Trefoil's Dylan of Donessle, became an American Boxer Club Sire of Merit (eight champions).

Missy's daughter, Ch. Donessle's Foxfire, was the dam of nine champions including two Sires of Merit, Ch. Donessle's Crusader and American and Canadian Ch. Donessle's Diplomat, and a Dam of Merit, Ch. Donessle's Enchantress.

Enchantress was the dam of Ch. Donessle's Nightwind, owned by Nance and Richard Shields of Canonsburg, Pennsylvania, who won the Futurity Stakes and was Best of Winners at the 1980 American Boxer Club Specialty. Nightwind was the dam of the 1987 American Boxer Club Winners Dog and Best of Winners, Shieldmont's Judge 'N' Jury.

Crusader was the sire of American and Canadian Ch. Donessle's Cassino, who won the Futurity Stakes of the 1982 American Boxer Club Specialty. To date he has sired 23 Canadian champions and seven American champions, thus continuing the Donessle line of outstanding producers.

More than 150 dogs have carried the Donessle name. Of those, 43 are Canadian champions, 12 are American champions, and five are champions in other countries.

Frank and Betty Rouse take the breeding of Boxers very seriously. They try never to breed to a dog with major faults and always to see some puppies that the dog has previously produced. This is one of the reasons that Dr. and Mrs. Rouse make their annual pilgrimage to the American Boxer Club Specialty, no matter where it is held.

Donessle bitches have been bred to such great dogs as Int. Ch. Scher-Khoun's Shadrack, American and Canadian Ch. Scher-Khoun's Meshack, American and Canadian Ch. Grayroy's Minstrel Boy, American Ch. Benjomin of Five T's, American Ch. Arriba's Associate of Karjean,

Ch. Donessle's Nightwind being awarded Best of Winners at the 1980 A.B.C. Specialty show enroute to his American championship. Shown in the presentation are (from left) Carl A. Wood, judge Beatrice P. Goodman, handler Dick Baum and Club President Dr. Dick Mason.

Canadian Ch. Elharlen's Zipcode, a Ch. Salgray's Minute Man son, owned and bred by Eleanor Foley.

American Ch. Aracrest's Talisman and American Ch. Holly Lane's Prairie Chief.

Frank and Betty Rouse are quick to point out that their success has been made with the advice and counselling of fellow breeders, handlers and clients, many of whom have become very good friends.

ELHARLEN Boxers, Reg., *Mt. Uniacke, Nova Scotia*

In 1960, Eleanor Foley acquired a two-year-old fawn male Boxer sired by Ch. Hotspell of Blossomlea, a Ch. Jered's Spellbinder son. He won at numerous matches and took second in the Group at his first point show. The next weekend he fared poorly, and Eleanor began comparing him to the other Boxers being shown and to the Boxer standard. Despite his early success, the fawn male was never shown again.

Eleanor and her husband began looking for a good foundation bitch. First they purchased a Bang Away granddaughter but decided not to breed her. After more research and questioning, they decided on a bitch from Blossomlea kennels. She was sired by Ch. Salgray's Flying High ex Ch. Fireside Chat of Blossomlea. In time she became Ch. Bobby Pin of Blossomlea. The Foleys joined the Canadian Kennel Club and decided on a kennel name of Elharlen.

Bobby Pin was bred to a double Bang Away grandson, Ch. Chataway Dandy of Blossomlea, a Best in Show son of Chataway of Blossomlea. One champion bitch resulted from this litter.

Bobby was later bred to American Ch. Salgray's Fashion Plate, and that litter of three bitches produced one Canadian champion and one American champion. A repeat breeding produced Ch. Elharlen's Camanchero, who became a Best in Show winner. Another bitch from the litter, Elharlen's Camero, became the dam of the American Boxer Club Best of Breed winners and Best in Show winners, American Ch. Galanjud's Blue Chip and American Ch. Salgray's Bojangles.

Bred to Ch. Salgray's Ambush, Bobby produced Ch. Salgray's Double Talk and Ch. Salgray's Double Play, two more Best in Show winners.

Elharlen Boxers have produced 30 Canadian champions, three of them Best in Show winners, one American and Canadian champion, and six American champions including three Best in Show winners. Eleanor Foley usually handles her own dogs in the show ring and is a frequent visitor to American Boxer Club Specialty Shows.

HAVILAND Boxer Kennels, *Thornhill, Ontario*

In 1948, this kennel was established by Stan and Eve Whitmore with three bitches and one male, Ch. Beau Jangles of Showline, sired by American Ch. Baron of Brightwood.

To date, this kennel has bred over 150 Canadian champions, nine of

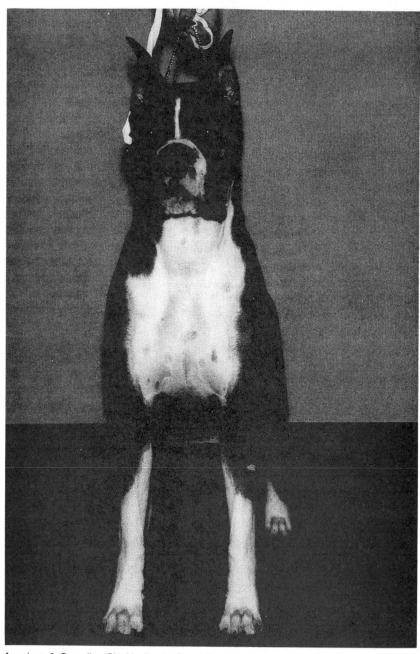

American & Canadian Ch. Haviland's Count Royal, owned and bred by Stanley and Eve Whitmore, was Canada's top-winning Boxer for 1977-79 and was a Canadian Sire of Merit as well.

whom have been Best in Show winners in Canada. Their most famous Boxer, American and Canadian Ch. Haviland's Count Royal, was handled by Mr. and Mrs. Whitmore to Top Dog in Canada in 1979.

The Whitmores have won the Canadian Breeder of the Year Award ten times. Some of the top winning Boxers in Canada owned by Haviland Kennels were Canadian Ch. Haviland's Gai Robin, Canadian Ch. Haviland's Rebel Rouser, American and Canadian Ch. Haviland's Count Royal, and American and Canadian Ch. Diamondaire's Dealers Choice.

Mr. and Mrs. Whitmore are both all-breed judges in Canada and judge frequently in the United States. Eve Whitmore has judged the American Boxer Club Specialty, which she considers a high honor.

Currently they have a kennel of 15 Boxers and still exhibit when time allows.

MEMORYLANE Kennels, *Ontario*

Miss Vera Bartol was born in Yugoslavia and emigrated to Canada in the early 1950s. She had always loved Boxers and formed a breeding partnership with a fellow countryman, Michael Millan. They bred and showed Boxers for many years, and the crowning success of this partnership was the legendary Int. Ch. Millan's Fashion Hint.

In 1970 Miss Bartol formed her own kennels, which she called Memorylane, and had great success breeding and showing champion Boxers. Among her kennel stars were Int. Ch. Memorylane's Fashion Escort, who was Best Puppy of the Year 1970 and became a Sire of Merit, American and Canadian Ch. Memorylane's Avenger, the No. 1 Boxer in the United States in 1975 and an American Sire of Merit with 12 champions, American and Canadian Ch. Memorylane's Zenith, and American Ch. Salgray's Argo of Memorylane.

Always a controversial person, Vera Bartol nevertheless made a great contribution to the Boxer breed in both Canada and the United States. Unfortunately she died of lung cancer in mid-1987 and was buried with the ashes of her favorite dog, Fashion Hint, on her chest.

MEPHISTO Boxers Reg., *Surrey, British Columbia*

In 1968, Walter and Monika Pinsker purchased their first Boxer, who, handled by Walter, became Ch. Haviland's Gold Rebel.

Mr. and Mrs. Pinsker then decided to breed their own champions, so they purchased Ch. Scher-Khoun's Autumn Concerto, an outstanding fawn bitch who was not only their foundation bitch but ranks among the top producing bitches in Canada. Thus, in 1969, Mephisto Kennels were founded.

Autumn Concerto produced ten champions, four of whom, American, Canadian, and Bermudian Ch. Mephisto's Vendetta, American, Canadian,

Bermudian, and Mexican Ch. Mephisto's Stakkatto, American, Canadian, and Norwegian Ch. Mephisto's Intermezzo and Canadian Ch. Mephisto's Battlecry, won over 28 Best in Show awards in three different countries.

Shortly after acquiring Autumn Concerto, Walter and Monika Pinsker purchased an equally outstanding brood bitch, Ch. Verwood's Lollipop, a brindle Fashion Hint daughter. It is believed that this bitch set a world record by producing 12 champions. One of them was the noteworthy Triple Ch. Mephisto's Soldier of Fortune, sire of over 100 champions, winner of 24 Bests in Show and Top Dog in Canada.

This remarkable success was the result of linebreeding Concerto and Lollipop to the outstanding Fashion Hint and his equally prolific son, Shadrack. Continued crossbreeding of the progeny from the afore-mentioned four Boxers led to the breeding which Walter and Monika Pinsker think is their finest and most important achievement, American, Canadian, and Bermudian Ch. Mephisto's Vendetta.

Both Monika and Walter are extremely proud of the fact that this truly outstanding dog's pedigree is reflected in the two top producers in the United States, Ch. Marquam Hill's Traper of TuRo and Ch. Doggone Ounce of Gold, and that he has passed his showmanship on to Ch. TuRo's Cachet, Ch. Wagner Wilverday Famous Amos, and Ch. DJ's Mystique of Galaenjud, all outstanding winners in the show ring.

The Mephisto Kennel has rarely had more than five Boxers in residence, but they have produced 45 champions in seven countries, many of whom are double or triple champions. Walter and Monika Pinsker continue to strive to improve the quality of their dogs and their present stud, Canadian Ch. Mephisto's Zorro of LeBlanc, shows every promise of carrying on the tradition set by his impressive ancestors.

Monika Pinsker has always run the kennels while Walter concentrated on showing and exhibiting the dogs. However, their daughter, Michelle, has taken over handling responsibilities in recent years and is the youngest handler ever to win an all-breed Best in Show award with a Boxer in Canada. Michelle's handling has allowed Walter Pinsker to devote more time to judging. He is licensed to judge the entire Working, Herding, Terrier and Hound Groups, and has officiated at shows in the United States, Mexico, Southeast Asia, Africa and Europe.

MILLAN Boxers (formerly of Toronto)

Born in Yugoslavia, Mike Millan emigrated to Canada in the 1950s and one Christmas received as a gift a fawn male Boxer named Duke von Fritz. This began Millan's love affair with the breed, and he developed an intense interest in Boxers, visiting shows and kennels, talking with breeders and judges, all in an effort to find the best breeding stock. He soon met Mr. Jack Northover and was very impressed with his breeding. He purchased a

Ch. Bonnie Lee's Dancing Doll, a BIS winner and the dam of Ch. Haviland's Rebel Rouser. Her breeders were Scott and Nora McNair and she was owned by Stanley and Eve Whitmore.

Ch. Mephisto's Solider of Fortune, bred by Walter and Monika Pinsker and owned by Donna M. Cole, is the sire of 58 champions.

Ch. Mephisto's Vendetta, owned by Walter and Monika Pinsker, sired by Norwegian Ch. Mephisto's High Noon ex Canadian Ch. Scher-Khoun's Autumn Concerto. This dog became a champion in Canada, the US and Bermuda and sired 30 champions in turn.

115

flashy brindle bitch sired by Ch. Salgray's Flying High. He called her "Dusky," but she was registered as Gaymitz Jet Action. Mike admits she was always his favorite bitch.

Jet Action was shown by a young school boy of 16 years who finished her quickly. She soon became the first Canadian Boxer bitch to become an American champion and the first Canadian dog to become a triple champion.

Although advised against the breeding, Mike Millan decided to breed Jet Action to Ch. Salgray's Fashion Plate and the rest is history. The breeding produced Int. Ch. Millan's Fashion Hint, top Canadian sire of all time of all breeds with 127 champion get including 65 American champions. *The Kennel Review System* proclaimed him Top Sire in the Breed and the Working Group. He received the American Boxer Club award for producing the most champions in one year (18) and produced the most Best in Show winners. Fashion Hint was the American Boxer Club Sire of the Year from 1971 to 1974 and holds the American Boxer Club record for producing the most top producers, namely 11.

Now a resident of the Blue Ridge Mountains of Georgia, Mike Millan still has Boxers, though he rarely shows. However, his interest is just as keen, and his love of the breed is still strong. He is an American Kennel Club approved Boxer judge.

PINEPATH Kennels, Reg., *Fingal, Ontario*

In 1967, Jack and Cathryn Ireland obtained a fawn bitch, Balmar Queen Bee, from the late Catherine Lloyd of Balmar Kennels. This bitch was bred to Int. Ch. Scher-Khoun's Meshack, and, with the guidance of Shirley and Ben De Boer, the Irelands chose the best puppy to keep as their foundation bitch, Pinepaths Mini Bee.

This bitch was bred to Meshack's sire, Int. Ch. Scher-Khoun's Shadrack, and the Pinepath line began. Jack and Catherine Ireland have adhered closely to linebreeding with only occasional outcrosses when necessary.

In 1976, Ch. Pinepaths Sweet Gypsy Bee was Winners Bitch at the Georgia Boxer Specialty, but she was bred to Ch. Moon Valley's Sun N' Shadow before completing her American championship. This breeding produced the Irelands' first stud dog, Ch. Pinepaths Gemini. Gemini produced many champions in Canada and became a Canadian Sire of Merit. He sired American and Canadian Ch. Trimanor Fair Antionette and American and Canadian Ch. Trimanor Pinepaths Hudson Bay, a Canadian Sire of Merit.

Hudson Bay had an outstanding career for his short life. He finished with three majors and was Grand Sweepstakes Winner at the Central Indiana Boxer Club Specialty. He produced many champions including

American, Canadian & Bermudian Ch. Gaymitz Jet Action, by Ch. Salgray's Flying High ex Canadian Ch. Gaymitz Dash O'Fire. Bred by Mr. and Mrs. F. T. Northover and owned by Michael Millan, she was the dam of the celebrated Int. Ch. Millan's Fashion Hint.

Int. Ch. Millan's Fashion Hint, sire of 127 champions, was bred and owned by Michael Millan

American and Canadian Ch. Countrytimes Candy Apple. Hudson Bay's tragic death at five years of age was caused by a commercial weed killer.

Pinepath Kennels is currently campaigning American and Canadian Ch. Acadias Consquistador, a Hudson Bay grandson bred by Brian and June Cross. He has proved himself an owner's dream, starting in the show ring with outstanding wins at 10 months. In 1985 and 1986 he was the top winning Boxer in Canada, and in the latter year he was the No. 6 Working dog in Canada. He is also a multiple Best in Show winner.

Over 45 Boxers with the Pinepath prefix have finished their championships in Canada, and Pinepath stud dogs have sired eight American champions. Jack and Cathryn Ireland breed two litters per year and enjoy showing their own dogs. In recent years they have handled many American dogs to their Canadian championships. Jack Ireland enjoys judging matches and has judged a number of Boxer Sweepstakes in the United States.

SCHER-KHOUN Kennels, Reg. *(formerly of Toronto)*

Shirley De Boer's first contact with Boxers was in 1947 when she was working for a veterinarian. Mr. and Mrs. Spencer Weller, well-known German Shepherd breeders, had just imported a Boxer from the Mazelaine Kennels and brought the puppy to the clinic for examination. Shirley fell in love with the breed and later bought a puppy from the Wellers.

Mr. and Mrs. Weller's approach to breeding had a tremendous influence on Shirley and was later adopted by the Scher-Khoun Kennels.

In 1947, along with the Wellers and several other breeders, Shirley became a Charter Member of the Boxer Club of Canada.

Scher-Khoun Kennels was registered in 1957. It was named after the famous Afghan hound, Ch. Shirkhan of Grandeur, but the Canadian Kennel Club misspelled it when they issued the certificate.

Shirley and her husband, Ben, purchased their foundation bitch, Canyonair's Teacher's Pet, whom Shirley handled to her Canadian championship. They then bred Teacher's Pet to Ch. Captain Lookout of Thorhall, and she produced an outstanding litter, which included Ch. Tagwood's Bronze Silhouette. Bronze Silhouette was bred to American Ch. Canyonair's Man-on-Fire and produced Ch. Scher-Khoun's Fire Imp.

Fire Imp was in turn bred to Jean Grant's Ch. Standfast of Blossomlea. Standfast's background included Spellbinder and Bang Away bloodlines. A bitch from this litter, Ch. Scher-Khoun's Apricot Brandy, was bred back to her sire, Standfast, and she produced Ch. Scher-Khoun's Carousel.

In the ten years since the beginning of the Scher-Khoun breeding program, each of the four generations of bitches was an improvement over the previous generation. This was one of the breeding principles adopted by

Ch. Pinepath's Gemini with his breeder/owner Jack Ireland. Shown here at nine months, Gemini distinguished himself as a sire with 15 champion offspring.

American & Canadian Ch. Acadia's Conquistador, a grandson of Hudson Bay, bred by Brian and June Cross. This dog is a BIS winner and was the top-winning Boxer in Canada for 1985-86.

Scher-Khoun Kennels and was achieved through the concentration of bloodlines through linebreeding and in-breeding.

Carousel was bred to Int. Ch. Millan's Fashion Hint, whose pedigree included Salgray and Blossomlea dogs, and in 1967, Canada's Centennial Year, Int. Ch. Scher-Khoun's Shadrack and Int. Ch. Scher-Khoun's Syncopation were born. Both dogs quickly finished their American and Canadian championships.

Shadrack's adult show career led him to become Canada's Top Dog of all breeds for two consecutive years, 1969 and 1970. He also had an impressive American show career, where he was successfully campaigned at Boxer specialties. He won Best of Opposite Sex and Best of Breed at American Boxer Club regional shows.

Shadrack was a prepotent sire, producing 56 Canadian champions and 44 American champions. Eleven of his American champions became Sires or Dams of Merit, including Int. Ch. Scher-Khoun's Meshack and Int. Ch. Scher-Khoun's Abednego. Shadrack, Meshack, and Abednego sired more than 80 American champions, including numerous Sires and Dams of Merit. Many of them went on to win top honors in the show ring in various countries throughout the world.

Besides the Boxers mentioned, the Scher-Khoun Kennels also bred such outstanding dogs as American and Canadian Ch. Scher-Khoun's Coquette (Winners Bitch at the American Boxer Club Specialty), American and Canadian Ch. Scher-Khoun's Delegation, Int. Ch. Scher-Khoun's Electioneer, Canadian Ch. Scher-Khoun's Autumn Concerto, Canadian Ch. Scher-Khoun's Blue Beau (Best of Breed at the Boxer Club of Canada Specialty), and many more.

Ben De Boer states that Scher-Khoun Kennels has been a satisfying experience where a breeding strategy was followed according to plan. Their goal was to produce Boxers good enough to win at American Boxer Club shows and who could pass on their outstanding qualities to their offspring. That goal having been achieved, Shirley and Ben De Boer no longer breed Boxers. They make their home in Montreal, Quebec, and enjoy giving advice to up-and-coming breeders, as well as passing judgment in the ring.

Germany

During the six years of World War II, dog breeding in Germany changed drastically. Because the Army needed service dogs, breeders were supported with food rations for working dogs. However, in return for their rations the breeders were required to breed only dogs of high quality and good temperament. The military reviewed dog shows once or twice a year and only the soundest dogs were bought. These dogs had to have strong nervous systems, good hearing, and the ability to scent well. Any dogs not meeting these standards were deprived of food rations.

American & Canadian Ch. Scher-Khoun's Shadrack strongly impacted the breed as a sire with 56 Canadian and 44 American champions to his credit.

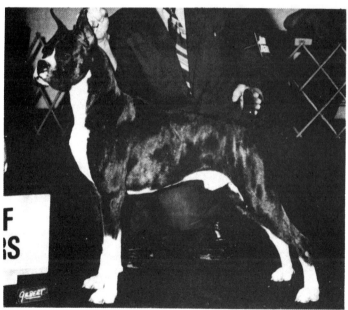

American & Canadian Ch. Scher-Khoun's Meshack, bred and owned by Ben and Shirley De Boer. A Shadrack son out of Int. Ch. Scher-Khoun's Syncopation, he has inherited his sire's ability as a producer. His record stands at 28 champions.

Ch. Xanthos v. Bereler Ries, Sch.H.III, by Bruno v.d. Morsback, Sch.H.I ex Queen v. Bereler Ries, Sch.H.III.

Agave vom Okeler Forst, Sch.H.III, FH, AD, by Ch. Xanthos v. Bereler Ries ex Bonny v.d. Pfennigebrücke.

Ch. Utz v. Bereler Ries, Atibox winner, Champion of the Year and Club Champion, was sired by Bruno v.d. Morsback, Sch.H.I ex Queen v. Bereler Ries, Sch.H.III.

122

Another innovation was the practice of breed selection. Dogs were examined for health, size, weight, chest expansion, bones, muscles, hind- and forequarters, head shape, nose, forehead, color of eyes, teeth and other features. All these qualities were listed in a *Breed Selection Book,* the first of which appeared in 1941, with 54 Boxer males and 49 bitches listed. Only these Boxers could be bred.

The second *Breed Selection Book* appeared in 1942 with 39 males and 29 bitches. Breed selection continued for two more years, but the books were not published.

Along with qualifying for breed selection, the dog also had to win a training badge which required strong temperament and character. To earn a badge, the dog was required to defend his master from attack, hold the attacker from moving, and ignore shots or other disturbances.

Fortunately the Boxer qualified well under these severe tests, and eventually the better dog breeders welcomed the system. While many dogs suffered badly from lack of food, the Boxer, as a breed, improved dramatically during the war years.

Philip and Friederun Stockmann came through the war with 11 bitches. Their prized stud dog, Rolf v. Vogelsberg, survived his military service and was returned to the Stockmanns. He went on to win high honors again in the show ring. Philip Stockmann died in July 1946.

When visiting the United States in 1949, Frau Stockmann was offered two puppies by Dr. and Mrs. Harris. She picked a beautiful bitch, Goody Goody, and her kennel mate, a male, Abra Dabra of Sirrah Crest. Dr. Harris paid all the expenses to send the dogs home with Frau Stockmann so Lustig's blood could return to Germany.

When Frau Stockmann visited the Mazelaine Kennels, she chose a dog sired by Ch. Mazelaine's Zazarak Brandy ex Mazelaine's Handmaiden. He was sent to Frau Stockmann at the age of four months and became the 1950 German Reichssieger (equivalent of Jahressieger or Champion of the Year) at the age of 18 months. His name was Czardas of Mazelaine, and he was the very first foreign-bred Boxer to win a German Sieger title. Czardas sired the 1954 Bundessieger (Champion of an All-Breed show, similar to Westminster) Quickli Von Dom, a brindle. Despite his success in Germany, Czardas was later sold to Allan Dawson in England, because many Germans considered him too small and would not use him for breeding. Mr. Dawson eventually sold him to an American army officer, who brought him back to the United States.

Frau Stockmann died in 1973, but what a legacy she left Boxer breeders all over the world. Through her art, her sculpture, her dedication, and even her mistakes, the modern Boxer evolved. Her life was not an easy one and she faced many hardships. Parting with some of her greatest dogs must have been heartbreaking, but this sad necessity allowed the rest of the world to share the great Von Dom line.

Boxers remained in good hands in Germany, and shows were plentiful after the war. It would take an entire book to list the many great champions and successful breeders as well as a history of the breed. There are some excellent books on the subject written in German.

Photographs show the high quality of today's German Boxers. You will notice that great emphasis is placed on the headpiece, with a wide, square muzzle and a short nose with the tip of the nose higher than the root of the muzzle. White markings are becoming more popular in Germany but, happily, are not seen as often as they are in America.

Breeding System

The German Boxer Club has quite a different breeding system from our own. Rigid rules must be followed, or registrations cannot be made in the official Stud Books.

The Zuchwart (Breed Warden) is the supervisor in control of all breeding. Bitches cannot be bred before they are twenty months old, and they must be tested for temperament as guard dogs. Without this testing, dogs cannot be used for breeding. The Breed Warden is an experienced breeder, who will give advice on the kind of stud dog to complement your bitch. Each breeding must be witnessed and certified by a club member.

The Breed Warden visits the breeder shortly after whelping and verifies the number of puppies and their colors. He also notes any stillborn puppies and any culls. The Breed Warden may no longer require culling, but he may make recommendations. The Breed Warden visits the puppies again after weaning and records any whites, checks, soft palates, monorchids, cryptorchids, or any other defects. These findings are then published in the *Boxer Blätter*. Tails are still docked in Germany, but ear cropping was banned as of January 1, 1987.

Exhibiting in Germany

Most of the German Boxer clubs own or lease their own club houses and grounds where meetings, social functions, and training take place on a regular basis. Most of these clubs are well equipped, and the members work hard and give a lot of support. Training for Schutzhund and Working Trials is encouraged, because it is required of the top show dogs.

There are many shows in Germany and the rest of Europe, but by far the most prestigious is the ATIBOX (Association Technique International du Boxer), an organization to which most European countries belong. It takes place every three years in a different country and is judged by four judges usually coming from other countries. The ATIBOX titles are awarded to the best dog and the best bitch of each color, the best junior dog, and best junior bitch.

The dogs are shown in European fashion on long, loose leads. This is a

Cas Van Worikben, famous sire of World Ch. Casper Van Worikben, bred by Piet van Melis, Holland.

World Ch. Casper Van Worikben, holder of every European title for which he was eligible. He was bred and owned by Piet van Melis.

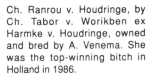

Ch. Ranrou v. Houdringe, by Ch. Tabor v. Worikben ex Harmke v. Houdringe, owned and bred by A. Venema. She was the top-winning bitch in Holland in 1986.

125

more relaxed way of showing without any stacking of the dogs. However, there is a good deal of double handling at times, and Boxers are often baited against each other as if they were terriers. Little attention is paid to gait, and it is not even mentioned in the German standard. Nevertheless the ATIBOX is a wonderful opportunity to see Boxers from so many countries. The writer was fortunate to attend the 1985 ATIBOX show where Boxers from 26 nations were exhibited. Americans were received graciously and royally treated.

The German Klubsieger (Club Champion) award is difficult to obtain and much coveted. The dog or bitch must be over 15 months old and must win three certificates under three different judges at shows controlled by the Munich Boxer Club. The dog or bitch can be in the Open, Working or Champion classes, but the number of entries must be more than 75. There are approximately 40 of these club shows per year, sometimes two on the same day. However, a period of at least 12 months must elapse between the winning of the first and third certificates.

In addition to earning three certificates, the dog must also pass the "Korung" before winning the third certificate. This is a test of character as well as conformation and type. Before qualifying for the Korung, the dog must pass a guard dog test, which includes tracking, manwork, and obedience, plus a test of stamina proving that the dog can cover 20 kilometres at a speed of 10 to 12 kilometres per hour, with only two pauses. In Germany, the title of Champion applies to the total dog.

Holland

Before World War II, Dutch breeders imported many grand specimens of the breed from Germany. These included progeny of Ch. Dorian v. Marienhof, Ch. Lustig v. Dom, Sigurd v. Dom and other pillars of the breed. Although few in numbers, Dutch breeders were enthusiastic about the Boxer and started with the finest of lines.

The Complete Boxer book by Milo G. Delinger states that 1,010 Boxers were registered in the Stud Books for the years 1946 and 1947, which shows the care and dedication Dutch breeders gave to their dogs during the War years.

One of the best-known breeders and judges from Holland was Peter Zimmerman, who will always hold a high place in history of the breed. He bred Boxers under the kennel name of Von Haus Germania for some 40 years and died in 1975. Zimmerman began with Idella V. Pfarrkirchen, a daughter of Ch. Lustig v. Dom, who became the foundation bitch of the Von Haus Germania Kennels. Later, he imported a Bang Away son from the United States, a Lustig son from Italy, Witherford's Satans Touch from Pat Withers of England, Good News of Skelder from Joy Malcom of England, and many more dogs.

126

American & Japanese Grand Ch. Treceder's Progression, whelped
August 1962, owned by Mr. Shigeru Nakamura.

American, Canadian, Japanese & Bermudian Ch.
Jacquet's Urko, the sire of
45 Japanese and 10 American Champions. Urko, also
an International Molossar
Champion with 3 CCs, is
sired by American Ch.
Happy Ours Fortune de
Jacquet. He is owned by Dr.
H. Nakazawa and R. Tomita.

His first champions were sired by Leoncillo's Alf, who produced Champions Fix, Faust and Favoriet. Faust was sold to England and Favoriet spent time there by accident. The fawn bitch, Favoriet von Haus Germania, somehow became lost in Holland and was befriended by a soldier who took her to Germany. Later, she was taken to England and passed through quarantine under the name of Liebe von Germania. Joan Dunkels and Hilary Gamble discovered her and contacted Peter Zimmerman, who went to England in 1947 and took her back to Holland.

The strength of Von Haus Germania Kennels lay in its bitches, particularly Zenith, her daughter Oracle, and Sonya.

Peter Zimmerman judged all over Europe and many times in England, including Crufts. He was well known and respected in the United States.

One of the best-known current breeders is Piet Van Melis of Van Worikben Kennels. The pedigrees of his Boxers go back to Peter Zimmerman's lines. Piet Van Melis bred World Champion "Casper van Worikben," one of the most famous Dutch Boxers, who won every title in Europe and was featured in magazines all over the world.

Another famous breeder is Jan De Vries, whom the writer had the pleasure of meeting at the ATIBOX show in 1985. He bred the 1985 top bitch Hannina V. Adeltrots. Other top breeders who should be mentioned are J. Vermeulen, J. V. Wijck, G. V. Assen, and G. V. Leusen, all of whom have produced top winning dogs.

The Nederlandse Boxer Club was formed in 1904. In 1984 it celebrated its 80th year by publishing a Nederlandse Boxer Club Jubilee Book covering the history of the Boxer in the Netherlands. It is written in Dutch but contains many photographs of top Boxers both past and present.

Japan

Prior to World War II, there were very few Boxers in Japan. When the War ended, American armed forces personnel brought about 50 Boxers with them to Japan, but these were mostly pets. The first Boxer was registered in Japan in 1952.

In 1956, Mr. and Mrs. David Daw of Tokyo imported Ch. Mazelaine's Captain Jinks from Mazelaine Kennels in the United States. Mr. and Mrs. Daw spent a great deal of time and money trying to improve the breed in Japan. Through their efforts and those of a handful of other dedicated Boxer lovers, the breed gradually became more popular. Captain Jinks was used for breeding and shown to Best Dog in Show in Tokyo. His birthdays were celebrated every year by lavish parties given by Mr. and Mrs. Daw. He died at the age of 10½ years in August, 1962.

Several other imported American champions became trend setters in Japan. These included Ch. Canzonet's Minute-Minder, owned by Mr. Ichiyama, whose offspring dominated the Japanese Boxer ring throughout

American Ch. Omega's Special Edition of Sam-El, by Ch. Aracrest's Talisman, was purchased by Dr. Nakazawa in 1984. A Best in Show winner in Japan, he quickly became the top-winning Boxer in his adopted country.

Japanese Ch. Jacquet's Todd going Best King in Show. In 1987 he was the top-winning Boxer in Japan and #8 All Breeds. Todd is owned by Dr. H. Nakazawa and Richard Tomita.

129

the early 1960s. In fact, it was common to find his progeny winning all the first place awards in each category. However, the arrival of Ch. Treceder's Progression, owned by Mr. Shigeru Nakamura, brought welcome competition.

After Ch. Treceder's Progression stole the scene in 1964, Mr. Nakamura imported Ch. Treceder's Happy Hiker (sired by Ch. Oliver's Custom Cut ex Ch. Treceder's Laughter) and the Treceder reign began. Treceder descendants compiled an unmatched string of wins over the rest of the decade.

When Mr. Peter Delano, who handled for the Treceder Kennels in the United States, visited Japan, he pointed out to the breeders that their Boxers were too small. Once again, Japanese breeders turned to American lines to improve their stock.

Dr. Hideaki Nakazawa, a veterinarian, imported Ch. Interlude's Jon-Jon, Ch. Salgray's Rose of Tralee, and Ch. Indian Bend's Red Cloud, all of whom brought needed size and substance to Japanese lines.

In 1981, Dr. Nakazawa visited the Jacquet kennels in Paramus, New Jersey, and became co-owner of Jacquet's Urko. After gaining his American championship, Urko was sent to Japan.

Up until this time, Boxers had not been successful in Japanese Group competition. Urko changed all that. He took Best in Show awards wherever he was shown, and sired over 50 champions in Japan before returning to the United States. They called him "super dog" in Japan—and with good reason.

Later Dr. Nakazawa bought Ch. Jacquet's Dancing Star, who became Japan's top winning Boxer bitch of all time. In 1984, Dr. Nakazawa purchased Ch. Omega's Special Edition of Samel (sired by Ch. Aracrest's Talisman) and showed the dog to five Bests in Show and seven Group I's. He quickly became the top Boxer in Japan and his offspring have garnered many Best of Breed awards.

Dr. Nakazawa believes that inter-relations between American and Japanese Boxer breeders should be encouraged. He feels this will lead to a better understanding of the breed and to the continued breeding and exhibiting of top quality Boxers in Japan.

Scandinavia

To accurately trace the development of Boxers in Scandinavia, we must consider the area as two separate units. For breeders and exhibitors of dogs, Scandinavia is Norway, Sweden and Finland.

The reason is quarantine restrictions. Until the early 1970s, dogs could travel freely between all the Scandinavian countries, but, when Denmark joined the European Common Market, it had to open its borders to all the other member countries. As a result, the three other Scandinavian

American Ch. Merrilane's Salute to April, by Ch. Merrilane's April Holiday. Owner: Paul Scott, Norway.

Paul Scott

American, Canadian & Norwegian Ch. Mephisto's Intermezzo, sired by Int. Ch. Millan's Fashion Hint ex Canadian Ch. Scher-Khoun's Autumn Concerto. Owners: Eva & Paul Scott and Jorunn Mæland, Norway. *Paul Scott*

Int. Ch. Formula Miller, B.I.S. Winner, sired by Canadian & Norwegian Ch. Mephisto's High Noon ex Formula Merlyn. Breeders: Eva & Paul Scott. Owner: Jørn Sevre, Norway. *Paul Scott*

countries closed their borders to Danish dogs and enforced a four-month quarantine. It should be pointed out that Norway, Sweden and Finland were at that time, and still are, free of rabies.

Danish breeders therefore have free access to shows and more importantly to all top breeding stock throughout Europe. As a result, they have tapped many outstanding German and Dutch lines. Their Swedish, Finnish and Norwegian colleagues, on the other hand, have to rely upon their own stock for breeding unless someone imports breeding stock with the considerable extra cost of a four-month quarantine. The only country outside Sweden, Finland and Norway from which a dog can be imported without being quarantined is the United Kingdom, which is also rabies free. That is probably why the English influence is so much in evidence today.

In the history of Boxers in Scandinavia, all three countries have had their golden eras. Starting in Norway, where the first Boxer arrived in 1907, it stretched into the 1930s. The scene was dominated by Mr. L. Eyv. Dahl and his famous Kerberos line, which was inherited and further developed by the late Mr. Jan Berggrav. Mr. Dahl was a personal friend of the Stockmanns of Germany, and he was held in great respect as one of the foremost authorities on the breed.

Sweden saw the first Boxer registered in 1909, but it was not until the early 1940s that their heyday began. Outstanding among the early Swedish breeders was Mr. H. A. Fogelberg, whose Rolands line outshone most of the others. There is hardly any Swedish-bred Boxer today who cannot be traced back to his famous Ch. Rolands Kadett.

The first Finnish Boxer was registered in 1912, but there was hardly any serious breeding until after World War II, when Mrs. Aili Rinne came on the scene with her Borealii Boxers. In a few years she created such a line that, in 1956, Mr. Bernh. Schmitz, then President of the German Boxer Club, went on record in "Dog World" claiming the Finnish Boxer to be the most typical in the world.

The popularity of the Boxer breed in Scandinavia has varied considerably over the years. Norway is the only country showing an increase in present registration of between 400 and 500 annually, which places the Boxer in the top twelve in popularity. Sweden and Finland have both experienced downward trends. Finland registers about 200 annually, which is way down from the figure of 442 in 1974. In Sweden the downward trend is even more evident with 700 Boxers registered annually as against 2,400 in 1974. In neither Sweden nor Finland does the Boxer place in the top twenty breeds.

Scandinavia does not have a point system to measure show wins or record sires and dams of merit. In Scandinavia, a champion Boxer must not only win three challenge certificates but also has to pass a rather severe working dog trial. This restricts the number of champions finished annually to a very few. It also explains why Scandinavian breeders prefer to publicize the number of challenge certificates won. The rules are presently being changed so that the working trial for Boxers can be replaced by a mentality test, which does not require the same amount of arduous training.

All three Scandinavian countries are members of the Federation Cynologique Internationale (The International Dog Federation) and are therefore required to use F.C.I.'s basic standard, which is the same as the standard of the German Boxer Club.

In Scandinavia, one can hear breeders talk of three different types of Boxers, the German, the American, and the English. In fact, each country has gone through German, American and English periods. Generally speaking, the German periods were before World War II, the American periods from the mid-1960s to the end of the 1970s, and the English period since the quarantine.

It should be noted that the pillars of the breed are more or less the same dogs in all three countries.

American Ch. Havana of Sirrah Crest arrived in Sweden in 1950. He was not used at stud extensively but left his mark in Norway and Finland as well as Sweden.

Another early import from the United States, who made a great impact in Finland, was Boxella's Lafayette. Although not a top winning dog, his place in history was assured when he was chosen as a foundation for a nationwide multi-generation breeding plan by the Breed Council of the Finnish Boxer Club. Thereafter he was used extensively at stud.

In the late 1960s, a very influential dog was imported into Sweden. He was American Ch. Treceder's Mighty Dark. He was considered a very striking dog and became a dominant sire, leaving his mark on the breed throughout Scandinavia.

In the early 1970s, American Ch. Wedge Hollow's Sam's Son arrived in Finland to become the second step in the breeding plan of the Finnish Boxer Club. He was later taken to Sweden where, in 1974, he became the top winning dog of the year in all breeds.

Norway, too, had its share of American influence through the importation of My-R's Side Car. He became a Norwegian champion and was a very dominant sire but unfortunately met an accidental death at an early age. Canadian Ch. Mephisto's High Noon, although imported into Sweden, left his mark mainly through his sons in Norway and Finland. American and Canadian Ch. Mephisto's Intermezzo was imported into Norway by Mr. and Mrs. Paul Scott and Jorunn Maeland, and his influence was mainly in that country.

Other U.S. imports are too numerous to mention, and, for the same reason, it would be impossible to try to list the English imports. Suffice to say that Norway has been inclined to favor the Seefeld kennels (Pat Heath) while Finland has leaned more to the Marbleton line (Mary Hambelton).

"Sarah" at three months with friend—a daughter of Ch. Mephisto's Intermezzo   *Paul Scott*

Int. Ch. Larun Good Grief, by Ch. Mephisto's Intermezzo ex Larun Elektra. Bred by Mrs. Unni Vestrheim, Lillestrøm, Norway. Owner: Paul Scott.   *Paul Scott*

Finnish Ch. Dubraza's Waterproof, by Ch. My-R's Side Car ex Dubraza's Burdaresheba—one of the most successful sires in Finland for many years. Breeder: Mr. Lasse Luomanen.

In Sweden, Witherford Boxers (Pat Withers) used to be preferred by some breeders while others chose to go to Gremlin Boxers (the late Marion Fairbrother).

There have been a few German and other European imports during the past two or three decades but none have left any significant progeny to date.

Leading breeders in Sweden are the Marion's Kennels of Bengt and Anders Haernman. They have been breeders of quality Boxers for many decades and imported American and Swedish Ch. Treceder's Mighty Dark.

The top winning Boxer breeders of 1986 were Mr. and Mrs. Christer Petersson and their Ploy's Kennels. Their line is based on American and Swedish Ch. Treceder's Mighty Dark, with some Salgray blood thrown in for good measure.

In Norway, the foremost Boxer breeder is Mr. Paul Scott and his Formula Kennels which goes back to the English Wardrobe line combined with American and Canadian stock. Formula was the top winning Boxer kennel in Norway for a decade.

For the past five years, however, the top winning honors have gone to the Larun Kennels of Mrs. Unni Vestrheim. Her breeding goes back to American and Canadian Ch. Mephisto's Intermezzo combined with Boxella's Jeremiah.

In Finland, the most consistently winning dogs are bred by the Dubraza's Kennels of Mr. Lasse Luomanen. His line is richly endowed with American blood as his top sire was Finnish Ch. Dubraza's Waterproof, a son of Norwegian Ch. My-R's Side Car.

Another Finnish kennel worthy of mention is Mrs. Taimi Eckhardt's Eckbran. Based on Boxella's Lafayette and American Ch. Wedge Hollow's Sam's Son, she has been producing high quality Boxers for the past twenty years.

Mr. Rodney Lindroos, a well-known Finnish breeder and respected judge of Boxers, now residing in Sweden, states that "not one single top winning Boxer of today can be mentioned because if you mention one, you would have to mention several dozen others of equal quality. For the time being, the Scandinavian Boxer can match the competition almost anywhere in the world, but unfortunately there are not any super stars like Bang Away or the Fabulous "F" puppies.

As a note of interest, mention should be made about cropped ears. A dog with cropped ears can be shown in Norway provided it was born before January 1, 1977. You can exhibit a dog with cropped ears in Sweden and Finland provided it comes from a country where cropping is permitted.

South African Ch. Filou von Nassau-Oranien, Sch.H.I, 1980 German Jahres Jugendsieger, imported by John Clarke and Marlien Heystek. Breeder: Mr. Willibald Wendel, Germany.

South African Ch. Jakkalsdans Knight Rampant, sired by South African Ch. Filou von Nassau-Oranien, Sch.H.I, has been successful in the show ring and is producing Champions. Owner/ Breeder: Marlien Heystek.

138

South Africa

In September, 1946, the first Boxer was registered with the South African Kennel Union. He was Vejland's Hector of Denmark, owned by Roy Henwick. The first dog to attain a championship under South African Kennel Union rules was Gaykell Dandy, owned by Mr. Williamson.

In 1948, Kelvin B. Clegg imported a brindle bitch, Bladen's Nora Belle. Mr. Clegg then went to England and purchased three Boxers from Mr. Allon Dawson. They were Stainburndorf Martini, a 20-month-old fawn bitch, Stainburndorf Revenge, a line-bred Stainburndorf Zulu son of eight weeks, and a ten-week-old brindle bitch, Westmorland Witchcraft. In 1949, Martini whelped a litter of nine puppies sired by Hector. Only one puppy survived, and she became the first South African-bred Boxer to be registered. She was a fawn known as Pellindaba of N'Duna.

Mr. Clegg took Nora Belle to England and bred her to Zulu. After they returned, she whelped three dogs and two bitches. One bitch, Jewel of N'Duna, became the first South Africa Boxer to become a champion. Her brother, Chaka of N'Duna, became the first South Africa dog to sire a champion, Ch. Lili Marlene of N'Duna.

In 1949, Mr. Clegg imported Freeman Ozark Jerris, a Lustig daughter, from Jean Grant in Canada. She was followed a year later by Herald of Blossomlea.

1960 was a very important year, as the Federation of Boxer Clubs of South Africa was established. The intent of this organization was to provide a controlling body, based on democratic principles, for the Boxer breed in South Africa. Until that time all Boxers were registered with the all-breed controlling body, which has never permitted the registration or exhibition of dogs with cropped ears. The majority of Boxer owners wished to decide on cropping themselves, but some remained with the all-breed body.

At present the Federation comprises six affiliated Boxer clubs with a membership of approximately 650. Some 250 of these are registered breeders. The organization has a governing body composed of elected delegates representing all the Boxer clubs. Administrative matters are handled by an elected executive committee, assisted by panels of judges, breeders, and trainers.

In popularity, Boxers rank about fifth or sixth of all breeds in South Africa. About 1,500 puppies are registered annually. Every year ten to twelve breed championship shows are held in various parts of the country. Entries range from 60 to 100. To date 15,000 Boxers have been registered in the official Stud Book, of whom 152 were champions by the end of 1986.

In order to qualify as a champion, a Boxer has to win 12 points, including one major, under various judges, in more than one province. At least two points must be awarded after the age of 27 months for a male and

21 months for a bitch. A litter must also be produced before the title is awarded.

A breed rally is held every two years at which a panel of breeders evaluates progeny groups as well as individual dogs for conformation and working ability. Obedience classes are given by most clubs, and Boxers are trained in all three phases of Schutzhund.

Very few countries have a program like South Africa for training judges. Before a provisional judge can even attend lectures on the breed, he must pass a written test on ring stewarding and have had stewarding experience. Later, he must take written examinations on the history of the Boxer, skeletal and surface anatomy, basic genetics, the standard, and ring procedure. Additionally the provisional judge must make written reports on dogs and shows. Two members of the Panel of Judges assess reports after watching the provisional judge in action. It is not easy to become an accredited judge of the Boxer breed in South Africa.

To its great credit, the Federation has established a broad genetic base for the Boxer in South Africa. It has achieved this through the judicious importation of high quality Boxers representing many of the best producing bloodlines in the world.

English and S.A. Ch. Stainburndorf Dandylion of N'Duna was bred by Allon Dawson and imported by Kelvin Clegg in 1954. He was sired by Stainburndorf Frohlich von Dom ex Stainburndorf Babette. He is regarded as a cornerstone of the breed in South Africa. By the time the Federation was founded, he had sired several champions and, as a veteran, produced one Federation champion as well.

Int. Ch. Maurane's Bel Ami von Wiking Blue, Sch.H.I, was acquired from Frau Stockmann in 1958 by the late Mr. Maurice Vane. He gained his international championship in Germany and his South African championship on the Kennel Union circuit. Campaigned again after the Federation was formed, he unfortunately won only 10 points before he died. He sired many South African champions, and his name appears in the pedigrees of many top winning and producing Boxers in Europe. He was sired by Primus von Dom ex Herta von Feldhaid.

American and S.A. Ch. Beaulaine's Parlay of Gezira became the Federation's first champion in 1961. He was imported by Mrs. Louise de Young in 1959 and sired by the famous Bang Away of Sirrah Crest ex American Ch. Beaulaine's Fantasy. He proved to be a powerful stud force in South Africa and sired seven Federation champions.

American and S.A. Ch. Flintwood's Places Please of Strathmere was imported by the late Mr. Basil Allen and proved to be another powerful stud. Sired by American Ch. Barrage of Quality Hill ex American Ch. Sans Souci of Kresthallo, he was bred by Dr. Lloyd Flint. He produced eight champions in South Africa and one in the United States.

Canadian and S.A. Ch. Jandaire's Justice of Peace was imported in

1968 by Louise and the late Elsabe van Aswegen. He was a great-grandson of Places Please and was a very successful show dog winning Best of Breed eight times at championship shows. He sired 16 champions, making him the top producing sire of the Federation to date.

American and S.A. Ch. Aracrest's Courier of Holly Lane was imported by Mark Steele in 1975. Bred by Mr. and Mrs. J. McGriskin of Canada, he was sired by the illustrious Int. Ch. Millan's Fashion Hint ex Can. Ch. Jocolu's Charming Fashion, a Fashion Hint daughter. He gained his South African championship by winning four majors in four straight shows. He is the sire of one American and nine South African champions and the grandsire of four of the Federation's eight top producing bitches.

Wiking vom Schütting was imported as a puppy by Franz and Ute Füglister in 1978. He was bred by the German breeder and judge, Mrs. Karin Rezewsky, and sired by Int. Ch. Enok vom Schütting ex World Ch. Julie vom Schütting. Wiking is closely linebred on the legendary Int. Ch. Witherford Hot Chestnut. He has produced 11 champions to date with many pointed progeny being campaigned. He has also won the Three Wings Sire of the Year award for five consecutive years.

S.A. Ch. Arriba's Pieta of Beckleavale was imported as a youngster by Lea and Hannes Pelser in 1980. Bred by Dr. Ted Fickes, he was sired by American Ch. Arriba's Crescendo ex Merrilane's Banner to Arriba. He has had a meritorious show career, going Best of Breed nine times at championship shows. To date he has produced one champion and has several youngsters with points.

S.A. Ch. Filou von Nassau-Oranien, Sch.H.I, won the 1980 Junior World Championship and the 1980 German Jahres Jugendsieger title (Youth Champion of the Year) before being imported by John Clarke and Marlien Heystek. Bred by Mr. Willibald Wendel, he was sired by Ch. (VDH) Valentino von Schatzkastlein ex Ratze von Heidelch and is linebred on top winner and producer Ch. Carlo von Henningshof. He was co-winner of the Sire of the Year Award in 1986 and has produced four South African champions and one Spanish champion. He has also won a Best in Show and has many pointed youngsters being campaigned.

S.A. Ch. Aracrest's Ipsofacto was imported by Mark Steele in 1983 when only a few months old. He was bred by Norah McGriskin and sired by American Ch. Salgray's Market Wise ex Aracrest's Rhinegold. He shows promise of leaving his mark on the breed and reinforces the earlier Salgray influence. He is the sire of two Federation champions and has many pointed progeny.

Some prominent breeders in the Federation should be mentioned.

BALLYDUFF. John and Fran Clarke of Pretoria have been extremely active members of the Boxer fraternity ever since 1967. John is a past chairman of the Federation and at present is chairman of the Northern Boxer Club. He is a member of the Federation Executive, the Panel of

Judges, and the Panel of Trainers. Fran currently chairs the Executive, in addition to being a member of the Panel of Judges and the committee of Northern Boxer Club.

Their breeding program was initially based on stock linebred from Jandaire's Justice of Peace and continued with the introduction of some of the finest American and European bloodlines. They have produced 14 champions to date, plus a Spanish champion, Ballyduff's Fury, who has won several Best in Show awards at large international all-breed shows in Europe.

In partnership with Marlien Heystek, the Clarkes imported a number of Boxers from Europe. Best known of these is Ch. Filou von Nassau-Oranien, Sch.H.I, the sire of Ballyduff's Fury.

BECKLEAVALE. This Johannesburg kennel was established in 1977 with three foundation bitches obtained from the late Basil Allen. These three full sisters sired by Ch. Strathmere's Riding High ex Strathmere's Amalis of Charmwood, all became champions.

Although the kennel is registered in the name of Lea Pelser, it is very much a joint effort between her and her husband, Hannes. Hannes is also active at committee level, serving on the Federation Executive, the Eastern Transvaal Boxer Club committee and the Panel of Breeders.

The Pelsers received the 1986 Breeder of the Year award and bred the 1986 Dam of the Year, Beckleavale's Mon Cherie of Monalea, sired by American Ch. Wesan's Duke of Dixieland and owned by Sue Smit.

They have imported several Boxers from the United States and one from Europe. Best known of these is Ch. Arriba's Pieta of Beckleavale, who has had a highly successful show career with nine Best of Breed awards. The Pelsers have bred three champions so far, with a host of pointed youngsters being campaigned.

THE CLEGG FAMILY. Kelvin (now residing in the United States), Yvonne and son Christopher represent four decades of intense involvement with the Boxer breed. Boxers carrying their various kennel names (N'Duna, Hedderley and Charmwood) appear in the pedigrees of numerous Federation champions.

One of their many imports was Ch. Allena's Chemain, who arrived in whelp to American Ch. Warlord of Cherokee Oaks. That litter produced Ch. Allena's Siovain, one of the top winning bitches in the history of the Federation with seven Best of Breed awards won at championship shows. Chemain is also the granddam of two of the Federation's top producing bitches, Strathmere's Amalia of Charmwood and Jakkalsdans Siovain's Pride of Charmwood, both bred by Christopher Clegg.

Kelvin, Yvonne and Christopher are all accredited judges of the breed and have served on various Federation committees and panels over the years.

DA CUNHA. Louis and Elsabe van Aswegen registered their kennels

South African Ch. Gypsy Coquete of 100% U.S. bloodlines, winner of numerous Bests in Show and the dam of 40 puppies during her breeding career. Owned by Hannes and Lea Pelser, Johannesburg, S.A.

South African Ch. Strathmere's Honey Girl of Beckleavale combines the best of Strathmere Kennels and Beckleavale Kennels. Owners: Hannes and Lea Pelser, Johannesburg, S.A.

143

South African Ch. Tambay's Inkost, sired by Wiking v. Schütting ex Wienerwald's Flying Lady. Owners: Frank and Ute Fuglister, Midrand, S.A.

in 1961 and bred twelve champions. Elsabe's ill health forced them to cut back on their activities, and she died in 1985. They were breeders and owners of a whole gallery of outstanding Boxers, probably the best known of which was their imported Canadian and S.A. Ch. Jandaire's Justice of Peace. Many of his progeny are also producing well, among them Ch. Pantabeth's Make Way, who is the sire of ten champions.

DRUM ROCK. Mark Steele of Johannesburg has been an eminently successful breeder since 1975 when he imported American and S.A. Ch. Aracrest's Courier of Holly Lane. Courier is the sire of one American and nine Federation champions, including Ch. Drum Rock's Glory Be, 1984 Dam of the Year and producer of four champions, and Ch. Drum Rock's Tiny Girl of Eldoret, 1985 Dam of the Year.

Two other Courier granddaughters, Ch. Kia Ora's Royal Velvet of Drum Rock and Wienerwald's Flying Lady of Tambay, produced three and four champions respectively.

Mark Steele has imported several other Boxers from the United States. His most recent was Ch. Aracrest's Ipsofacto, who is also showing promise as a prepotent sire. Drum Rock has produced thirteen Federation champions.

ELDORET. The most successful breeder and exhibitor of Boxers in the Cape Province is Emma Meades, who has been registered as a breeder since 1970. Her two most successful Boxers to date are both bitches. Ch. Da Cunha's Lilla-Anne of Eldoret, bred by Elsabe van Aswegen, had a highly successful show career with two Bests of Breed and five Best of Opposite Sex awards at championship shows. The other bitch, Ch. Drum Rock's Tiny Girl of Eldoret, bred by Mark Steele, is the dam of two champions and many pointed youngsters. She won the 1985 Dam of the Year award. Emma Meades of Kimberley has bred three champions to date.

JAKKALSDANS. Current Federation secretary, Marlien Heystek, has been involved with Boxers since 1976, when she received a Boxer puppy as a gift. This bitch became a champion and dam and granddam of champions and pointed youngsters.

Marlien is an accredited breed judge, a committee member of the Northern Boxer Club, and chairperson of the Panel of Breeders.

Co-owner of German import Ch. Filou von Nassau-Oranien, Sch.H.I., she has bred three champions from him. One of these, Ch. Jakkalsdans Knight Rampant, has to date been awarded Best of Breed seven times at championship shows. His half brother, Ch. Jakkalsdans Fire & Ice, has had four Best of Breed awards. He has sired one champion and has several pointed progeny being campaigned.

Rembrandt van de Aakant was imported from the Netherlands as a puppy in 1980. Sparingly used, he has produced two champions and some promising youngsters. To date there are six Federation champions with the Jakkalsdans prefix.

STRATHMERE. This kennel was established by the late Basil Allen of Johannesburg in 1960. Allen produced a total of thirteen champions, many of whom were multiple Best of Breed winners and prepotent sires and dams. Strathmere bitches formed the foundation of some of the most successful kennels of today, such as Drum Rock and Beckleavale.

Top producers of this kennel were American and S.A. Ch. Flintwood's Places Please of Strathmere, who sired eight South African champions, and the bitch, Strathmere's Amalia of Charmwood, who produced four champions.

Mr. Allen was a highly respected judge of the Boxer in South Africa.

TAMBAY. As a breed judge, trainer, member of the Executive and secretary of the Northern Boxer Club, Ute Füglister is another very active member of the Federation. Her husband, Frank, shares her enthusiasm and is a committee member and the catering manager.

One very important dog of the Tambay kennel is Wiking vom Schütting, imported in 1978. He is certain to go down in the history of the Federation as one of the all-time great sires, with 11 champion offspring.

Tambay is really a small hobby kennel with rarely more than five or six Boxers at one time. Their success in such a short time has been remarkable. The Füglisters have bred six champions and also campaigned another German import, Aralie von Okeler Forst, to her title. They live in Midrand, which is halfway between Johannesburg and Pretoria.

United Kingdom

Around 1911 or 1912, the first Boxer was imported into England. She was a daughter of Remos vom Pfalzgau named Jondy. Remos was a son of Hugo von Pfalzgau, one of the Flock and Meta von der Passage progeny. He had a sensational show career in Germany. On the occasion of his first defeat, however, his owner took him home and shot him! No one knows what happened to Jondy, and there is no record of offspring.

In 1932, Miss P. M. Rogers imported a bitch in whelp named Cilly von Rothenberg who became the first Boxer registered with the Kennel Club. One of Cilly's pups was registered as Riverhill Racketeer, and the Misses P. M. and F. M. Rogers became the first recorded Boxer breeders in the United Kingdom.

In 1936, the first class of Boxers was exhibited at Charles Cruft's Jubilee Show. There were nine entries in the class. The winner was Willy I Von Brandenburg, owned by Mrs. I. M. Graham.

In 1936, Mrs. Cecil Sprigge imported Gretl von der Boxerstadt from Germany. She arrived in whelp to Hansel von Biederstein. From this litter came the first recorded British-born champion, Horsa of Leith Hill, a brindle, who gained his title in 1939. He was owned by Mrs. H. Caro, first president of the British Boxer Club.

The famous English Ch. Gremlin Summer Storm—top winner of 33 Challenge Certificates, bred and owned by Marian Fairbrother.

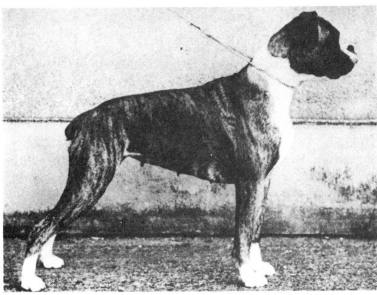

English Ch. Wardrobes Miss Sable, by English Ch. Winkinglight Justice, bred by Mrs. Wilson Wiley and owned by Mrs. Norrington. One of the many winning Wardrobes dogs.

Around this time, Mr. Allon Dawson, who had purchased his first Boxer from Mrs. Sprigge, began importing Boxers from Germany and founded his famous Stainburndorf Kennels. One of his imports was Burga von Twiel, in whelp to the famous Lustig. Allon Dawson did much to bring the Boxer to the public eye and establish its popularity in Britain.

Championship shows were not held during World War II, and certificates were not issued by the Kennel Club. There were a few small shows held, but the Kennel Club forbade travelling more than 35 miles to any show.

In 1938 Boxer registrations numbered 82. By 1947, they increased to 1,422. In 1956, registrations hit an all-time high of 7,000. 1985 saw registrations at 5,321.

In 1938 Elizabeth Montgomery (later to become Mrs. Somerfield) purchased a puppy sired by Fritz of Leith Hill ex Gretl von der Boxerstadt. She named her Annaliese, and she was the first of the famous Panfield Boxers. Previously there had been Panfield Great Danes. In 1940, Elizabeth Montgomery purchased the dam Gretl von der Boxerstadt, a golden brindle bitch.

In 1947, the Boxer scene received a big boost when Mr. and Mrs. John Wagner visited England. Jack Wagner judged the British Boxer Club's championship show, with 110 Boxers making an entry of 349. Wagner awarded one challenge certificate (three are required to obtain a championship) to a brindle bitch, Panfield's Serenade, handled by Mrs. Marian Fairbrother. Serenade was sired by Juniper of Bramblings (son of Stainburndorf Zulu) ex German import Alma von der Frankenwarte, a daughter of Lustig von Dom. Later, Serenade became the first post-war champion and the first British-born Boxer bitch to become a champion in the United Kingdom. She won five challenge certificates.

Jack Wagner awarded the challenge certificate in dogs to Ch. Monarchist of Maspound (sired by Mutineer of Maspound, a son of Stainburndorf Zulu ex Marienlyst of Maspound), handled by Tom Horner and owned by Mrs. Guthrie.

Serenade's dam, Alma von der Frankenwarte, was acquired by Panfield Kennels, because her owner was drafted into the Army. Three friends (Mrs. Elizabeth Somerfield, Mrs. Marian Fairbrother, and Miss Mary Davis), all starting out in Boxers, contributed £5. each to pay for her.

Serenade produced the top winning sire, Ch. Panfield's Tango, who became the first post-war British-bred male champion. Thus Panfield became the earliest successful breeder of Boxers in the United Kingdom and regularly produced champions through the line started by Alma.

In 1949, Tango was bred to Serenade and produced Ch. Panfield's Ringleader (eight challenge certificates), who succeeded his father as top sire for several years.

When Elizabeth and Stafford Somerfield visited the Wagners in

English Ch. Wardrobes Clair de Lune, by Ch. Wardrobes Hunters Moon ex Bartondourne Dainty Lady, bred by Miss Day and owned by Mrs. W. Wiley. She won 31 Challenge Certificates.

English Ch. Mitsuko of Maspound, by English Ch. Winkinglight Viking, owned and bred by Mrs. K. Guthrie.

Texas, they were given a flashy brindle male, Texas Ranger, brother of the fabulous Ch. Bang Away of Sirrah Crest. Texas could not be shown in England because of his cropped ears. He was also a monorchid (only one descended testicle), but he sired a number of champions for Panfield and other kennels. Major Somerfield states that "strangely enough he sired fewer monorchids than any of our entire stud dogs. There must be some explanation, but we never understood what it was."

Allon Dawson's Stainburndorf kennels flourished after the war, and he continued to import dogs from Germany. He did not finish a Stainburndorf champion until 1953, but he helped to keep the breed alive during the war and always remained an enthusiast of Boxers. His famous Stainburndorf Zulu figures prominently in early pedigrees.

Mrs. Marian Fairbrother founded her Gremlin kennels in 1939 and the first Gremlin champion was finished in 1949. He was Ch. Gremlin Sungari, sired by Ch. Panfield Tango ex German import Gremlin Bossi von Rhona. Mrs. Fairbrother's most famous dogs were Ch. Gremlin Inxpot (seven challenge certificates), Ch. Gremlin Inkling (24 challenge certificates), and the top winning Ch. Gremlin Summer Storm (33 challenge certificates).

In 1958, Mrs. Fairbrother formed a partnership with Mr. Martin Summers and his Summerdale kennels. That same year, Mrs. Fairbrother visited the United States and purchased from Donald Starkweather, Rainey Lane's Sirrocco, who was to sire 13 champions. On the same visit, she judged the Heart of America Specialty show in Kansas City and awarded Best of Opposite Sex to a senior puppy, Rancho Chiquito's Yanna.

Mrs. Fairbrother, with co-author Peggy Thomson, wrote one of the best books on the Boxer, *Boxer Blarney*, which is used by the American Boxer Club's standard committee. She has also judged all over Europe and had the honor of being the first overseas judge to be invited to officiate at the American Boxer Club Specialty show in 1962.

In the 1950s, Mrs. Hullock founded the Winkinglight kennels. Her stock was founded on the imported Ch. Holger von Germania. A fawn bitch, Ch. Orburn Kekeri, was the first Boxer to win Best in Show at a championship show in 1949. Mrs. Hullock bred a line of strong stud dogs which included Ch. Winkinglight Justice, sire of seven champions, and Ch. Winkinglight Viking (13 challenge certificates), who sired five champions. Viking was the first male Boxer to win a Best in Show at an all-breed show.

In the early 1950s, Major Douglas Bostock put Burstall Boxers on the map with a long line of champions. His first was Ch. Burstall Delight, who won 11 challenge certificates. He was sired by Ch. Panfield Ringleader ex Burstall Gremlin Torni, a daughter of Collo von Dom, bred by Frau Stockmann.

Major Bostock did not hesitate to import quality dogs from Europe or from the United States. One of his more influential imports was Rob Roy of Tomira, who sired many champions. Rob Roy was sired by American Ch. Mazelaine's Keynote ex American Ch. Mazelaine's Zenith. He also imported two daughters of Ch. Bang Away of Sirrah Crest. One was Beaulaine's Bonadea, a fawn, in whelp to Ch. Mazelaine's Gallantry, and a brindle, Kirsten of Tomira, in whelp to Ch. Avi's Independent Watchman.

Major Bostock was president of the British Boxer Club for many years. When he died, the Burstall Boxers were disbanded.

In 1951 Mr. and Mrs. Wilson Wiley of the famous Wardrobes Kennels finished their first Boxer, Ch. Wardrobes Alma of Greenovia, sired by Ch. Panfield's Ringleader ex Awldogg Veronica. The Wileys' greatest strength was in their bitches. They finished 27 champions and broke all existing records for the breed. Ch. Wardrobes Miss Mink, a fawn bitch, was their first Best in Show winner and went on to win three more Bests in Show amassing 27 challenge certificates. This was a record for 16 years, until her great granddaughter, Ch. Wardrobes Clair de Lune, won 31 certificates. Actually, many fanciers preferred Miss Mink's sister, Ch. Wardrobes Miss Sable, winner of eight challenge certificates and an excellent producer. However, she lacked Miss Mink's showmanship, which is so essential in keen competition.

Wardrobes Boxers completely dominated the show scene from 1956 to 1967 when they won 171 challenge certificates and produced 27 British champions.

In the United Kingdom, champions are not exhibited in a separate class but compete in the open classes and have to be beaten to win the challenge certificate or "ticket." Other obstacles are the enormous Boxer entries, anywhere from 100 to 300, and the limited number of championship shows, under 30 all-breed shows and around 12 Boxer specialties.

Another point of interest is that dogs can be entered in more than one class and a written critique is given on the first two dogs in every class and published in weekly dog newspapers. Most breeders and owners handle their own dogs in the show ring.

Mrs. Joan Dunkels and Mrs. Hilary Gamble of Breakstone Kennels are remembered as leading breeders who brought the Dutch influence into the United Kingdom. They imported the Dutch Ch. Faust Von Haus Germania and Helios von Haus Germania, both bred by Mr. Peter Zimmerman. They sired many champions and left their mark on the breed.

When Frau Stockmann judged the British Boxer Club's show in 1950, she gave the challenge certificate and Best in Show to Fenella of Breakstones, sired by Dutch Ch. Faust von Haus Germania ex Christine of Breakstones (of Von Dom breeding). Frau Stockmann judged 180 dogs in 26 classes with a total entry of 447, the largest to that date.

No list of early winners can be complete without including Ch. Mitsouko of Maspound, sired by Ch. Winkinglight Viking ex Marney of

English Ch. Panfield Ringleader, by English Ch. Panfield's Tango ex English Ch. Panfield's Serenade—leading sire in the U.K. after World War II.

English Ch. Ackendene Willy Wagtail, sired by English Ch. French Spice of Witherford. Owned and bred by June Grover. Willy was Best of Breed at Crufts in 1976 and 1977.

Maspound and bred by Mrs. K. Guthrie. He was a splendid show dog who made a lasting impression on all who saw him in the ring. Mary Hambleton and Sheila Cartwright both consider him the most outstanding Boxer they have seen. Unfortunately, he never sired a litter and was said to be sterile.

Before listing some current winning breeders, mention should be made of such kennels as Peggy Knight's Swanfield, Bill Malcolm's Valabeau, Mrs. Llewellyn Davies' Delapoer, Peggy Ingram's Bockenden, Dr. McKellar's Makreen, Mr. Makinson's Wilsiclea, the late Felicia Price's Felcign, the late Jane Heath's Starmark, and the late Mrs. Thornley's Cherryburton.

In 1980, *Progressive Axonopathy* of Boxer dogs (P.A.) hit the breed hard in the United Kingdom. P.A. is a heredity disease affecting the nervous system. With amazing speed, the Boxer Breed Council issued a large, six-page leaflet on the disease, which listed known carriers.

Decisive action followed and is to be commended. Working with veterinarians, the council evaluated current stock and checked pedigrees for known carriers. Within a very short time, the disease seemed to have been eradicated, but the mystery has never been solved as to how it penetrated the breed in the United Kingdom. In 1988, cases of P.A. were reported in Norway and Sweden. They were traced to British carriers.

The Breed Council's pamphlet on P.A. is available by writing to the Secretary of the British Boxer Council, whose address is available from the Kennel Club, 1-4 Clarges Street, Piccadilly, London W1Y8AB, England.

Several very successful kennels were forced to make painful sacrifices and had to begin all over again with new stock. That they had the enthusiasm to do so after such a bad experience, is admirable. However, some of them very quickly climbed back into the limelight, which shows their tenacity and dedication to the breed.

Principal Boxer Kennels in the United Kingdom

ACKENDENE Boxers, *Church Farm, Taunton, Somerset, England*

After several years of only moderately successful breeding, an unexpected stroke of luck allowed June Grover to purchase Tatiana of Shelaghdare, sired by Ch. Winkinglight Viking ex a daughter of Ch. Panfield Ringleader. A fellow joining the Royal Air Force had to sell her for £5.

Tatiana was bred several times to Ch. Wardrobes Wild Mink and the most noteworthy offspring was Ackendene Fair Comment, who became the foundation bitch of the kennel. Fair Comment was bred to the American import, Raineylane Sirrocco, and this produced the first Ackendene champion, Royal Fern.

Ch. Ackendene Royal St. John was the next champion of note. He was sired by Ch. Ackendene Royal Fern ex Ackendene Spinning Coin. He won nine challenge certificates, many reserves, and a Group placement. Ackendene Royal Gloss was bred to her great-grandsire, Royal St. John, and produced Ch. Ackendene Royal Streaker of Zondora, a group winning dog owned by Mrs. P. Queen.

June Grover kept breeding promising puppies until the dog of her dreams appeared. The famous Ch. Ackendene Willy Wagtail, sired by Ch. French Spice of Witherford ex Ackendene Flirtybird, won nine challenge certificates, a Working Group and was reserve at Crufts under Mrs. Elizabeth Somerfield.

Willy Wagtail was the sire of the sensational Ch. Antron Prize Guy, winner of two Groups, a Best in Show and Reserve Best in Show with his first and second challenge certificates.

Having visited the United States and Europe, Miss Grover admits to liking dogs from both continents and admires good qualities, whatever the background. As a judge, she is popular and respected. She thinks the secret of successful breeding is not taking things too seriously, accepting the disappointments, and always looking ahead to that fabulous stud dog that will someday come upon the scene.

BRAXBURN Kennels, *Glasgow, Scotland*

As a young teenager, Joan MacLaren saw a film about a new breed which featured the great Ch. Warlord of Mazelaine. Her enchantment with the character and appearance of the Boxer was immediate and has never changed. However, it was not until 1949 that a brindle Boxer bitch joined the family.

It was through Boxers that Joan met her husband, the elder son of the famous Viewpark Scottish Terrier family. Both keen lovers of all animals, they founded a boarding kennel which is their livelihood and have kept and bred a fairly wide range of livestock.

Their first champion was Ch. Braxburn Flush Royal, sired by Gremlin Winkinglight Vigilent, whom they finished in 1954. He produced Ch. Braxburn's It's Dinah-Mite and Ch. Braxburn Waza Waza.

American, British, Dutch and German bloodlines have been successfully incorporated into the Braxburn line. They have bred a total of five champions, several Irish champions, and at least 12 more Boxers who achieved top awards but were not campaigned. Both Braxburn males and bitches have produced champions for other people.

Joan MacLaren admits that breeding is only their hobby, but a serious one. Winning is regarded as an endorsement of their care and aptitude. Occasional ventures into the show ring are used to compare Braxburn Boxers with the top winners in the breed and to evaluate stock from other kennels. This enables them to decide the direction future breeding should take.

Best in Show winner English Ch. Marbelton Dressed to Kill, shown with Best of Breed Cup won at Crufts 1986.

English Ch. Marbelton Drunken Duncan, sired by English Ch. Dressed to Kill ex English Ch. Wanderobo Hurly Burly of Marbelton. Named Top Boxer of 1986 by Cotswold Boxer Club.

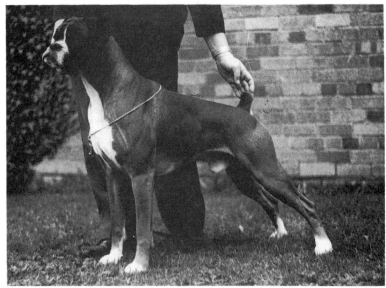

English Ch. Rayfos Cock Robin, bred and owned by Philip and Barbara Greenway, top winning fawn male in British Boxer history.

Int. Ch. Seefeld Picasso at six years. This celebrated Boxer won 24 Challenge Certificates and sired over 75 Champions. Owned and bred by Pat Heath.

Both Joan and her husband are judges but prefer the European system, which they feel allows time for an in-depth assessment of each dog and a more natural form of presentation. Joan MacLaren judged Crufts in 1984.

MARBELTON Boxers, *Aughton, Lancashire, England*

Mary and John Hambelton's first bitch was Waylands Top Trick of Marbelton, sired by Ch. Winkinglight Justice ex Texas Flare of Jacinta. They bred her to Ch. Witherford Dawn Sky and produced their first champion in 1963, Marbelton Top Mark. He sired their first Crufts Best of Breed winner, Ch. Marbelton Double O Seven.

Ch. Marbelton's Top Mark also sired Ch. Marbelton Desperate Dan. Dan won Best of Breed at Crufts in 1971 under Pat Withers, in 1973 under Felicia Price, and in 1975 under Tom East. He acquired 29 challenge certificates, a record only beaten by Marian Fairbrother's Ch. Gremlin's Summer Storm.

Ch. Moljon Dream Again of Marbelton, sired by Dutch import Dandy von Starenschloss of Marbelton, Sch.H.I, won the bitch challenge certificate at Crufts in 1984 under Marian Fairbrother.

Ch. Marbelton Dressed to Kill, a Dandy grandson, won the breed at Crufts in 1986 under Joey Royle. Dressed to Kill also won Best in Show at two all-breed shows, one at Birmingham with an entry of 21,000 dogs. He has also taken the Group on six occasions. Mary Hambelton once refused an offer from Norway of £10,000 for him.

Ch. Marbelton Drunken Duncan, sired by Dressed to Kill, won the Top Boxer of the Year award in 1986 at the Cotswold Boxer Club.

Ch. Marbelton Desperate Dan won the Champion of Champions trophy in 1975 and 1976, and Ch. Marbelton Dressed to Kill won the same award in 1986.

When Ch. Marbelton Desperate Dan was listed as a carrier of P.A., Mary Hambelton's world seemed to fall apart, but she has climbed back to the top again with Ch. Marbelton Dressed to Kill. In 1987 she had the honor of judging Boxers at Crufts. Marbelton Boxers has bred 18 English champions and over 30 overseas champions.

RAYFOS Kennels, *Grantham, Lincolnshire, England*

Philip and Barbara Greenway had their first success with Ch. Rayfos Rainmaker, sired by Sheafdon Medallist ex Astree Summerdale Merry Tune. Rainmaker won 13 challenge certificates.

Philip Greenway then decided to become a professional Boxer handler, and, over the next 10 years, he finished many champions for Rayfos Kennels and his clients.

When the Greenways moved to Grantham, Lincolnshire, Philip

retired from professional handling. They resumed their breeding program based mainly on Ch. Norwatch Glory Boy of Rayfos, who proved to be a good sire of winners including Ch. Ice Maiden of Rayfos and Ch. Rayfos Cock Robin. Cock Robin became the top winning fawn male in the history of British Boxers.

Cock Robin was retired from showing after winning Best in Show at the British Boxer Club Specialty Shows in 1985 and again in 1986, when there was a record entry of over 500 Boxers.

Rayfos Kennels has also bred Lakeland Terriers for approximately 17 years. In 1984 they were the only kennel to be top breeders in two breeds (Boxers and Lakeland Terriers) and were in the lead again in 1987.

SEEFELD Boxers, *Biddersham, Somerset, England*

In 1957 Pat Heath purchased her foundation bitch from Monica Norrington. She was Seefeld Radden Rosina, sired by Ch. Wardrobes Red Sash ex his full sister Ch. Wardrobes Miss Sable. In 1959, she purchased Seefeld Radden Rembrandt, a half brother to Rosina, sired by Felcign Faro ex Miss Sable.

Rembrandt sired Ch. Seefeld Holbein, C.D.Ex., who not only sired champion get but became the only champion Boxer in the United Kingdom to qualify at championship show working trials.

Rosina was bred to the American import Wardrobes Delhart's Mack The Knife, sired by Ch. Jered's Spellbinder, and produced Ch. Seefeld Musk Rose. Musk Rose was bred to Holbein and produced the legendary Ch. Seefeld Picasso, who became the top sire of all time in the United Kingdom. He acquired 24 challenge certificates, produced 15 British champions and over 60 champions overseas. He won 16 Best in Show awards and many Groups at championship shows in the United Kingdom and Ireland. He also won a reserve in the Working Group at Crufts. It should be noted that there are not four placements in the Group in the United Kingdom but only first and reserve.

Picasso was all-breed Dog of the Year in Ireland and Top Sire of the Year many times in the United Kingdom. His offspring have won Boxer of the Year in Norway, Boxer Bitch of the Year in New Zealand (27 challenge certificates), championships, Groups, and Bests in Show at all-breed shows in Malaya, West Indies, Australia, New Zealand, Norway and India.

In 1974, Pat Heath imported Norwegian Ch. Cavaljes Herakles of Seefeld, sired by Norwegian Ch. My-R's Sidecar. He combines the lines of Salgray with My-R and Boxella breeding and has sired eight champions. Seefeld Kennels had Ch. Salgray's Minute Man at stud for seven months after he completed his quarantine en route to Australia. He sired 13 litters and has many winning progeny in the United Kingdom.

Since 1966, Pat Heath has judged in 13 different countries including

American Ch. Salgray's Minute Man, who stood at stud at Seefeld Kennels after quarantine before continuing to Australia.

Int. Ch. Seefeld Art Master, by Int. Ch. Seefeld Picasso ex Marven Marcasite, owned by Pat Heath and bred by Mrs. Banks.

Specialties in Canada, Holland, Sweden, Norway, Australia, New Zealand and the United States, where she judged the dog classes and Best of Breed at the American Boxer Club Specialty Show in 1977.

SKELDER Boxers, *Blandford Forum, Dorset, England*

Joy Malcolm won her first challenge certificate with Lifeline of Skelder at the British Boxer Club show under Mr. Peter Zimmerman. She continued to breed and garner many challenge certificates and reserves but did not finish her first champion, Felcign Saffron Velvet of Skelder, until 1968. In 1969, she finished another bitch, Ch. Farfield Mayfly of Skelder. In 1974, Ch. Scallywag of Skelder, sired by Donovan of Skelder ex Snarestone Newcast of Skelder, finished with four challenge certificates and four reserves.

Burning Bright of Skelder was bred to Ch. Starmark Sweet Talkin Guy (winner of 17 challenge certificates) and produced the biggest winner for Skelder to date, Ch. Skelder Burnt Almond, winner of 20 challenge certificates and 12 reserves. The same breeding produced Ch. Skelder Scorching, Joy Malcolm's first male champion, who won ten challenge certificates and nine reserves.

Other champions have followed in regular succession, and many Skelder dogs have become champions in Singapore, Australia, South Africa and Trinidad.

Skelder kennels maintains less than a dozen Boxers, of whom the eldest is usually around five years of age. Joy's husband does not care for house dogs, so she places her older ones, including champions, in good homes rather than have them live out their lives in kennels. They are always welcome to return for visits and frequently do so. Joy Malcolm has been judging in the United Kingdom and abroad for 20 years now and had the honor of judging Crufts in 1988.

STEYNMERE Boxers, *Harwell, Oxfordshire, England*

Bruce Cattanach inherited his love of Boxers from his mother, whose first Steynmere Boxer was born in 1945. He was attending Edinburgh University when his mother became ill, and her dogs had to be placed. Dog breeding led Bruce Cattanach into genetics, first at the Department of Agriculture, Newcastle, and then to the Institute of Animal Genetics, Edinburgh. He continued his studies in the United States for five years while he attended dog shows in Tennessee and California. Before returning to the United Kingdom in 1969, he and his wife, Margaret, purchased a new foundation bitch for Steynmere, Black Rose of Cherokee Oaks, a granddaughter of Ch. Treceder's Shine Boy and Ch. Cochise of Cherokee Oaks.

160

English Ch. Skelder Burnt Almond, by English Ch. Starmark Sweet Talking Guy ex Burning Bright of Skelder, shown with owner/breeder Joy Malcolm in 1978.

English Ch. Skelder Scorching, brother of Burnt Almond, winner of 10 Challenge Certificates and leading Boxer in the U.K. for 1979.

Black Rose, a brindle, was quarantined for twelve months due to a rabies scare. Subsequently she was bred to Ch. Seefeld Picasso and produced the first Steynmere champion, Ch. Steynmere Ritzi Miss, winner of four challenge certificates. Ritzi Miss was bred to Ch. Seefeld Goldsmith and produced Ch. Steynmere Summer Gold. Her second breeding to Pirol v. Belcane produced Ch. Steynmere Golden Link.

Ch. Steynmere Night Rider, sired by Australian Ch. That's Right of Panfield ex Ch. Kalendars Gold Mink of Steynmere, is currently one of the most influential sires in the United Kingdom. He has sired six champions, including group winners Ch. Norwatch Brockbust (29 challenge certificates) and Ch. Trywell Twelfth Night (20 challenge certificates) and Best in Show Winner, Ch. Garnet Gelert of Steynmere.

Over the years Steynmere has produced six British champions and others who have won challenge certificates or reserves. Steynmere Star Turn is an Australian champion. All but two of these dogs have been homebred, and those two were sired by Steynmere stud dogs. The kennel is kept quite small with only one or two breeding bitches and males at home. The Boxers are all basically house pets.

Dr. Cattanach's first judging assignment was in 1955, and he has judged at several breed club open shows with record entries. He has also judged two championship shows in Ireland and two in Norway, including the prestigious Norsk Kennel Club Show. Dr. Cattanach has judged two shows in New Zealand and one in Australia and judged Boxers at Crufts in 1989.

Bruce Cattanach has been highly involved in the investigation and control of P.A. in Boxers and is currently working on kidney problems in Cocker Spaniels and Soft-Coated Wheaten Terriers.

TYEGARTH Boxers, *Worplesdon, Surrey*

When Int. Ch. Gaymitz Jolly Roger was in England for about six months, he sired puppies ex Palex Talk of the Town and Sheila Cartwright kept one, Tyegarth the Tatler. He was a monorchid but threw many entire males. He was bred to a Tyegarth bitch and produced Tyegarth Old Fashioned. Old Fashioned was bred to Ch. Gremlin Summer Storm and produced two excellent litters. The first contained Ch. Tyegarth Famous Grouse and the second Ch. Tyegarth Glenmorangie of Jenroy.

Ch. Tyegarth Famous Grouse won 11 challenge certificates, 10 reserves, and a Group first. He was proved to be a great stud dog, siring 12 British champions and several more overseas. Many of his offspring have also sired champions. Grouse has won the British Boxer Club Sire of Merit Trophy for five straight years since 1983. His son, Ch. Faerdorn Pheasant Plucker, owned by Sue Harvey and Rodney Hughes, won the breed at Crufts in 1981 under Major Somerfield. Another son, Ch. Tyegarth Blue

English Ch. Steynmere Night Rider, by Australian Ch. That's Right of Panfield ex English Ch. Kalendars Gold Mink of Steynmere, owned and bred by Dr. and Mrs. Bruce Cattanach.

Australian Ch. Steynmere Star Turn, by English Ch. Steynmere Night Rider ex an English Ch. Steynmere Golden Link daughter.

English Ch. Tyegarth Famous Grouse, by English Ch. Gremlin Summer Storm ex Tyegarth Old Fashioned—winner of the British Boxer Club's Sire of Merit Trophy from 1983 for five straight years. Owner/breeder: Sheila Cartwright.

English Ch. Tyegarth Brainduster, by English Ch. Tyegarth Famous Grouse ex Biloran Little Claret—Challenge Certificate winner at Crufts 1985. Owner/breeder: Sheila Cartwright.

Kiwi, owned by Mrs. A. Portlock and Mr. V. Zammit, won the breed at Crufts in 1987 under Mary Hambelton. His daughter, Ch. Tyegarth Double Whisky, won in 1982, and another daughter, Ch. Tyegarth Brain Duster, won in 1985. Grouse is a dominant brindle sire.

Sheila Cartwright is proud of the lifespans of her Boxers, some of whom have lived to be 16 and 17 years of age. She is also a breeder of champion Bulldogs with whom she has also had great success in the show ring.

WINIWUK Boxers, *Stonehouse, Gloucestershire, England*

This kennel is owned by Ivor and Marion Ward-Davies. It all came about because of a severe illness contracted by Mrs. Ward-Davies and her wish to have a dog to keep her company while convalescing. Ivor had developed a keen interest in the Boxer during his service in Germany with the Royal Air Force. He had seen them used as guard dogs and admired their common sense and courage. So it was that a Boxer became Mrs. Ward-Davies' companion. Both Mr. and Mrs. Ward-Davies believe that they owe that dog a great debt as it provided an interest that helped her recover.

The Ward-Davies showed their pet briefly in 1954 until one judge explained that their handsome dog was not a great show prospect. They then decided to look for some good foundation bitches. In 1957, they bought two Panfield bitches descended from Rainey Lane's Raffles, Ch. Southdowns Rector, and Mazelaine's Texas Ranger (the monorchid brother of Bang Away)—all American bloodlines.

They bred Panfield Blonde Princess to Rainey Lanes Ch. Sirrocco and produced Ch. Summerdale Stormkist, their first champion, who was shown by Marion Fairbrother.

On a trip to the United States, the Ward-Davies were overwhelmed with the hospitality and kindness of American breeders, particularly Margaret Krey. They acquired a young brindle male, Kreyon's Back in Town, whom they called "Mack." This dog was sired by Int. Ch. Scher-Khoun's Shadrack ex Ch. Kreyon's Firebrand.

Mack sired four English champions, including Ch. Kinbra Uncle Sam of Winuwuk. Sam won 13 challenge certificates including Best in Show at the British Boxer Club championship show and was retired at an early age. He was the top male Boxer in 1977 and sired two English champions as well as champions overseas.

On a judging trip to the U.S.A., Mr. and Mrs. Ward-Davies bought Milray's Red Baron of Valvay, a monorchid who sired fewer monorchids than any of their other stud dogs.

Baron was bred to a Mack daughter, Goodness Gracious of Winuwuk, and produced the outstanding bitch, Ch. Winuwuk Good Golly. Golly won

English Ch. Kinbra Uncle Sam of Winuwuk, sired by Kreyon's Back In Town, top English male 1977.

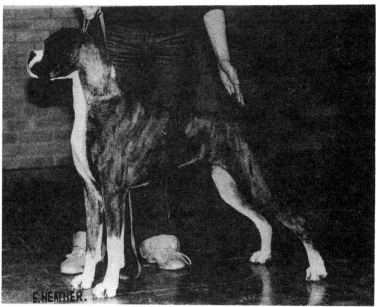

English Ch. Winuwuk Good Golly, winner of 25 Challenge Certificates, the record for a brindle bitch in the U.K.

Int. and World Ch. Witherford Hot Chestnut, the first puppy to go back to Germany where the breed originated. A big winner and producer who lived to age 13. Bred by Pat Withers and owned by Karin Rezewski.

25 challenge certificates and 20 reserves, making her the record holder for a brindle Boxer bitch in the United Kingdom. She has been the British Boxer Club's Champion of Champions twice and was Top Winning Boxer in the United Kingdom in 1980.

The next Baron daughter of note was Ch. Wrencliffe Lets Try Again ex Wrencliffe Sweet Pepper, a daughter of Ch. Kinbra Uncle Sam of Winuwuk. Try Again was Top Winning Boxer in 1981 and joint Top Bitch with Golly in 1982.

Mr. and Mrs. Ivor Ward-Davies have judged in the United Kingdom, Australia, United States, Sweden, Holland and Ireland. They feel that the debate over type (American, German, English, etc.) is overemphasized. Dogs who impressed them on their foreign assignments were Boxers that were winners in their own countries. Therefore, they both feel that the type gap is not as wide as believed.

WITHERFORD Boxers, *Corfton, Salop, England*

Pat Withers chose the prefix "Witherford" about 1951 and, in 1955, finished her first Boxers, Ch. Witherford Sweet Talk and Ch. Witherford Crystal Clear. Crystal Clear was the result of linebreeding and was the cornerstone of all subsequent Witherford breeding.

With a few carefully chosen outcrosses (never very far out), the line has been carefully maintained. This is probably one of the few kennels that has certificate-winning two and a half year olds whose pedigrees go back unbroken to the foundation bitch (six generations in 32 years).

Witherford has produced ten British champions and has exported dogs who became champions in the United States, Canada, New Zealand, Japan, India, Italy, Germany, Sweden, Norway, and Finland.

Pat Withers is particularly proud of Int. Ch. Witherford Hot Chestnut, the first Boxer puppy to go back to Germany, where the Boxer originated. He was purchased by Karin Rezewski and produced 35 champions and many other big winners. He lived to be 13 years old.

Pat Withers has judged Crufts and many other championship shows and has had many European assignments. She judged in Israel recently and has judged 12 times in Germany, being the only English judge to be invited more than once.

English Ch. French Spice of Witherford, by English Ch. Witherford Cool Mango ex Lynpine Polly Pare Kins, bred by Mr. and Mrs. Charles Walker and owned by Pat Withers.

5

The Boxer Standard

To describe a breed so that even the layman can form a good idea of it is very difficult.

Professor Dr. E. Hauck

THERE ARE REALLY only two Standards for the Boxer These are the Standard approved by the American Kennel Club and the Standard of the German Boxer Club adopted by the F.C.I. (*Federation Cynologique Internationale*). Other countries use basically one or the other of these Standards with some slight differences.

The American Boxer Club recently changed the Standard to comply with the generalized format required by the American Kennel Club, to which all breed standards must ultimately adhere. Similar to the reformatted English Standards, details of each feature of the dog are set out and are easier for quick reference and study. The English Standard is much shorter than the American or German Standards.

At present, Australia, which has followed the English Standard, is in the process of writing a new Standard. The English wish to revise the Boxer Standard but so far cannot reach agreement on the changes.

The English Standard differs, of course, regarding ears as cropping is not permitted. Also eyes are stated as "Dark rims with good pigmentation showing no haw," as in the German Standard—this was once included in the American Standard. Weight is specified as "Dogs approximately 66-70 lbs; Bitches approximately 55-60 lbs." Weight is not specified in the American Standard.

The Canadian Standard for Boxers is almost the same as the American Standard.

The greatest difference between the American and German Standards is that gait is not mentioned at all in the German version. Both Standards are presented herein.

OFFICIAL STANDARD FOR THE BOXER
approved by the American Kennel Club, 1989

General Appearance

The ideal Boxer is a medium-sized, square built dog of good substance with short back, strong limbs, and short, tight-fitting coat. His well-developed muscles are clean, hard and appear smooth under taut skin. His movements denote energy. The gait is firm, yet elastic, the stride free and ground-covering, the carriage proud. Developed to serve as guard, working and companion dog, he combines strength and agility with elegance and style. His expression is alert and temperament steadfast and tractable.

The chiseled head imparts to the Boxer a unique individual stamp. It must be in correct proportion to the body. The broad, blunt muzzle is the distinctive feature, and great value is placed upon its being of proper form and balance with the skull.

In judging the Boxer, first consideration is given to general appearance to which attractive color and arresting style contribute. Next is overall balance with special attention devoted to the head, after which, individual body components are examined for their correct construction, and efficiency of gait is evaluated.

Size, Proportion, Substance

Height: Adult males 22½ to 25 inches; females 21 to 23½ inches at the withers. Preferably, males should not be under the minimum nor females over the maximum; however, proper balance and quality in the individual should be of primary importance since there is no size disqualification.

Proportion: The body, in profile is of square proportion in that a horizontal line from the front of the forechest to the rear projection of the upper thigh should equal the length of a vertical line dropped from the top of the withers to the ground.

Substance: Sturdy and in balance with the individual. Males larger boned than their female counterparts.

Head

The beauty of the head depends upon harmonious proportion of muzzle to skull. The blunt muzzle is one-third the length of the head from the occiput to the tip of the nose, and two-thirds the width of the skull. The head should be clean, not showing deep wrinkles (wet). Wrinkles typically appear upon the forehead when ears are erect, and folds are always present from the lower edge of the stop running downward on both sides of the muzzle.

Expression: Intelligent and alert.

Eyes: Dark brown in color, not too small, too protruding or too deep-set. Their mood-mirroring character combined with the wrinkling of the forehead, gives the Boxer head its unique quality of expressiveness.

Ears: Set at the highest points of the sides of the skull are cropped, cut rather long and tapering, raised when alert.

Skull: The top of the skull is slightly arched, not rounded, flat nor noticeably broad, with the occiput not overly pronounced. The forehead shows a slight indentation between the eyes and forms a distinct stop with the topline of the muzzle. The cheeks should be relatively flat and not bulge (cheekiness), maintaining the clean lines of the skull, and should taper into the muzzle in a slight, graceful curve.

Muzzle: The muzzle, proportionately developed in length, width and depth, has a shape influenced first through the formation of both jawbones, second through the placement of the teeth, and third through the texture of the lips. The top of the muzzle should not slant down (downfaced), nor should it be concave (dish-faced); however, the tip of the nose should lie slightly higher than the root of the muzzle.

The nose should be broad and black.

The upper jaw is broad where attached to the skull and maintains this breadth except for a very slight tapering to the front. The lips, which complete the formation of the muzzle, should meet evenly in front. The upper lip is thick and padded, filling out the frontal space created by the projection of the lower jaw, and laterally is supported by the canines of the lower jaw. Therefore, these canines must stand far apart and be of good length so that the front surface of the muzzle is broad and squarish. Viewed from the side, the jaws show moderate layback. The chin should be perceptible from the side as well as from the front.

Bite: The Boxer bite is undershot; the lower jaw protrudes beyond the upper and curves slightly upward. The incisor teeth of the lower jaw are in a straight line, with the canines preferably up front in the same line to give the jaw the greatest possible width. The upper line of incisors is slightly convex with the corner upper incisors fitting snugly back of the lower canine teeth on each side.

FAULTS: Too broad in skull, cheekiness. Wrinkling too deep (wet) or lacking (dry). Excessive flews. Muzzle too light for skull. Too pointed a bite (snipy), too undershot, teeth or tongue showing when mouth closed. Eyes noticeably lighter than ground color of coat.

Neck, Topline, Body

Neck: Round, of ample lenth, muscular and clean without excessive hanging skin (dewlap). The neck has a distinctly marked nape with an elegant arch blending smoothly into the withers.

Topline: Smooth, firm and slightly sloping.

Body: The chest is of fair width, and the forechest well defined and visible from the side. The brisket is deep, reaching down to the elbows; the depth of the body at the lowest point of the brisket equals half the height of the dog at the withers. The ribs, extending far to the rear, are well arched but not barrel-shaped.

The back is short, straight and muscular and firmly connects the withers to the hindquarters.

The loins are short and muscular. The lower stomach line is lightly tucked up, blending into a graceful curve to the rear. The croup is slightly sloped, flat and broad. Tail is set high, docked and carried upward. Pelvis long and in females especially broad.

FAULTS: Short, heavy neck. Chest too broad, too narrow or hanging between shoulders. Lack of forechest. Hanging stomach. Slab-sided rib cage. Long or narrow loin, weak union with croup. Falling off of croup. Higher in rear than in front.

Forequarters

The shoulders are long and sloping, close-lying, and not excessively covered with muscle (loaded). The upper arm is long, approaching a right angle to the shoulder blade. The elbows should not press too closely to the chest wall nor stand off visibly from it.

The forelegs are long, straight and firmly muscled and when viewed from the front, stand parallel to each other. The pastern is strong and distinct, slightly slanting, but standing almost perpendicular to the ground. The dewclaws may be removed. Feet should be compact, turning neither in nor out, with well-arched toes.

FAULTS: Loose or loaded shoulders. Tied-in or bowed-out elbows.

Hindquarters

The hindquarters are strongly muscled with angulation in balance with that of the forequarters.

The thighs are broad and curved, the breech musculature hard and strongly developed. Upper and lower thigh long. Leg well angulated at the stifle with a clearly defined, well "let down" hock joint. Viewed from behind, the hind legs should be straight with hock joints leaning neither in nor out. From the side, the leg below the hock (metatarsus) should be almost perpendicular to the ground, with a slight slope to the rear permissible. The metatarsus should be short, clean and strong. The Boxer has no rear dewclaws.

FAULTS: Steep or over-angulated hindquarters. Light thighs or over-developed hams. Over-angulated (sickle) hocks. Hindquarters too far under or too far behind.

Coat

Short, shiny, lying smooth and tight to the body.

Color

The colors are fawn and brindle. Fawn shades vary from light tan to mahogany. The brindle ranges from sparse, but clearly defined black stripes on a fawn background, to such a heavy concentration of black striping that the essential fawn background color barely, although clearly, shows through (which may create the appearance of "reverse brindling").

White markings should be of such distribution as to enhance the dog's appearance, but may not exceed one-third of the entire coat. They are not desirable on the flanks or on the back of the torso proper. On the face, white may replace part of the otherwise essential black mask and may extend in an upward path between the eyes, but it must not be excessive, so as to detract from the true Boxer expression.

FAULTS: Unattractive or misplaced white markings.

Disqualifications

Boxers that are any color other than fawn or brindle. Boxers with a total of white markings exceeding one-third of the entire coat.

Gait

Viewed from the side, proper front and rear angulation is manifested in a smoothly efficient, level-backed, ground-covering stride with powerful drive emanating from a freely operating rear. Although the front legs do not contribute impelling power, adequate "reach" should be evident to prevent interference, overlap or "sidewinding" (crabbing). Viewed from the front, the shoulders should remain trim and the elbows not flare out. The legs are parallel until gaiting narrows the track in proportion to increasing speed, then the legs come in under the body but should never cross. The line from the shoulder down through the leg should remain straight although not necessarily perpendicular to the ground. Viewed from the rear, a Boxer's rump should not roll. The hind feet should "dig in" and track relatively true with the front. Again, as speed increases, the normally broad rear track will become narrower.

FAULTS: Stilted or inefficient gait. Lack of smoothness.

Character and Temperament

These are of paramount importance in the Boxer. Instinctively a "hearing" guard dog, his bearing is alert, dignified and self-assured. In the show ring, his behavior should exhibit constrained animation. With family and friends, his temperament is fundamentally playful, yet patient and stoical with children. Deliberate and wary with strangers, he will exhibit curiosity but, most importantly, fearless courage if threatened. However, he responds promptly to friendly overtures honestly rendered. His intelligence, loyal affection and tractability to discipline make him a highly desirable companion.

FAULTS: Lack of dignity and alertness. Shyness.

THE STANDARD FOR THE BOXER
approved by the Munich Boxer Club (No. 144b F.C.I.)

Drawn up in still valid form in 1905, this Standard was thoroughly revised in 1920. In 1925 black and white Boxers were excluded, in 1938 checks (parti-colours).

1. General Appearance: The Boxer is a medium-sized, smooth-haired, sturdy dog of short, square build and strong bone. The musculation is clean (dry) and powerfully developed and stands out plastically (pliantly) through the skin. The movements are lively and full of strength and nobility. The Boxer should not appear plump or heavy, lean or racy.

2. Head: The head imparts to the Boxer a unique, individual stamp. It must be in good proportion to the body and should appear neither too light nor too heavy. The skull should be as lean and angular as possible, without salient cheeks, the muzzle as broad and massive as possible. The beauty of the head depends on the harmonious proportion between the muzzle and the skull. From whatever direction the head is viewed, whether from the front, from the top or from the side, the muzzle must always appear in correct relationship to the skull, that is, it must never seem too small. It should be clean (dry), showing neither wrinkles nor dewlap. Folds normally appear on the forehead when the ears are erect and they are always indicated from the root of the nose running downward on both sides of the muzzle. The dark mask is confined to the muzzle and must be in distinct contrast to the colour of the head, so that the face will not have a sombre expression.

The muzzle is powerfully developed in all three dimensions, thus it must not be pointed or narrow, short or shallow. Its shape is influenced first through the formation of both jawbones, second through the placement of the teeth in the jawbones and third through the quality of the lips.

The two jawbones do not end in a perpendicular plane in front, but the lower jaw protrudes beyond the upper and curves slightly upward. The Boxer is normally undershot. The upper jaw is broad where attached to the skull and maintains this breadth, except for a very slight tapering to the front. Thus both jaws are very wide in front. The canine teeth should be as widely separated as possible, the incisors (6) should all be in one row, with no projection of the middle teeth. In the upper jaw they are set in a line curving slightly forward, in the lower jaw they should be in a straight line. The bite is powerful and sound, the teeth set in the most normal arrangement possible.

The shape of the muzzle is completed by the lips. The upper lip is thick and padded, filling out the frontal space created by the projection of the lower jaw and is supported by the fangs (canines) of the lower jaw. These fangs must therefore stand as far apart as possible and be of good length so that the front surface of the muzzle becomes almost square, forming an obtuse angle with the topline of the muzzle. The lower edge of the upper lip rests on the edge of the lower lip. The repandous part of the lower jaw, with the lower lip, called the chin, must not rise in front of the upper lip, but even less may it disappear under it. It must, however, be plainly perceptible when viewed from the front as well as from the side, without protruding and bending upwards as in the Bulldog. The teeth of the lower jaw must not be visible when the mouth is closed, neither should the Boxer show its tongue when the mouth is closed.

The top of the skull is slightly arched, not so short as to be rotund, nor too flat, nor too broad and the occiput not too pronounced. The forehead forms a distinct stop with the topline of the muzzle. The bridge of the hose should not be forced back into the forehead like that of the Bulldog, nor should it slope down, however. The proportion between the length of the nose and that of the skull is as one (1) and is to two (2). The tip of the nose lies somewhat higher than the root of the muzzle. The forehead shows a suggestion of furrow which, however, should not be too deep, especially between the eyes. The cheeks are powerfully developed to correspond with the strong bite, without protruding from the head with too bulgy an appearance. They should preferably taper into the muzzle in a slight curve. The ears are set on high, are cropped to a sharp point, fairly long, without too broad a shell and are carried perpendicular. The eyes are dark, not too small or protruding and not deep set. They disclose an expression of energy and intelligence, but should not appear gloomy, threatening or piercing. The eyes must have a dark rim. The nose is broad and black, very slightly turned up, the nostrils wide, with the naso-labial line between them.

FAULTS: Lack of nobility and expression, sombre face, unserviceable bite due to disease or faulty tooth placement, Pinscher or Bulldog head, drivelling, badly cropped ears, unpigmented third eyelid, showing teeth or tongue, light (bird of prey) eyes, sloping topline of the muzzle (downface), snipy bite or muzzle too light, brown, flesh-coloured or pink nose.

3. Neck: Round, not too short and thick but of ample length, yet strong, muscular and clean cut throughout, without dewlap. It runs down to the back in an elegant arch with distinctly marked nape.

FAULTS: Dewlap.

4. Body: The build is square. The profile or outline, that is a horizontal line over the back and two vertical lines, the one touching the forechest in front, the other the ischiatic bones in the rear, form with the ground level a square. The torso rests on sturdy, straight legs with strong bones.

5. Chest and Forequarters: The chest is deep, reaching down to the elbows. The depth of the chest amounts to half the height of the dog at the withers. The ribs are well arched but not barrel shaped, extending far to the rear. The loins are short, closed and taut and slightly tucked up. The lower stomach line blends into an elegant curve to the rear. The shoulders are long and sloping, close lying but not excessively covered with muscle. The upper arm is long, forming a right angle to the shoulder blade. The forelegs when seen from the front must be straight, stand parallel to each other and have strong, firmly articulated bones. The elbows must not press too closely to the chest wall nor stand off too far. The forearm is perpendicular, long and firmly muscled. The pastern joint of the foreleg is short, clearly defined but not distended. The pastern is short, slightly slanting but stands almost perpendicular to the ground. Feet are small with tightly arched toes (cat feet) and hard soles.

FAULTS: Too broad and low in front, loose shoulders, chest hanging between the shoulders, hare feet, hollow flanks, hanging stomach, turned legs and toes.

6. Back: The withers should be clearly defined; the whole back short, straight, broad and strongly muscled.

FAULTS: Carp (roach) back, sway back, thin, lean back, long, narrow sharp sunken-in loins, weak union with croup.

7. Hindquarters: Very strongly muscled, the musculation hard as a board and standing out very plastically (pliantly) through the skin. The thighs are not narrow and flat but are broad and curved. The breech musculation is as strongly developed.

The croup slightly sloped, with a flat arch and broad. Tail set on high rather than too low, tail docked and carried upward. The pelvis should be long and, in bitches especially, broad. Upper and lower thigh long, hip and knee joint with as much angle as possible. In a standing position the knee should reach so far forward that it would meet a vertical line drawn from the hip protuberance to the floor. The hock angle about 140°, the lower part of the foot at a slight slope of 95-100° to the floor, thus not completely vertical. Seen from behind, the hind legs should be straight. The hock joints clean, not distended, with powerful heels, the toes normally slightly longer than in front but similar in all other respects.

FAULTS: Falling off or too arched or narrow croup, low set tail, overbuilt (higher in back than in front), steep, stiff, insufficiently angulated hindquarters, light thighs, cow hocks, bow or sickle legs, narrow heels, hind dewclaws, soft hocks, tottering, waddling gait, hare feet, hindquarters too far under or too far behind.

8. Height: Males 57-63 cm at the withers, Females 53-59 cm. The height is measured with the dog standing erect and the measurement is taken with a straightedge from the withers, along the elbow down to the ground.

9. Mass: A male of about 60 cm should be over 30 kg, females of about 56 cm should weigh about 25 kg.

10. Coat: Short and glossy, lying smooth and tight to the body.

11. Colour: The colours are fawn and brindle. Fawn occurs in various shades, from dark deer red to light yellow, the shades in between (red fawn) are, however, the most beautiful. The mask is black, but must be confined to the muzzle so that the face does not appear sombre or unfriendly.

The brindle variety has dark or black stripes running parallel to the ribs, on a fawn ground colour in the above shades. The stripes should be in distinct contrast to the ground colour, neither too close together nor too thinly dispersed. The ground colour must not be dirty and the two colours should not be intermingled (grizzled) so that the brindle markings disappear.

White markings are not to be rejected; they are often very attractive in appearance. Unattractive white markings, such as a completely or laterally white head, etc., are faults.

All Boxers with any other colour, as well as those with the ground colour more than one third replaced by white, are not according to the Standard.

12. Character: The character of the Boxer is of the greatest importance and demands the most solicitous attention. He is renowned from olden times for his great love and loyalty for his master and the whole household, his alertness and fearless courage as a defender and protector. He is harmless in the family but distrustful of strangers, bright and friendly of temperament at play, but fearsome when roused. He is easily trained due to his obedience, his self-assurance and courage, his natural sharpness and scenting ability. Because of his modesty and cleanliness he is equally desirable as a family dog and a guard, escort or service dog. He is honest and loyal, never false or treacherous even in his old age.

FAULTS: Viciousness, treachery, unreliability, lack of temperament and cowardice.

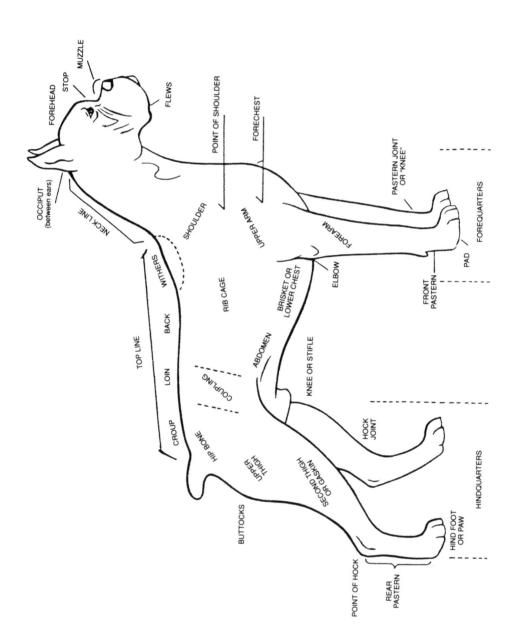

FOREHEAD
STOP
MUZZLE
FLEWS
POINT OF SHOULDER
FORECHEST
OCCIPUT (between ears)
NECK LINE
SHOULDER
UPPER ARM
PASTERN JOINT OR "KNEE"
FOREARM
ELBOW
BRISKET OR LOWER CHEST
WITHERS
RIB CAGE
FRONT PASTERN
PAD
FOREQUARTERS
TOP LINE
BACK
LOIN
COUPLING
ABDOMEN
KNEE OR STIFLE
HOCK JOINT
CROUP
HIP BONE
UPPER THIGH
SECOND THIGH OR GASKIN
BUTTOCKS
POINT OF HOCK
REAR PASTERN
HIND FOOT OR PAW
HINDQUARTERS

6

The Active Anatomy of the Boxer

by Frau Friederun Stockmann

(This is part of an article which was printed in the "Boxer Blätter," September 1961, translated and freely adapted by Mrs. Pat Withers.)

The Skeleton of the Boxer

First we look at the skull. This differs from those of other breeds by the short upper jawbone and the sharply steep forehead. The jawbones viewed from the front do not form a narrow bow, but are almost straight, and dictate the flat surface of the muzzle. Here it becomes quite clear that the broadening of the fang leads to an increase in incisors in the upper jaw. It does not stop at the usual six. Seven, even eight, incisors can sometimes be counted. I was told in England that on numerous occasions more than seven incisors had been counted in lower jaws too, but I have no experience of this.

The skull is the brain box, which varies with different breeds in proportion to the body. It would be false to assume that a dog with a large head is more intelligent than one with a small one. Such a conclusion is as invalid in dogs as among humans. The brain is of no importance to us insofar as it has nothing to do with the external appearance. In order for a dog to be intelligent and capable of work, it must, however, have a healthily developed brain and spinal cord. . . .

The neck has seven vertebrae. Of these seven, two are the ones which interest us most. They are different in appearance from the others, and they allow free movement of the head. In the noble, beautifully swung head of the Boxer they can be clearly observed as the turning point of the neck.

There follows eight vertebrae which form the withers. On the upper side, they have long vertical points which are there to form a firm base for the strong neck and back muscles. In addition, they have sockets and hollows on the sides in which rest the heads of the ribs in a movable position. These cannot be felt from the exterior as they are covered with muscle.

The five vertebrae which follow are those of the back. Their characteristic is that they show a step, like a change in shape until they join the loins. They too have hollows for the ribs. I will return to these five vertebrae later.

The loin consists of five vertebrae, to which I will also return later. The croup consists of three vertebrae which are closely merged together in order to give a firm support for the pelvis. Tail vertebrae do not concern us as the Boxer is docked.

Thirteen pairs of ribs form the rib cage. It has the task of encasing the heart, lungs, and liver, the most important organs of any living being. For two-thirds of their length, the ribs are bone, but then they change to gristle which adheres to the breastbone. Of the last four ribs, three join in a single piece of gristle which joins them to the other ribs. The last is quite free.

The Bones of the Forehand and Hindquarters

With the forehand, we will start with the shoulder blade. This is a flat triangular bone. It is divided along its length by a bone ridge, which is a starting point for muscle. At the bottom end there is a round hollow for taking the spherical head of the upper arm bone. This angle between the shoulder blade and the upper arm is what produces the shoulder angulation.

The upper arm is a slim bone with a slight spiral shaped revolution. It runs from the shoulder blade slantwise towards the back and changes in size and position (angle) according to the breed. Near the ball at the head end is another small protuberance, which prevents the shoulder angle from opening too far. The lower arm consists of two long bones, the radius and the ulna. The radius is in front, the ulna at the back, and these form the structure of the elbow. The lower end of the upper arm has a groove, in which the elbow rests and glides back and forth giving the desired leverage.

The pastern consists of seven small bones. The most vital one is an important starting point for the tendons and serves as a lever in the action of the foot. The lower arm bone is supported on the largest of the ankle bones. The middle foot consists of five long slender bones which correspond to the human wrist. Four toes join them, each of which consists of three more bones.

What the shoulder blade is to the front, the pelvis is to the hindquarters. This is a large formation of three closely knit bones, which resembles a large hat brim with no crown. It is connected to the spine and, together with this, forms the croup.

The upper thigh bone, which resembles the humerus, is similarly joined to the pelvis by means of a ball and socket joint. There is great freedom of movement for the femur. At the lower end, it goes into the knee joint, which has a host of interesting characteristics. Here we see a bone at the lower end of which sits a ball, on top of which rests another similar bone, and they take over as the strongest shock absorbers of the entire body. At the front a flat disc of bone, the knee cap, looks after the maintenance of direction and prevents the limbs from stretching too severely. At the rear the maintenance is achieved through a bone protuberance.

The lower thigh is again formed by two bones. In old dogs these can fuse into one. The hock joint consists of seven small bones, the most important of which is the ankle protuberance, a long bone set on the fourth hock bone—it rises vertically to the heel at the hock point. The tibia and fibula are so fitted together that the movement of the ankle bone is that which achieves the best leverage. Just as in the pastern, there are five long slender bones which join the hock with four toes, also consisting of three bones each.

The skeleton is indeed a most incredible masterpiece . . . such as no human brain could have invented any more practically or more simply.

And now to the muscles. We see in the bone structure how nature has worked with such clever technique. The smallest bone is not superfluous or unskillfully attached. Each has its task and serves its movement. Nature tries again and again, after deviation from normal, to return to its original form, even when it only has the slightest possibility of doing so.

Those who have had the opportunity of seeing wild dogs have been fortunate enough to see correct construction, which is evidenced in their short backs and beautifully angulated shoulders and hindquarters. If these advantages have been partly lost in the breeding of pedigreed dogs, then this has happened by means of man's rape of nature. Man, who wanted to maintain or force some abnormality purely for fun or self gratification. Again and again, nature tries to strike the balance and mediate.

Take the Boxer head, for example. The inclination to shortening of the muzzle exists in dogs, otherwise it would not have been possible to breed Bulldogs, Pugs, Pekes, etc. However, this type of head must surely be undesirable in nature and must be a degeneration as a consequence of domestication. We do not find this short muzzle in wild canines, and, unless we take great care with breeding, it will be the head of the Boxer which, first of all, will revert to type and form by becoming longer and shallower with the muzzle lengthening and fining down. Dogs with heads which are much too short occur only rarely whereas long, flat heads are no rarity even with the best parentage.

Take cross-breeding Shepherd Dogs with Spitz breeds. These are the two breeds nearest to the original in type . . . and, [when they are bred to each other] it is hard to tell if they are thoroughbred or mongrel. But when [one of these breeds is] crossed with a Boxer, this problem never arises. In most cases from birth, or within 14 days, their long, flat head was clear proof of mixed mating. Grown animals leave one in no doubt as to their mixed parentage and, with the vast majority, there is not the slightest hint of the Boxer head.

Nature shows its determination to balance things out in many ways. For example, the well-known steep shoulder of the Fox Terrier is due mainly to the too-short upper arm bone (as with the Boxer). Nature attempts to compensate for this by the creation of the long, narrow shoulder blade.

Due to indiscriminate breeding during and immediately after World War I, the German Shepherd Dog was in danger of losing its length of back and tremendous angulation. Nature tended to revert to the wild form, even if the ability to indulge in the well-loved racing trot was greatly diminished.

Returning to the Boxer and taking the judges' reports from the turn of the century, we find that they concentrated solely on the hindquarters, back and bone. The one with the heaviest bone shone above all!

Perhaps it will be interesting to give our attention to bones and their structure. Throw a bone into the fire, and we see that it burns well, a sign that not only does the marrow contain a lot of fat but that this is also present in the porous part of the bone. Fire, however, destroys all other animal material. If we are careful, we can extract an apparently undamaged bone of purest white, but we are mistaken. What we now hold in our hands is a pure calcium formation which is brittle to the highest degree. We can destroy the calcium with acid. Think of the bones of the pickled herring which have become soft, or of the soft bone of meat in aspic jelly which one can bite through with no difficulty. In both cases the shape is maintained but the structure is changed.

In a living being, of course, neither heat nor acid can destroy the bones, but hunger and sickness can have their effect upon them. There is an old proverb which says that every baby costs the mother a tooth. This arises from the fact that the unborn child derives nourishment from the mother. When the mother cannot herself obtain an adequate supply, especially of calcium, from her diet, then she gives from her own reserves. So it is with the bitch and her puppies. If she is severely short of calcium and Vitamins A and D in her diet, she may well produce one or two litters of good puppies. The following litters, however, may well contain rickety puppies, since she has used up all her own reserves for the previous litters. These conditions can be treated, of course, but it is far better to prevent them by adequate feeding.

The quality of the bones is of utmost importance and perhaps their condition is even more important than their anatomical position. Thick, heavy bones are not of themselves a sign of good quality. It has been proven that such bones are often porous in structure and are not of steel and iron, as we like to describe them.

Comparing the bones of the wild animal with those of our domesticated ones, the advantage is always on the side of the wild animal. Today a Boxer is not placed solely because he has tremendous bone. We realize that they are simply the foundation on which the muscles are arranged, and I shall later show why it is not merely heavy bones which are so desirable.

The Muscles

The muscles are a fleshy elastic network which have the ability to expand or contract. They are permeated with nerves, which direct their work. They consist of two parts, the red, fleshy, active, working portion . . . and the non-active sinews that attach the muscles to the bones.

The dog is covered with muscles, which lie in various positions over one another. They can contract to about two-thirds of their length. By means of their position and attachment to the bones, they carry out the aforementioned lever action. The muscle activity affects the movement and support of the limbs. Without them, for example, the head could not be held up.

Usually, certain groups of muscles work together. The longest and strongest extend from the neck over the back to the croup. There is also a very strong and efficient muscle fixed on the side of the back and thigh. It is certain that broad, stronger muscles react much more slowly to all kinds of impulses than thin ones of the same length. They may be late starters, but, in spite of weak initial speed, they have more power and can help to overcome greater resistance.

Because the heart loses its efficiency, there is a decrease in the activity of an aging dog. Since in nature everything balances out, however, the less muscles are used, the more they shrink. This is best seen when a limb has been rested as the result of injury. Here the fleshy part of the muscle changes back into sinew. This muscle disappearance is characteristic of the aging dog, and it is often only the fat which gives the impression of rounded form.

We have spoken of harmony in nature which ordains everything in a practical and purposeful way. So it is with the muscles and bones. Coarse bones give rise to broad, heavy muscles. They give the animal its character. We have definite proof in our dogs of yesterday opposed to those of today. The old time Boxer, muscle-bound and heavy boned, full of tremendous power, was very calm but tired easily and aged quickly.

The present-day dog, which has lost the coarse weight as well as the paunchiness and sponginess in the body thanks to a finer bone and muscle structure, is livelier and has more stamina. It does not age so quickly but now has a more excitable nature characteristic of dogs with light bones and thinner, quicker-reacting muscles. It lies, therefore, in the hands of the breeders to keep the Boxer in his most beautiful form and the one which is most efficient for our purpose.

We come now to the most important point, the shoulder. Previously, far more attention was given to this part of the anatomy than is given today. It has become neglected due to the entirely different mode of living prevalent today. Whether the owners live in town or country, the dog is no longer called upon to run beside the horse and carriage or even the bicycle.

Today in the country, one is wary of letting a dog run loose in case of stock chasing, and very few owners have the time to take dogs for long walks. Therefore, the dogs don't get enough exercise. Lucky exceptions are the hunting dogs and the shepherd dogs, if they haven't become purely pets.

We should not take the view that our dogs have no need for stamina, because they are practically never in the position of having to run 40 kms. at one go. Let us forget, too, the convenient excuse that it can manage to do what it has to do even with a steep shoulder and that stamina is, after all, only a matter of training. . . . We must regard our Boxer as a working dog, and we must not cease to strive for correct construction and immaculate gait.

When you see a good and bad jumper together, take the trouble to compare their construction. My dog, Heiner van Zwergek, had an ideal head, neck and forehand but was unfortunately weak in the rear. In spite of this, he was a persevering runner who could easily cover 40 to 50 kms. (25 to 30 miles) accompanying a bicycle. His lady kennel companion, Warthe von Dom, was hardly able to move after 10 kms. The bitch was in no way exhausted. The cause lay in her very steep shoulders, which incompletely absorbed the shocks in running and jumping. One could see that every step hurt her like a hiker who marches in boots which are too tight. Both dogs had the same upbringing, with a lot of free running. Here the failure of one dog was not in the training but in the forehand deficiency.

The three drawings of forehands will show what has to be accomplished by the front, and the tasks for which it was created: (1) the task of weight bearing; (2) the absorption of shocks in walking, running or jumping; (3) the propulsion of the front when turning; and (4) helping to maintain balance.

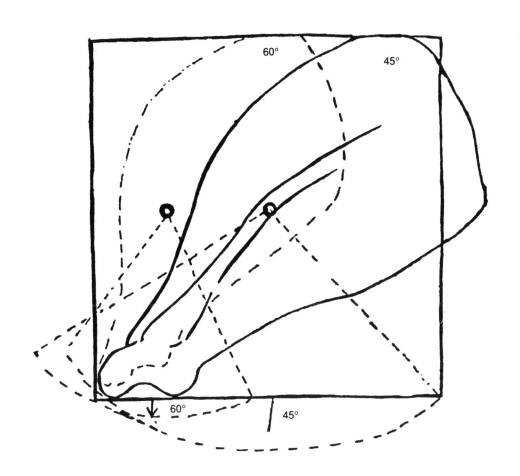

The basis of the front is the shoulder blade. Most breeds call for a long, sloping or well-laid-back shoulder blade. These all say the same thing by and large. In order to see which is the most practical and efficient position for the shoulder blade, we must examine the illustration in order to determine its usefulness as a carrier.

The shoulder blade is able to work by means of connected muscles, particularly the long ones which create motion, and the wide ones which create power. As we have seen that the muscles fit the bones which they serve, we can appreciate that a correspondingly long, wide shoulder blade is desirable. . . .

In the drawing, two shoulder blades are shown. The first is at an angle of 45° to the ground, and the other is at an angle of 60° to the ground. You can see that the 45° blade is much longer, and, because of its length, it has a much more highly developed ridge for the onset of long and powerful muscles. Assume that the triangle of dotted lines represents the field of force which the shoulder blade can generate. The small circle in the center is the axis on which the blade turns. You can easily see how much greater is the efficiency of the 45° blade. It can accomplish two and one-half times more than the one of 60°.

The further a limb can stretch out the greater becomes its efficiency, and here the 45° blade proves itself. Just as the flight of a bullet describes an arc, so every step of the dog, in whatever gait he uses, does the same. The arc begins at the moment of raising and ends with the setting down of the foot. To see this clearly we must look more clearly at the shoulder blade. This is a flat, triangular bone which has at its lower end a socket-like hollow joint. A small, bony protuberance prevents the joint from opening too wide and removes the danger of the upper arm springing out of the socket. The ridge of bone which runs the full length of the shoulder blade can be clearly felt with the fingers. Place the dog in a normal position, and, drawing a line as a continuation of the ridge down to the ground, you will see the reach of the foreleg. This will be at its greatest in a blade of 45°.

Let us now look at the illustrations. This shows the normal step forward with a correctly positioned shoulder blade. Here two forces are at work which cause the forward drive, the force of weight and the mechanical drive of the hindquarters. If the reach is insufficient, as in the illustration depicting a 60° position, the dog has to help itself by other means. It therefore steps shorter and steeper onto the ground, consequently causing a greater shock. This shock is taken first of all by the pastern, and then the whole shoulder formation suffers with it. This fault in a riding horse would bring every rider great discomfort and, in a very short time, would bring about the breakdown of the animal in the forehand.

The dog has another way to compensate for this fault. It can use its forearm muscles to a greater extent. Then the forelegs will be lifted for a longer time and higher into the air than in a normal gait, producing the

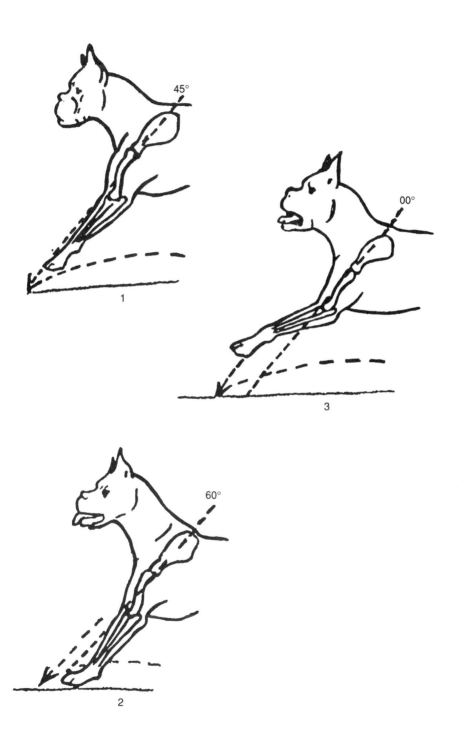

so-called high stepper. For a time, it was an action very highly valued in coach horses as an elegant and conspicuous gait. They were nearly always horses, however, which, due to their construction, covered too little ground.

Both these gaits which I have described use up a great deal of energy and lessen the speed. The dog can also attempt to balance the fault in the front by straining the hindquarters and covering it up with greater thrust. This leads to a less efficient rocking horse gallop, which, as with the horse, has its advantages going downhill but loses them again going uphill. For a dog with this build, it is better not to produce any great speed, since the faulty front will also limit the efficiency of the rear.

The Correctly Balanced Forehand

Drawings A, B and C show the shoulder when the dog is standing in the correctly balanced position. Here a comparison between A and B is very interesting. In Figure A, the very sharp angulation is caused by the long upper arm bone, and this is the shoulder found in the German Shepherd Dog. Here the long, sloping pasterns have to compensate in order that the ball of the foot can stand, as it must, under the center of gravity, despite the very great angulation.

Figure B shows the correct shoulder placement for the Boxer with the line going straight through to the ground at the point of the center of gravity.

Figure C is the usual shoulder for a Terrier, but this is no longer a rarity in our breed. The angulation here fails, not through a faulty positioning of the shoulder blade, but because the upper arm bone is too short. It is completely unbalanced, and dogs who possess this construction can never achieve satisfactory results in either speed or endurance.

How has it come about that faulty shoulders have taken over, where at one time it was very rarely seen? Perhaps we can find the answer in a very interesting paper on the German Shepherd Dog written by Rittmeister von Stephanitz concerning construction. In this, he states that he throws out every oversized animal, since, inevitably, with the increase in height, an upright shoulder occurs.

Over the years, we have raised the height of our dogs from 45 cm. (18 inches) to 62 or 63 cms. (24 to almost 25 inches), believing that working dogs should be of this size. It is well known that with every advantage comes a disadvantage, and it is perhaps as well to remember that the Boxer is a medium-sized dog.

The pasterns because of their structure are not suited to a lever action. The bones are too short, and contracting and expanding muscles are totally missing. Instead, the pastern has a certain ability to move backwards and

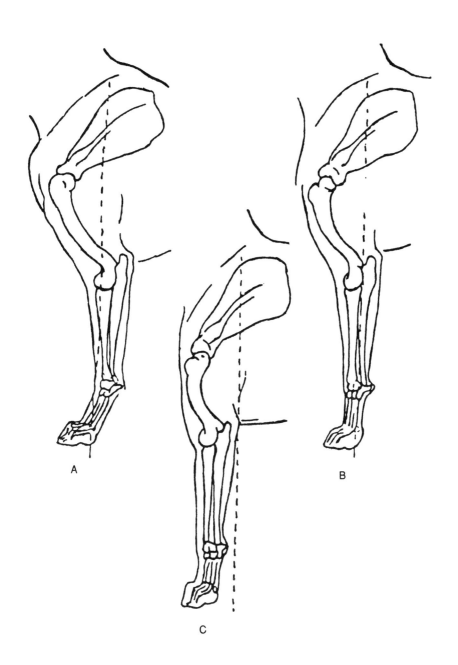

A

B

C

forwards. Therefore, the main role of the pastern is to absorb the shock in walking. A short upright pastern will not fulfill this task as well as a slightly sloping one.

Comparing Pictures A and B, upright pasterns are more suitable for bearing weight and the slightly sloping one, as required for the Boxer, is more suitable for absorbing shocks.

The pastern seen in Picture C is usually found with constructional faults in the bone above (shoulder, humerus). Because of its length and degree of slope, the foot does not come under the center of gravity. In this pastern the tendons must, to a large extent, take over the work of the bones. Animals so constructed are less efficient and will quickly break down in front.

Regarding the feet, Picture 1 shows the desired cat foot and 2 shows the hare foot. The advantage of the cat foot is that it is compact and closed. It therefore offers more resistance to injury, and lameness occurs more rarely.

The hare foot is not in itself a constructional fault. It has longer bones and for this reason it can effect great leverage for fast runners. It is found in racing dogs and in wild animals such as the hare and the fox. In accordance with the law of levers, such a foot accelerates the speed but tires more quickly. The ball or sole of the foot plays quite an important part in the absorbing of shock in walking.

Picture 3 shows a flat foot. Here the angulation of the individual toe joints has been lost, and neither absorption nor leverage can be exerted. The ball of the foot has no room to develop. This foot is inferior in beauty as well as in efficiency. It is undesirable in any breed.

We are not yet finished with the front. The breed standard says that the shoulder shall be close lying and not too heavily muscled. Why the last bit? It gave me a lot of trouble as a raw beginner. We have already seen how each bone fits precisely into the next, just as the muscles do. Now, behind the shoulder lie a few very important and powerful muscles. If the exterior of the shoulder is too heavily muscled, then the ones behind the shoulder will be correspondingly powerful and thick. This will push the upper half of the shoulder blade away from the rib cage, which in turn will force the joint between the shoulder blade and the upper arm back against the rib cage, and finally push the elbow joint out. From this arises the wide front and the so-called loose shoulders, which should really be described as being out at the elbow. Here the straight column-like support is broken, as can be seen in Figure A. Figure B shows the normal position and correct stance.

Continuing with the standard requirements, the front legs must be straight when looked at from the front, stand parallel to one another and have firmly-made bones. You will see this in Picture 1. The center of gravity lies right in the middle of the chest and is born equally by both sides. This is a correctly constructed dog at rest.

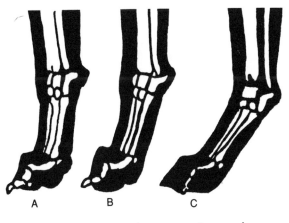

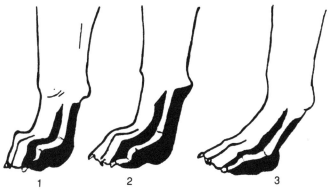

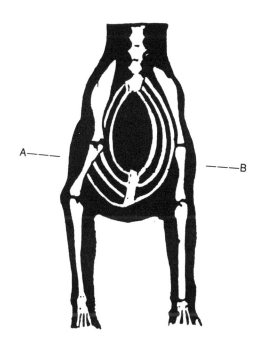

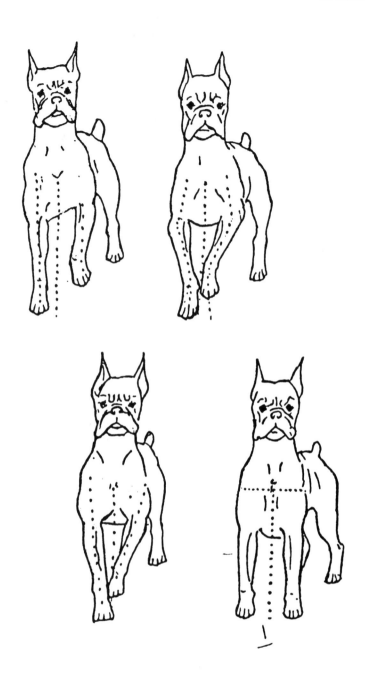

As the dog begins to move, he lifts one foot. In order to maintain his balance he must transfer the weight of his body to the other side. In many standards, the dog is called to move its fore limbs vertically to the ground at all times. Indeed, you do see this gait in broadly-built, slow dogs. It can also be seen in the show ring, particularly in America, when the dog is held and moved on a very tight lead, the head held high, thereby giving the animal a support which enables him to maintain his gait more easily.

A dog moving freely, however, will always have the urge, the faster he goes, to break away from this vertical gait. It is more advantageous for him, instead of constantly shifting the weight from right to left, to effect the balance by trying to place the feet as far as possible under the center of gravity. It would remind you of the tracks of the fox. It leaves only one row of tracks, but it nevertheless belongs among the quickest of animals. Such a gait should not be considered faulty as, with normal construction, the feet never touch or brush against each other.

If the dog's body was a box with wheels which never left the ground, then such niceties would be unnecessary; but as we have seen, the dog has to support its entire weight with three, two or sometimes only one limb, according to its particular gait at the time. This requires the most efficient use of the virtues of the dog. With crooked bones, a Chippendale-type front, or too wide a chest, a dog will never be able to reach a high performance of either speed or endurance.

The Hindquarters

There is a great difference between the functions and purposes of the fore- and hindquarters. If we press hard down on the withers of the dog, it will offer such strong resistance that it will be difficult for an adult to force the Boxer down. However, if we press on the dog's rear, the dog will yield or at least arch its back high and endeavor to unload part of the weight onto the shoulders.

With this example, the difference between the two halves of the body has been demonstrated. The front and shoulders are for weight bearing and supporting the body, while the hindquarters have the opposite duty— namely to bring the body out of a position of equilibrium. Their task is first and foremost to drive the body forward and only secondarily to absorb blows and shocks of movement. See illustrations of the relationship of front and rear angulation.

In contrast to the front which joins the body in a comparatively moveable way, the hindquarters are firmly bound to the body by means of the pelvis, which is firmly grown into the spinal column. Above all, it is the angle at which it is positioned which interests us most.

We demand in a Boxer a short, straight back. That does not mean, however, that it should look like a line drawn with a ruler as is sometimes seen in badly touched up photographs. Just as the withers can be seen in the shoulders, so a slightly sloping croup should be observable in the quarters. The drawings show a more horizontally positioned pelvis which can be described as a stiff or flat croup. The flat pelvis must put more strain on the back, and this can easily cause a yielding behind the shoulder blades. One drawing shows a croup which is more sloping, and this is the one which has proved to be the most useful and advantageous.

If you look at the femur or upper thigh bone in Picture 1, you will see that this bone fits into the pelvis and that it is shorter than the same bone shown in Picture 2. You will see, too, that the angulation of the knee joint (stifle) is therefore much less, and this then continues down to the hock angle. If we then take into account that the length of the muscles corresponds to the length of the bones, then we shall see that in Picture 1 there is much less room for muscle than there is in Picture 2.

Drawing C illustrates the action of the hind leg. It stretches itself forward, touching the ground with the ball of the foot (C-1). The whole foot touches the ground; now the thigh has reached the point of smallest contraction (C-2). The body is driven upwards and forwards, the foot still does not leave the ground, but the weight is now carried by the toes (C-3), and the thigh is now once again expanded. The driving force created by the hindquarters is in relation to its length during the duration of the step. The contraction of the thigh begins at both joints, knee and hock.

It is desirable, therefore, to lengthen the upper thigh bone (femur) in order to get a well-angulated stifle joint, but here an old law of nature creates difficulties. As we have already seen, the extreme shortening of one bone means the lengthening of the one next to it, and vice versa. A lengthening of the femur would mean a shortening of the lower thigh bone, and this would defeat the object. We can only achieve a well-angulated stifle without any disadvantages when the pelvis is correctly positioned at a slope of 30° to the back line. The usual tendency is for the femur to be at an angle of 45° to the back line, so a well-angulated stifle is therefore very important for the construction of the remainder of the limb. The lower thigh goes down from the knee to the hock, which is identical to the ankle in man. The length of the two bones (tibia and fibula) in the lower thigh is of great importance, since it determines the length of muscle and tendon which is important for the whole hind leg. The muscle is attached to the femur, runs along the lower thigh to the hock and is attached there on the heel bone projection.

This muscle must create a balance with the power of the lower leg, in which bones and tendons are much shorter. These must, above all, have the power to support and stretch the hock. In the case of over-angulation of the hindquarters, known as sickle hocks, the joints lack ability to stretch themselves fully, as the muscles which move the hock have insufficient room to contract, or the cartilages are too highly developed.

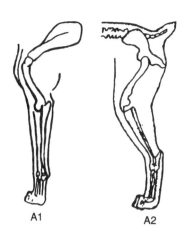

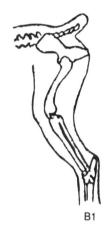

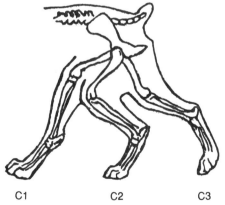

The animal with sickle hocks always wants to put its hind feet under the body's center of gravity. In order to balance out this over-angulation the hock should be short and not stand high off the ground. Hindquarters with a sloping pelvis, not too long a femur, good knee angle, long lower thigh bones and a well-angulated hock will be the most efficient form of hind leg. They possess the greatest lever action and stamina.

An American judge once said, "If you want to judge the whole dog by only two parts of its body, then look at the shoulders and the hocks and see if they are in order—if these two are correct, then the whole structure is harmonious."

We will look at the hindquarters once more, this time from behind. Figure D-1 shows us the correct hindquarters with the hind legs standing vertical to the ground. D-2 shows bowed legs that do not stand directly under the center of gravity. They are unconstructive and therefore faulty. D-3 is the opposite. Here the heels are too close together. Their support is even less than D-2, and this, too, is very faulty. D-4 shows the hind feet too close together, usually caused by a turning out of the knee joints. D-5 shows a position which a free running or standing dog will rarely take up, but it is one which is frequently seen in the show ring.

A dog which is aggressive and strains hard at the leash shows the driving power of the hindquarters. By means of such a brace, the dog can easily lift its front feet from the ground using only the collar and lead as a frontal support. A similar thing is to be seen in Figure E except that the hindquarters are sketched from the side. With the front placed higher and the quarters in a crouching position, it will be difficult to properly assess the true arching of the back and the flatness or otherwise of the croup. In addition, the angulation can often appear much better or much worse than it really is. To accurately assess the dog's structure, the feet must be placed under the center of gravity of the body.

The back feet are smaller, but longer than the front feet. Look again at Figure C and you will see that the toes have to take over part of the leverage as seen in C-3.

We now come to the most important part of the dog's body, the spinal column. The backbone joins the fore- and hindquarters and is the bearer of the rib cage and the abdomen, thereby supporting the most important life organs of the dog. For dog breeders, the "back" is a collective term meaning the whole line from the withers to the tail. Anatomically, however, it is quite different.

The spinal column is divided into different sections, as already explained in detail earlier. All the vertebrae points are needed as bases for muscles, and it is no wonder that those of the withers should be particularly well developed, as they are the support foundation for the long back muscles and for the entire shoulder muscle network. It is therefore understandable why high withers should be desirable. This should not be confused with apparently high withers created by an upright shoulder.

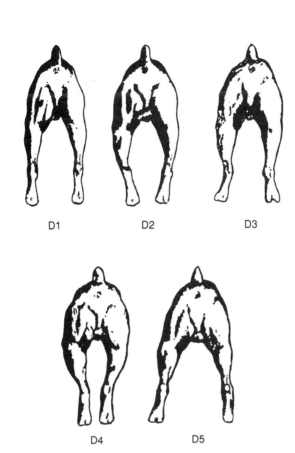

D1   D2   D3

D4   D5

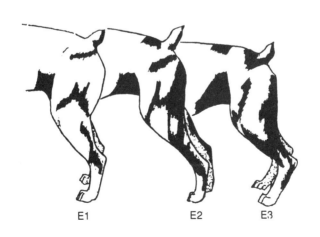

E1   E2   E3

197

The muscles of the loin and croup are fixed for the most part on the small bone projections of the back and loin vertebrae.

Many would not believe the part played by the head and neck in the forward movement of the dog. In the first place, these simplify the maintenance of equilibrium by helping to shift the center of gravity from right to left according to which foreleg moves into action.

In running, the dog will stretch his head and neck far forward, thereby shifting the weight on to the front and so achieving greater speed. On stopping suddenly the dog throws its head back into its neck, thereby shifting the weight to the back which is taken by the hindquarters and acts as a counterweight.

We will now look at sketches 1-5. The Boxer standard says that the withers shall be clearly defined, the whole back, short, straight, broad and very muscular. Now most people imagine a back like the one shown in drawing No. 1. This is a back which rarely occurs in reality. The Americans try to achieve this by their method of ring handling and forcing the tail up and forward. For decades, all our photographers have contributed their utmost to this illusion.

The natural form of the spinal column is that of a slightly arched bow. It stands without any real support and rests only on the croup and the vertebrae of the back which are joined onto the rib cage. This part of the body must carry by far the greatest weight, including the intestines and, in the pregnant bitch, an entire litter. It is easy to understand that an arched "carrying bow" has anatomical and constructional advantages.

In many breeds a slightly arched loin is called for and is not regarded as in the least faulty. Picture 2 shows such a structure (slightly exaggerated for easy identification). Here the slight arching arises from the fact that the vertebrae at the lower end are slightly smaller than those higher up—it is the same method by which the bridge or arch builder lays his stones.

Another kind of arched back can arise through weakness, kidney disease, worms, etc. Here the loin is arched up by the dog, but, as it doesn't have the correspondingly constructed vertebrae, it is possible that they will be stretched on the upper side further than is natural. A lengthy continuation of this condition can bring about a change of position of the cartilages between the individual vertebrae, and a permanent fault can arise as in Picture 1.

Picture 4 shows the true roached back. This starts at the withers and runs right through to the root of the tail. The wheel or roach back compensates in racing dogs where an otherwise flat pelvis would prevent the dog from bringing its hind legs far enough under the body during great speeds.

The so-called saddle back seen in Picture No. 5 is undoubtedly the worst of all the shown structural faults of the back. This nearly always increases with progressing age. The muscles are often weak and less efficient, and the neck is without nobility. This back gravely impairs the animal's working efficiency.

Any machine is useless if the motor which drives it is weak or built in such a way that it cannot fully achieve maximum efficiency. The motor of the living being is the heart and the important organs in its vicinity. The body is divided into two halves, the rib cage with the heart and lungs, and the abdomen with the stomach, small and large intestines, and the bladder. The rib cage is divided off by the diaphragm, one of the most important muscles in the body. The diaphragm is in two parts. It begins close behind the rib cage, on the loin vertebrae, runs in a slight inward curve and finishes on the breastbone.

The diaphragm has its important functions. It protects the heart and lungs, it serves as a bellows, and it creates the vacuum that, in an emergency, helps the dog to breathe without raising the ribs. It is clear that the shape of the rib cage has a far-reaching significance for the work of the heart and lungs. One should assume that the wider and deeper the chest, the better it would be since space is enormously valuable. However, we have heard that too great an expansion to the sides is undesirable because of the shift of position of the equilibrium. For this reason, the space must be obtained through greater depth. In addition, the arching of the ribs is very important, and a flat rib, lacking spring, is very undesirable, although the Boxer should never have a barrel rib.

The line of the belly should slope upwards from the breastbone. The region of the kidneys or the loins should be barely arched, be packed with powerful muscles, and appear as wide as possible when seen from above. The lower line of the loin should be drawn up in an elegant curve.

It will now be clear why it is that a most beautiful dog is also a most useful and efficient one. An animal whose lines and contours are harmoniously blended is the one who will, in speed and endurance, always give the best performance.

Pay attention to the angulation of the shoulders and quarters of your dogs. These are failings which we thought had been overcome years ago but today become more and more prevalent.

We do not want to turn the Boxer into a racing dog, but it has been proven that without losing substance, a well-constructed animal can have that free, ground-covering movement which is the most functional of all his assets.

7

Judging the Boxer

(Extracted from the book of the same title by Enno Meyer)

HOW DO WE CHOOSE the best Boxer? We look for one that is the embodiment of refined power and substance and active mobility.

His head should carry the hallmark of type, the perfectly proportioned square skull which may be slightly rounded on top, but whose squareness is carried out by rather flat cheek muscles. Above all, the muzzle must have sufficient width. Actually, at the outermost point of the well-padded flews, it should parallel the width of the skull.

When we examine the dentition of this muzzle, we find the upper incisors in a rather wide, slightly concave row. And when the outer and upper incisors fit closely behind the lower canines, it usually determines the correct length and width of muzzle and gives the chin the necessary, slight upturn. The ears, properly trimmed and carried with perfect upright symmetry, contribute to the alert air characteristic of the breed.

The brown eye, not too light or too dark, but luminous in the dark mask, does much to impart the true Boxer expression, that noble, kindly yet determined outlook, which promises a courageous but sensible character.

The head should rest upon a strong, columnar neck, very clean-cut and showing no dewlap. The proper length and arch adds nobility to its carriage.

The body and legs of the dog should give the impression of a square. This requires a short back, into which the neck melts gracefully. The gaily carried tail adds emphasis to the energetic outline of the dog.

The deep chest should reach to the elbows of the forelegs. Incidentally, this measurement is equal to the proper length of the foreleg from the elbow to the ground. The ribs should be well arched, though not barrel-like. The loin on a body of this length should be relatively short. The front legs should be perfectly straight, with not the least turning out of the elbows. Viewed from the side, they should show only a slight slant at the pasterns, and should be finished with tight, closely knit feet.

The hindquarters are most important, since they furnish the major portion of the dog's dynamic muscular activity. Almost any Boxer can, if he chooses, clear a six-foot barrier from a standing jump. Therefore, these powerful muscles are never bunchy but invariably possessed of the elasticity of a high jumper.

Proper angulation of the hindquarters is also most important, as it influences the stance and carriage of the dog. It ought not to be overdone or underdeveloped. If the various bones of the hindquarters are of correct length and structure, and the animal is sound and healthy, correct angulation and stance ordinarily follow.

After careful weighing of all structural qualifications, there still remains the final test of mobility, observing the gait as the dog comes toward you and goes away and, if necessary, from the side as well. This gait should typify the easy movement of the trained athlete, indicating a slight spring of the flexible muscular development.

After going over our Boxer minutely for the purpose of comparing each feature to the standard, we should then consider the part played by his general appearance. First, the coat must be fine and glistening, indicative of excellent health and condition. It should be of good, clear color in any of the various shades of golden fawn, rich red or brindle, with deep golden preferred. The dark shades are not quite as desirable since the black striping on brindles should be clearly defined. On all Boxers, however, the dark mask is imperative.

While the favorite color seems to be a golden fawn, there should be no real color discrimination in judging. Both colors, the fawn and the brindle, are necessary in breeding operations if we are to maintain the desired depth of color. Continuous mating of fawn to fawn results finally in washed-out shades, while the same procedure with brindles can produce blacks. White markings add much to Boxer attractiveness provided they are not overdone, are evenly distributed, and do not exceed one-third of the ground color.

Following the procedure described herein, we go through our first class, the puppies, seeking one that will in some degree approach or promise perfection. Once we have found him, we weigh others against him until we have found our second, and so on through the class. Successively, each class is examined and the dogs rated, until at last we must decide upon one dog for our Best of Breed.

Since we now have before us Boxers of practically equal quality, the scales do not tip as readily. We now add a criterion we have hitherto not considered as vital in our adjudication of the classes. This is temperament, character, that indefinable qualification generally known as showmanship. Some dogs possess it to a remarkable degree, while other animals seem to lack it entirely. The dog which does possess it will be carried a long way toward the final award. Should he, in addition, have outstanding physical characteristics, then we have found our best Boxer.

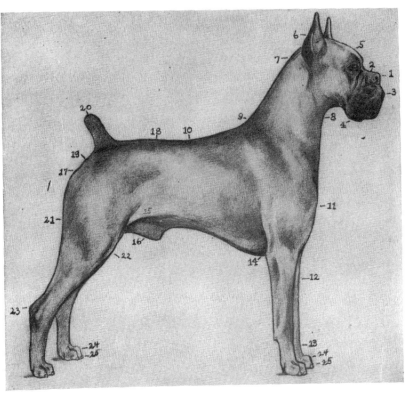

1—Nose	6—Ear	11—Chest	16—Penis	21—Thigh
2—Muzzle	7—Nape	12—Fore-arm	17—Ischium	22—Stifle
3—Chin	8—Throat	13—Pastern	18—Loins	23—Hock
4—Flews	9—Withers	14—Brisket	19—Anus	24—Toes
5—Forehead	10—Back	15—Flank	20—Tail	25—Claws

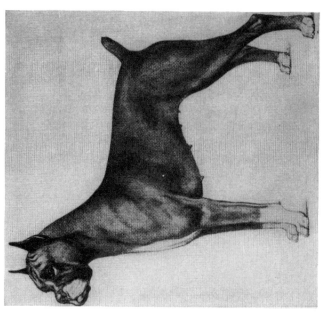

THE IDEAL MALE

Here we have the robust build indicative of the male, the distinct muscular development which, however, must not be exaggerated to such an extent as to mar the general smooth contour. Working dog structure demands that all component parts contribute to the exercise of required activities. The muzzle should be strong, but the skull not overdone since the active implements are in reality the powerful muscles which furnish motive power for the jaws, and these muscles should be fairly flat rather than bunchy. The strong neck must have sufficient length and suppleness, should fit into sloping shoulders, these into the well angulated upper arm, all synonymous with the correct front in a chest neither too wide nor too narrow. The front legs are parallel and of good bone; the pasterns are slightly sloping and the feet close.

THE IDEAL FEMALE

There is actually only a narrow margin of weight and height in properly balanced specimens of male and female, but the female must exhibit infinitely greater refinement by means of a smoother muscular development. In other words, the female, though not to be considered as lacking in strength, must have, above all else, the quality best described as femininity. While there is no provision for it in the standard, the female, on account of her maternal duties, should be allowed a slightly longer back than the male. Her back, however, is comparatively straight, with proper set-on of tail, the brisket reaching to the elbow, the body moderately tucked up, the hindquarters nicely angulated and the hocks strong. The legs are well boned but never clumsy.

204

STRAIGHT-STIFLED

The casual observer will have no trouble in spotting the faults of the dog portrayed in this illustration, for here are faults of a kind which come right out at you. No close study is needed to discern the poor quality, the atypical conformation and misfitting of the parts. The cloddy mold of the body has its usual accompaniment of pudginess and non-muscularity of loin, a condition frequently brought about by the straight stifle which cannot carry through real driving power. A stifle, straight to the point of exaggeration, coupled with a short back, can mean only one thing—a mincing gait, with its inevitable up-and-down, as opposed to flowing motion, when the animal is on the run. The neck is so devoid of arch that the head appears stuck on, while the poorly cropped ears do not enhance the general appearance.

OVER-ANGULATION

Here we have a dog of fair, over-all squareness but easily apparent faults, the most noticeable of which is over-angulation of the hindquarters. As a fault of conformation, this mars the general outline of the animal; more than that, it may impede the progress and staying power of the working dog not endowed by nature with a long, or fairly long, body. Couple with over-angulation the unfortunately flat feet shown in the illustration and we have two faults of mobility counting against the worker, as well as two faults of conformation militating against the stance and gait of the dog in the show ring. To a lesser degree, the profusion of wrinkle, and the dewlap, both constitute undesirable features which detract from the Boxer's characteristic neatness.

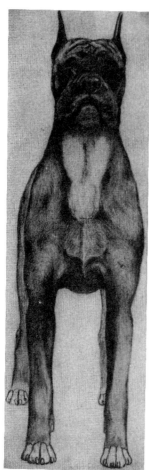

← FRONT VIEW
(Correct)

Viewed directly from the front, to greater degree perhaps than from any other vantage point, does a dog evidence characteristics of balance, particularly as regards those two balance-properties, station and substance. Here we find, first of all, the right proportion of over-all height to width. We see the right depth of chest as compared with width of chest; the right length of leg and comparative thickness and roundness of bone, from elbow to pastern to feet, with no suggestion of taper and equidistant throughout. The straight front, when accompanied by the correct slope of shoulder and the properly developed chest, is a thing of beauty which, in the presence of a well knit bony structure, spells admirable stance and commendable forepart gait.

FRONT VIEW →
(Incorrect)

Here we have two faulty builds, the one too narrow, the other too wide, both specimens typifying not faulty stance alone but, rather, the faulty structure responsible for faulty stance. In other words, no skilfull setting down of feet and legs could serve to hide these true structural shortcomings. In the narrow fronted dog, the same unfortunate inheritance, or actual lack of bone growth which resulted in the undeveloped chest, produced also long bones of the legs which did not grow straight to stand equidistant from each other. Instead, they bowed, or knock-kneed, a deplorable malformation. The wide fronted dog, though his legs are straight and equidistant, is just as far from standard. He is so out of balance as to be chesty; he is wider in front than he is behind, thus wedge shaped which a Boxer should not be.

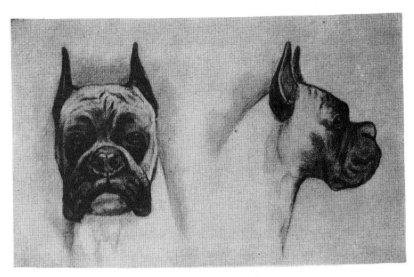

CORRECT HEAD

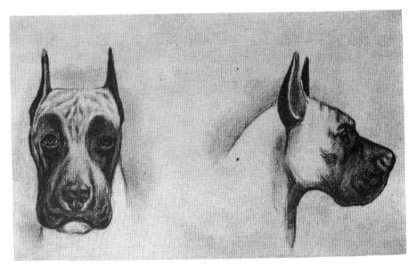

DANE-LIKE HEAD

The CORRECT Boxer head, as a whole appears muscular, for here lies the motive power for the jaws, yet it should in no way seem overdone. It is in balance when skull and foreface are in the right proportion. The skull is clean, the cheeks do not protrude, and there is no wrinkle save what may be occasioned by erection of the ears. In profile, the correct head shows relative length of skull and muzzle, the moderately rounded contour of the skull, the slight elevation of the nose and the proper depth of muzzle. In creating the DANE-LIKE head, Nature, in an effort to produce a level mouth through elongation of the maxillary, premaxillary and mandible bones, shoves skull and muzzle down to maintain a natural balance. The result is a head whose long cast, and small eyes and nostrils constitute the antithesis of everything desired in a Boxer.

INCORRECT PROPORTION

BULLDOG TYPE

On account of its INCORRECT PROPORTION of skull and foreface, this head is faulty, for the size of the muzzle is too small as compared with the size of the skull. The head, therefore, appears weak; the muzzle naturally lacks power and, as a rule, possesses no vestige of turn-up. And the light eye, improperly set, gives the face an expression quite foreign to the Boxer. In profile, this head looks even weaker because of the downward slope of the muzzle. In the BULLDOG TYPE of head, we have a reversion to one of the early progenitors of the breed—the flat Bulldog skull with profuse wrinkle, the stop receding into the skull with consequent abnormal shortening of the foreface. In profile, this head sometimes exhibits such marked turn-up as to expose the dentition of the lower jaw.

CORRECT NECK

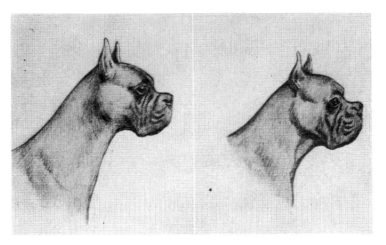

TOO LONG   TOO SHORT

The neck is an important feature of the show dog's anatomy, contributing greatly to symmetry and balance. Of ample length, it must be strong and muscular and slightly arched at the nape. Yet it must be clean, dry and devoid of dewlap or pendulous skin under the throat. Such a neck joins head to body in a continuously graceful line. The TOO LONG neck projects the head away from the body, thus destroying balance. It appears stringy because it lacks roundedness and arch. The TOO SHORT neck is least graceful of all, being almost invariably thick and too muscular. This neck, also, as a rule lacks arch while the dewlap, frequently observed in loose-skinned dogs, tends to make the head seem heavy and in that way to mar the harmony of the whole.

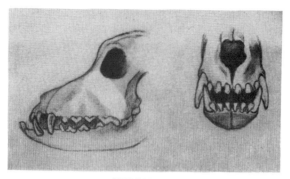

CORRECT BITE

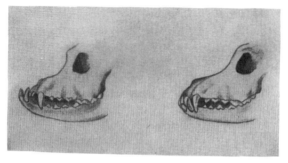

INCORRECT BITE

The dentition of the Boxer is an indicator of the correct construction and position of maxillary and premaxillary bones which constitute the upper jaw and the mandibles of the lower jaw. The correct bite consists of just enough protrusion of the lower jaw to permit the outer incisors of the upper jaw to pass behind the outer canines of the lower jaw. The front view discloses the desirable width of jaw together with even, regularly spaced incisors. In the diagram (lower left), we note too much length of underjaw leaving a gap between the upper incisor and the lower canine. Such a faulty mouth will, in its exaggerated form, show the teeth when the mouth is closed. The diagram (lower right), portrays what may be the perfect bite for some breeds but not for the Boxer, inasmuch as it would so change the contour and character of the head as to suggest a terrier cast.

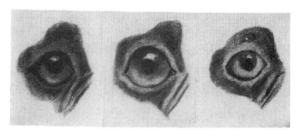

Normal   Large, Protruding   Small, Deeply set

THE EYE

Size, shape, setting and color share equal responsibility in creating the correct Boxer expression even though it is true that these qualities overlap in influence, each upon the other. The NORMAL Boxer eye is dark brown and luminous. It radiates energy, amiability and intelligence. It breathes trust as opposed to any semblance of craftiness or belligerence. The eye TOO LARGE is definitely not Boxer; ordinarily, it protrudes, and it has a vapid look which would indicate almost a lack of mental capacity. The SMALL, DEEPLY SET eye goes to the other extreme. If dark, it may have a threatening or piercing expression, foreign to the normal character of the breed. If it is light in color, it often incorporates a certain degree of shrewdness as if the dog must make up in cunning what it lacks in real brain power.

210

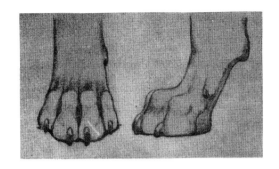

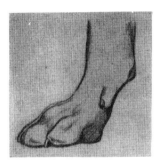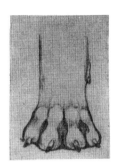

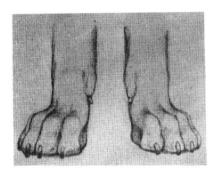

THE FOOT

CORRECT FOOT (Top) The correct foot is small, compact, with tightly arched toes and tough pads. Though described as a "cat's paw," the Boxer foot is as muscular as any other part of him, a feature which the "cat's paw" designation might seem to contradict. However, his is a graceful foot, never clumsy for all its strength. Viewed from the side, this foot is definitely square by virtue of its high-arched toes and strong ligaments. SPLAY FOOT (Center) The open, or splay foot, is one whose toes are spread and flattened. Whether the condition is an hereditary malformation, or whether consequent upon calcium deficiency, the fact remains that it is a weak foot incapable of prolonged effort. TURNED OUT FOOT (Bottom) The turned out foot, too, is undesirable in that it mars stylish stance in the show room and militates against endurance when at work.

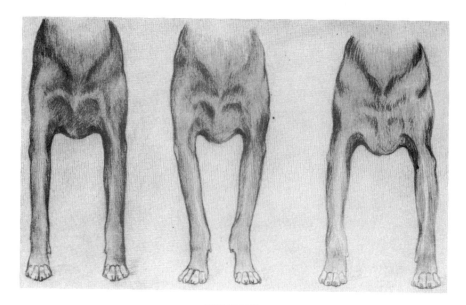

THE FRONT

In considering the front, we are concerned with more than legs and feet, bone and proportion, important as are these qualities in themselves. We are concerned, as well, with the legs as support for the body. Here we have three fronts, the one at the left correct with its straight, parallel forelegs, smooth, short pasterns and small, arched feet which together constitute sturdy underpinning for a powerful body. In the center view, the legs, in converging toward each other at the pasterns, can furnish only limited support, the appearance of weakness furthered by the narrow, undeveloped chest. To the right, we see another poor front caused primarily by shoulders so loose as to spread the front and thus rob the body of its rightful support.

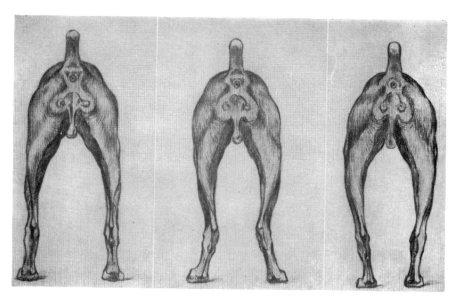

REAR VIEW

At the left, we have a commendable stance as viewed from behind. The overall proportion of height to width is good, while the pronounced musculation must play its part in the grace and sturdiness of the natural stand. The pelvis is broad, the thighs long, the hocks well let down and the same distance from each other as are the feet. In the center view, the hocks turn in, bowing the quarters and forcing the feet to turn out, thus affecting not alone stability but starting momentum. To the right, we observe a second faulty formation in the outward bowing of the thigh bones, caused primarily by weakness at the stifle to create a disagreeable stance and what must prove to be a waddling gait.

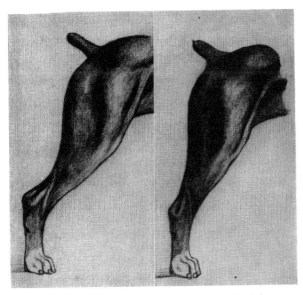

Ideal   Straight-Stifled

HINDQUARTER

The ideal hindquarter is first of all so strong that its muscles stand out through the skin; not bunchy, knotted or "muscled up," but seeming to flow with grace and rhythm even though the animal be absolutely still. For it is these muscles, in conjunction with the correct angulation of the bones, which furnish power for the drive and flexibility in motion. As here portrayed, it is the proportion of hip to hock, and hock to toe—roughly two thirds and one third—which means a sure and distance-eating reach and a powerful and long enduring drive. Contrast this ideal hindquarter with the one at the right which is comparatively straight-stifled, neither graceful nor characteristic. The muscular development seems good, but the definite lack in angulation cannot provide for proper leverage to stretch and flex the muscles, thus it must produce a stilted gait.

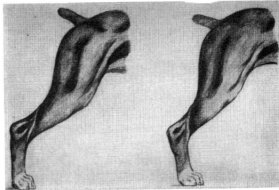

Over-Angulation   Set-Under Hock

HINDQUARTER

Exactly the reverse of the straight-stifled quarter is the over-angulation pictured at the left. The proportion of hock to toe is too great, and the quarter, as a sometime natural consequence, is stringy. There must be lost motion here, for muscles cannot deliver when impeded by such faulty angulation. The gait is almost sure to be loose, shifty, uncertain, and the effort entailed in producing it, extremely tiring. To the right, we see a hindquarter which appears really satisfactory in its muscularity, though markedly at fault through the set-under position of the hock. Such a build interferes with the propulsion of the entire hindquarter, the lack of power being evident even in the slack setting down of the foot.

213

THE BODY

Correct

The correct body impresses one first of all with its squareness, and then with its characteristic backline which, starting from the high point at the withers, comes down in a graceful but very slight curve across the back and on over the croup to the set-on of the tail. The deep chest reaches to the elbows, the well sprung ribs shorten as they approach the loin to produce a moderate tuck-up.

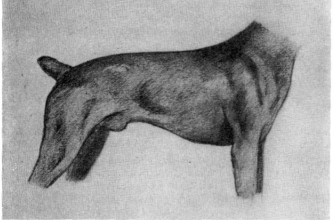

Long Back

Here we note the plain effect produced by the over-long back and the straight shoulder, this build often being accompanied by scant depth of brisket and a general deficiency in substance.

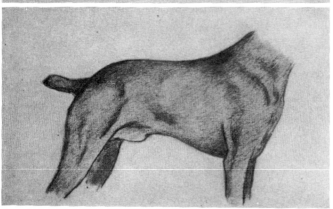

Slanting Croup

This model is conspicuous for its thoroughly atypical backline, its croup, or rump, being too markedly slanting and its tail set low.

CARP BACK

SWAY BACK

There are two extremely faulty formations which, though not often encountered in the show room, should be given space if for no other reason than to serve as a warning of what to avoid. In what is usually known as the CARP BACK, the backline is so convex as to dip at the withers and again at the tail. The general appearance produced is a hunching of the body, the antithesis of true Boxer mold, and it is often accompanied by the straight shoulder, improperly knit. The SWAY BACK is just as undesirable though it may spell weakness in even greater degree because it is part and parcel of undeveloped, straight-sided ribs and weediness throughout. In such specimens, the rump is usually over-built and the total ensemble that of an unsightly misfit.

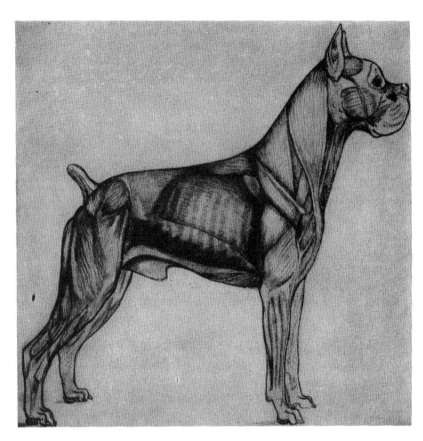

SUPERFICIAL MUSCLES

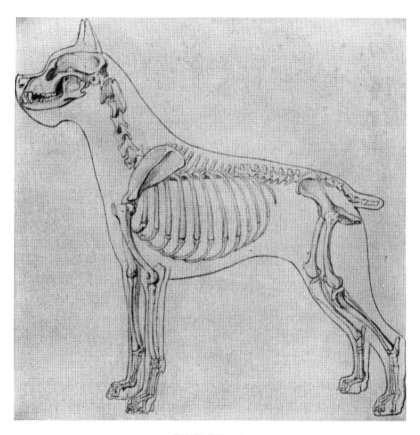

SKELETON

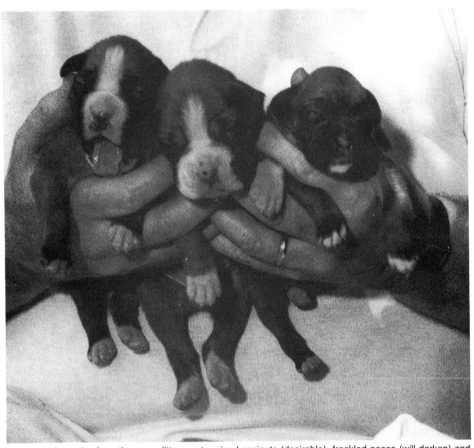

Ten-day-old puppies from the same litter—note raised occiputs (desirable), freckled noses (will darken) and wide white blazes which will narrow as heads broaden and develop.

8

Choosing a Puppy

IF YOU HAVE DECIDED on the Boxer as the breed for you, you should do some homework and prepare for the responsibility you are about to accept.

It would be wise to attend as many dog shows as possible to look at the Boxers. Talk to as many Boxer owners as you can, and ask plenty of questions. If you are not acquainted with anyone in the breed, contact the American Kennel Club, 51 Madison Avenue, New York, New York 10010. Ask them for the name and address of the secretary of the American Boxer Club. Write to the secretary asking for a leaflet on the breed and information on a local club or breeders in your area.

Now you are off to look at litters. Always make an appointment and, if you cannot keep it, please call and notify the breeder. If you know the color, sex and quality you want, tell the breeder, as he may not have your preference. White puppies or puppies with more than one-third white ground color do exist but are undesirable. Reputable breeders will not sell, give away, register, or breed them.

A breeder may let you look at a litter at four weeks, or he may ask you to wait until the puppies have had their first shots. It is advisable not to take the children when looking at litters. It is hard to leave without a puppy, and you may wish to look further. The more litters you see, the more differences you will notice, and the more you will learn about the breed.

Certain things will strike you immediately. Do the puppies look lively, alert, and healthy? Are the surroundings clean? If the dam is not with the puppies, ask to see her. She will give you some idea of what size the puppies might be, and you can assess her temperament. Remember that she will not be looking her best after whelping and nursing a litter.

Symmetrical white markings are always attractive, but remember the white blaze, white collar or white neck markings will shrink considerably as the puppy grows. If you are looking for a show puppy, try to select one with white markings. Remember, however, that the puppy is only a *potential* show puppy. No one can guarantee a champion.

Flashy puppies are so called because they have a white blaze running down between the eyes, possibly white shoes or stockings, a half or full white collar and a white chest. They are considered more attractive by many people, and flashy puppies definitely do better in the show ring. However, the so-called plainer puppy with a black mask and very little white on the body still has all the attributes of the breed and is equally as lovable. Plain puppies are usually sold as pets and sometimes at a lower price than the flashier puppies.

Take a good look at the puppy's eyes. They should not be light. When the eyes first open, they are usually dark blue. You should select a puppy with a dark rim around the eye. This is the third eyelid and white or pink color (unpigmented) is unattractive unless the dog has a very tight eye. The looseness of the eye cannot be seen or judged at a young age.

It is hard to judge the mouth at a very young age. It may or may not change as the head develops. It is very hard to be sure of a Boxer puppy's mouth until it is nine months old.

The unique headpiece of the Boxer can change more from birth to twelve months than any other breed. Nonetheless, the occiput (dome) of the puppy's head should be raised with a good wide muzzle. The stop (depression or step down between the eyes at beginning of nose) should be very obvious from side view. A longer looking head at this age is not objectionable.

Take a good look at the coat. It should be short, glossy and soft to the touch. A puppy should not have an exceptionally heavy coat, as this may or may not be lost with age.

Observe the bone on the puppies. Are they strong and do they have substance? Are the feet well-knuckled (catlike)? Have their nails been clipped?

If you are picking a puppy from six to eight weeks of age, the ears will probably have been cropped. Make sure that the breeder will assist you with maintaining the correct ear position. If the breeder cannot help, make sure your veterinarian is knowledgeable in this area. The ears must be given constant attention until they are erect. Natural growth and teething can make the ears sag.

Tails should have been docked and dew claws removed during the first week. Taut, hairless skin over the bone at the end of the tail is very

Ch. Eldic's Darius at two months, after ear cropping.

Another method of posting.

unattractive and is not necessary if the skin is cut with a flap. If you want a male show puppy, be sure he has two testicles. Sometimes the puppy will draw descended testicles up into the scrotum if it is very cold, or if he is continually prodded or handled. In some families, testicles do not descend until a later age (even after six months), so this is not necessarily a fault at this time. Although a puppy with one testicle may not be exhibited in the conformation ring, he can make a fine pet, and can be shown in obedience. He should not be used for breeding. If you have doubts, discuss the matter with your veterinarian.

If you want a show puppy, your purchase agreement should state that, if the puppy proves to be a monorchid (one testicle descended) or cryptorchid (neither testicle descended into the scrotum), the puppy will be replaced or the purchase price refunded.

If you have decided on a female puppy, you should decide now whether you want to spay or breed her. If you think you might breed her, discuss "breeding terms" with the seller. If you are not interested in breeding, most veterinarians recommend spaying before the first season to reduce the risk of several forms of cancer.

Once you have selected one or two puppies in the litter, it is time to judge them. Stand them up on a table, but make sure the surface has a good grip for the pup's feet. Pick up the neck behind the ears and let the front fall naturally. The feet may turn outwards a little, but this can correct itself. They should not turn inwards. The puppies should enjoy being handled.

Looking at the puppy from the side view should give you an idea of angulation and whether the puppy looks too long-backed. If you think he looks long, measure the other puppies' legs and backs to get proportions. You may find a lot of difference. Toplines are hard to judge at this age, as puppies wiggle and roach (hunch) their backs constantly.

Spend as much time as you can observing the puppies at play. Note how they approach you. A shy or nervous puppy should not be chosen, but one that comes bouncing towards you is not always the best one either. The cautious puppy who watches you and then comes over is often the most promising.

The size of the puppy is not too important at this age, as the smallest of the litter may grow to be larger than the other puppies. By all means spend as much time as you can questioning and listening to the breeder. Ask to see a copy of the puppies' pedigree. Visit as often as you can to observe the puppy and learn about raising a puppy.

Try to observe the puppy outside at play and note its natural stance. When a puppy is watching something of interest, it draws itself up into a natural alert pose. This is a perfect time to evaluate balance and angulation.

Temperament is very important, and puppies should be very outgoing at this age. They will be playing roughly with each other and with their dam, who will sometimes growl or shake a puppy. This is quite natural, and the dam is training them to accept discipline.

222

Seven-month-old pup in natural pose. Breeders: Paul and Linda Small.

Ch. Wagner Wilvirday Famous Amos shows his natural stance.

If there is anything about the puppy which you do not like, put off purchasing it. Miracles do happen, but a puppy with a great number of faults will seldom correct them all.

At four months of age, most Boxer puppies look terrible. Ears look too large for the head, fronts look too narrow, paws look too big for the body, and so on. They seem to be all legs with loose joints and muscles—like gangling teenagers, in fact. By six months of age, the puppies should be more in proportion. Ears are usually erect and temperament is developing. Test for temperament by clapping your hands and making noises, but do not frighten the puppy. The pup should stand its ground. If it has been properly socialized, it should still be very outgoing and affectionate. It should have style, hold its head proudly, be playful, curious and definitely mischievous.

Carefully go over the puppy on a table. Are the ears properly set? Are the brow and muzzle in proportion? Are the eyes tight? Is the stop developing? Is the mouth correct with no teeth visible when closed? (A very undershot bite can still correct itself, but as the months go by, there is less and less likelihood of this happening.) Good length of neck and well-angulated hindquarters should be noticeable at this age. The front will still look narrow but should look straight. Paws should be catlike. They may still turn out a little, but this can still correct itself.

The topline should be straight and firm. Check layback of the shoulders and position of the elbows. The depth of the brisket will still not be fully developed. Be sure the puppy does not drop off too much at the croup (the muscular area just above and around the set-on of tail). Does it carry its tail up?

Watch the puppy moving towards you and away from you. The legs should swing straight and true. Again examine the natural, alert stance.

By nine months of age, you will really know what you are buying. The whole body should be square and head in proportion to the body. You should see a picture of the dog-to-be. At this age, the bite probably will not become worse. A wry mouth (lower jaw twisted to one side) is definitely noticeable at this age. A very bad wry mouth will have teeth visible when the mouth is closed. The stop should be well defined and muzzle well developed but without excessive flews. Lip placement should be good. Both testicles should be descended into the scrotum.

Your dog should definitely be outgoing, alert, happy, and playful. The head should have taken on a chiseled look, and the body should look square. The pup should be showing his watchdog instincts by barking at strangers. The muzzle should have broadened, but the whole head can still develop up to two years of age.

If you are looking for a good show dog, this is probably the best age to buy, as you will have a much better idea of what the mature dog is going to look like. The breeder should have begun proper show training and may even have shown at matches and/or point shows. Of course, you must expect to pay more for a puppy at this age.

Lastly, please remember that there has never been a perfect Boxer. Every Boxer has faults, but you are looking for the one that comes closest to the breed standard. Take your time looking for just the right puppy, and be prepared to travel to look at litters. You will have a healthy dog a long time, and it will become a member of your family—so choose wisely.

When you purchase your puppy, you should receive a bill of sale, a health record, a pedigree, and the American Kennel Club application form which will enable you to obtain a registration certificate.

It is wise to have your puppy examined by a veterinarian within 48 hours. Should there be any medical problem, it is not so hard to return the puppy to the breeder. A reputable breeder usually advises you to do so.

If you want a pet Boxer and would like to spare yourself the trials of puppyhood, please consider adopting a Boxer from a Boxer Rescue Service. These services shelter and place Boxers who need homes.

To find out if there is a Boxer Rescue Service in your state, call the American Kennel Club and find out the current secretary of the nearest Boxer Club in your area. The secretary and reputable breeders in the vicinity should know the details. Both New Jersey and Connecticut have active Boxer Rescue Services, but there are many others throughout the U.S.A.

Breho Nightwatch demonstrates his gait at eight weeks.

Another Breho puppy strikes a show pose at only seven weeks.

225

Mr. and Mrs. Daniel Hamilburg's first Boxer, Ch. Sally of Grayarlin, bred by Jane Kamp (now Forsyth) and her partner George Pusey.

9

Grooming, Nutrition
and Training

ROUTINE GROOMING of the Boxer should be a special time for owner and dog. It is best to put the dog on a grooming table or some other solid surface. The puppy or dog should be taught that the grooming session is a time for business, not play. The Boxer should be handled gently so as not to hurt the animal in any way and so that it learns to enjoy being groomed.

Ears should be cleaned gently with a cotton swab to remove wax and dirt. Dry noses should be gently rubbed with Vaseline. Any slight discharge from the eyes should be cleaned. Teeth should be checked for irregularities, and tartar should be removed.

While the Boxer is on the table, check him all over for ticks or fleas. A good bath is the best way to rid the dog of fleas, followed by the washing of all bedding, blankets or pads. If you find fleas, place a flea collar in your vacuum bag to make sure that any fleas picked up off carpets or rugs will be killed. It can be transferred to new bags for the life of the collar.

Any cuts or grazes should be cleaned with an antiseptic. Anal glands should be checked by you or your veterinarian, particularly if the dog is dragging its hindquarters along the ground.

The Boxer's grooming requirements are few. Brushing twice or three times weekly should remove dead hair and loose skin particles. Brushing also stimulates the secretion of the natural skin oils that make the coat shine.

Boxers do shed moderately with the changing of the seasons. During this time, bathing with warm water will remove excessive hair. A dog that spends most of its time indoors will shed a little all year round. Some Boxers enjoy having the vacuum or the dustbuster used on them.

When the Boxer is an adult, grooming with a stripper blade is the best way to remove the dead hair but this should be done with care so as not to scrape the skin. A sisal grooming glove or hound glove is good for removing the last loose hairs.

Boxers are naturally clean dogs but do need baths occasionally. Excessive bathing is not recommended as this removes the natural oil in the skin. A wet towel will clean off most surface dirt. Waterless shampoo works well on mud and mess.

After brushing or bathing, the coat can be rubbed with a little grooming oil. There are numerous products available.

Nails should be clipped or preferably sanded down with an electric nail grinder every week. This is essential for the comfort of the dog and an attractive look. Be sure to avoid damage to the quick, which is visible on dogs with light nails, by holding the nail up to the light.

Show grooming requires all of the above and a little more, such as trimming around the ears, the tuck up, and hindquarters, to give a clean look. This is usually done with an electric trimmer and special scissors and is best taught by the breeder or a professional handler.

Nutrition

The adult Boxer best maintains his weight and health by eating two meals a day. Intestinal upsets can occur when a Boxer is fed only one large, heavy meal daily. Also, it is easier to cut down on the food for spayed bitches when they're served twice a day. If a spayed bitch or older dog is genuinely hungry, add cooked vegetables, particularly carrots, celery, or turnips which are high in fiber and will satisfy their hunger. Older dogs, like older people, can digest two smaller meals per day more easily.

New puppy owners should follow the diet used and advised by the breeders, and any changes should always be made gradually, otherwise severe diarrhea can result.

Commercial dog food is fine, but ingredients should be carefully checked to make sure it is a balanced diet of high quality. Meat can be added to the evening meal and alternated with cottage cheese, cooked eggs or yogurt. Only marrow bones should be given to the dog. Other bones can puncture the intestine.

Do not give your Boxer table scraps. Besides the fact that it is usually unwanted and inedible food, it is a bad habit to start feeding a dog from the table. You will not notice how bad the habit has become until you have guests.

Feed your Boxer at the same time every day and in the same place. This will assist with regular eliminations. Use non-toxic bowls and clean them thoroughly after each meal. Any uneaten food should be removed after 30 minutes. With a healthy Boxer, this will be an unusual event. In fact, Boxers can become obese if not watched carefully. This is unhealthy for any dog and can shorten its life.

To determine whether your dog is being fed a proper maintenance diet, weigh him at regular intervals. The easiest way to do this is to weigh yourself on the bathroom scale, then pick up the dog, see how much you weigh with the dog, and subtract the difference.

Vitamin supplements are essential during the growth period of the puppy, and many people continue daily use for the lifespan of the Boxer.

Some Boxers are subject to bile attacks. Bile is a fluid which is produced continuously by the liver. In some Boxers, as well as Great Danes and Doberman Pinschers, it is produced in excess at certain times—usually in the morning. The Boxer will not eat anything except grass, loud stomach noises can be heard, and the dog is in obvious discomfort until vomiting occurs. He then seems to recover very quickly, and he eats normally a few hours later. It is wise to give some yogurt or powdered yogurt after such an attack to put the flora back in the stomach.

During the winter, the heating of a house may make the dog's coat dry, and a tablespoonful of vegetable oil or wheat germ oil should be added to the evening meal.

Flatus (passing gas) can be an embarrassment for owners of some Boxers. It is best aided by the addition of charcoal powder or charcoal biscuits to the evening meal.

Training the Boxer

Before you buy your puppy, buy him a crate. It should be big enough for him to stand up and turn around in as an adult. While he is still a baby, you can block off half of it to make it cozier. This will be his own den where he sleeps and rests when you can't watch him. It will help you housebreak him and keep him from chewing your belongings when he is teething. In other words, it will keep him out of trouble—something Boxer puppies love to get into.

Start training your puppy the day you bring him home. Be gentle but firm. Remember that adorable bundle will grow into a big, strong dog, and behavior that is cute when the puppy is small will certainly not be funny when the dog is full grown. It is much easier to discipline and train a young puppy than a dog who weighs over fifty pounds.

Boxers are eager to please, and they respect training. Start with normal commands of "No," and "Off" for jumping up. If necessary, physically show the dog what you mean rather than repeating a command. Give lots of praise when the puppy does what you want.

By all means, take your Boxer to obedience classes so you can learn the right way to train him. Boxers can be obstinate and stubborn, but patience and consistency will make your Boxer a well-behaved companion.

If you are going to show your Boxer, you should start training him to stand still on a grooming table. Set him up two or three times a day for a few minutes, increasing the time as he grows and gets used to it. Always follow this training with lots of praise, a treat or play. Next you will need to leash train the puppy and teach him to gait in the way a Boxer is shown. Such training should be fun, and playing with the puppy during and afterwards is essential.

American & Canadian Ch. Trimanor Pinepath's Hudson Bay, bred and owned by Robert and Judy Jury.

10

The Character
of the Boxer

BOXERS are excellent watch dogs. Because of their keen hearing, the smallest noise puts them on alert. Their barking signals that someone or something strange is around, and they are not satisfied until they find out what it is. They are not nervous barkers and do not bark without reason.

When you live with a Boxer, you are safe from any kind of intruder. Any stranger would think twice before attempting to enter a home with a Boxer in it. It has the strength and size to take care of almost any situation. The Boxer is naturally cautious of strangers. A sound specimen ought to be rather distrustful but never vicious. In Germany, there is an old saying that "the Boxer fears neither death nor the devil."

On the other hand, the Boxer is very affectionate with his owners and family. Although cautious at first, he will quickly make welcome any friends of the family and give enthusiastic greetings thereafter.

Boxers are excellent with children and love to play. Being pushed, mauled, and teased does not seem to worry them. Children can dress them up, take their toys, and even sit in their crates; and the dogs tolerate it well.

I have taken several Boxers to local schools for educational programs. At first, the children are afraid because of the cropped, erect ears and the size of the dog. However, when he gently puts his paws on me and licks my

Robert Crane and Jacquet's Elizabeth share a "loving."

Beaufront's What The Dickens with L. J. and Nicholas Gibbs.

232

face, I know he has captured more hearts. Soon the children demand to be kissed, too.

The breed has an uncanny sense of knowing when to behave. At a nursing home, they will quietly greet older people in wheelchairs or walkers as though they were used to it every day. With a Boxer head in his lap looking up with soulful eyes, an older person will often say, "This dog understands me."

Boxers are meticulously clean and spend a great deal of time washing themselves like cats. In fact, nothing bothers them more than to get their white socks or stockings dirty.

Boxers like to run and enjoy exercise and long walks. A good game of football or tag delights them. The writer had an old champion male who took to being a country gentleman at the age of eight years. He stalked, pointed, and flushed birds, and caught and killed numerous rabbits, pheasants, and mice. He kept up this practice until he was over 12 years of age.

Toys fascinate Boxers, and they will spend hours playing with them. They enjoy the company of other dogs, and the intrigue of their games is amazing. You can never be bored if you own more than one Boxer.

Boxers are gregarious by nature. They love people and want to be with them rather than outside by themselves. This is why they often are not good kennel dogs.

The Boxer is very sensitive to the mood of his owner and can be very quiet and still when someone is ill or busy. The writer recalls a young cousin in Brazil, who was critically ill. Her faithful Boxer never left the end of her bed except to relieve himself, and he would not eat. Her mother sat by the bed watching and praying for the fever to break and finally fell asleep. When she awoke, she found the fever had broken and hastened to tell her husband. However, he already knew because the Boxer had wakened him and then had taken some food.

The Boxer is a natural clown and loves to entertain. He can be taught many tricks and loves to have you laugh at him.

Great as a guard dog, service dog, or guide dog, the Boxer has proved his worth time and time again. He may require a little more training due to his obstinate streak, but, once trained, he never forgets anything. You can teach him to do almost anything, but there is a proper way to do so. You must ask, ask again, and then allow him to do it.

A Boxer can converse with you, if you take the time to learn his language. He will tell you in no uncertain terms when dinner is late, and can give the dirtiest look should you offend him. He likes nothing better than to go to sleep touching you, be it with his paw on your foot, his head on your lap, or his whole body on your bed, if allowed.

If you are looking for a placid dog, do not buy a Boxer. He is always ready for action and eager for something new to learn. If you leave for 15 minutes, you will be treated to a welcome as though you had returned from a trip to the Orient. Any Boxer can wiggle so that you think he is coming right out of his skin. They do it even at 13 years of age! The most amazing thing about Boxers is the way they grow old with such grace, paying little attention to the passing of years and retaining puppy traits until the day they die.

Once you have had a Boxer, it is difficult to replace him with another breed. The late Danny Kaye once remarked that his family never owned dogs, only Boxers.

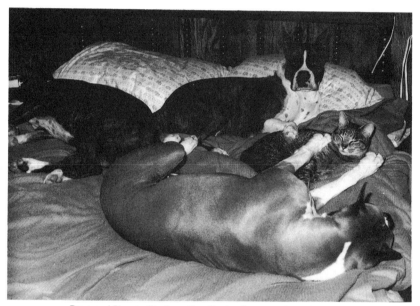

Boxers of Brenda Stuckey allow the family cat to share the bed.

11

The Boxer at Work

Obedience

Obedience competition is divided into three levels, each with its own title. The levels are Novice, Open, Utility, and the corresponding titles are Companion Dog (C.D.), Companion Dog Excellent (C.D.X.), and Utility Dog (U.D.). There are also tracking tests offering Tracking Dog and Tracking Dog Excellent titles.

Novice work is the basic obedience necessary to make any dog a good companion. It comprises heeling on leash, standing for examination, heeling off leash, the recall exercise, the long sit and long down. Every Boxer should have this basic obedience training, which should become a part of his everyday life even if he does not enter competition.

The Open class comprises seven exercises: heeling off leash, dropping to the ground on recall, retrieving on flat ground, retrieving over a high jump, the broad jump, the long sit and the long down with handlers out of sight.

The Utility class consists of silent hand signals, scent discrimination tests, directed retrieve, directed jumping and group examination.

To obtain any of these titles, the dog must earn three qualify scores of at least 170 points out of a possible 200.

In 1937 the first Boxer to obtain a C.D. title was High Spot Major, bred by Paul Ladin and owned by Mr. G. E. Zimmerman. 1939 saw the first Boxer obtain a C.D.X. title. This was Coquette v.d. Stuttgarter, owned by Mr. and Mrs. Glenn W. Studebaker. The first U.D. title was earned by a

Boxer in 1940. It was Harry of Hinshenfelde, who was handled by his owner/trainer, John A. Brownell.

Obedience teams became popular, and an all-Boxer team competed at the Westchester K.C. show in 1954. The four Boxers were Chardythe's Pacemaker, U.D., owned and handled by Judson L. Streicher (later president of the American Boxer Club), Imperial of Hinshenfelde, C.D.X., owned and handled by A. J. Schneider, Mozart Sonatina, U.D., owned and handled by Laura A. Dale, and Huck Hill's Goe Gander, owned and handled by Harry Hollestscher.

Joseph A. Galassi (a past president of the American Boxer Club) worked his own Boxers in competition as well as becoming a well-known obedience instructor. His dogs, Trooper, C.D.X., and Scooter, C.D.X., were part of the New Jersey Boxer Club's team and were never defeated in any competition against other teams. Joe regrets there are not more Boxers in obedience today but attributes it to the fierce competition from top scorers in other breeds, which discourages a lot of Boxer owners from competing.

Champion Yaboo of Tulgey, owned by Mr. and Mrs. George Goff, obtained a U.D. title in 1942 combining mental aptitude with physical beauty. Alma of Skole Gate won her U.D. in 1946, and later her U.D.T. She was bred by Mr. and Mrs. George Russell and owned, trained and handled by Mrs. Evelyn S. Rawcliffe, now living in Florida. At the American Boxer Club show in 1947, Alma, or "Bambi" as she was called, scored a perfect 200 in Utility. Mrs. Rawcliffe recalls that Bambi was known as one of the fastest working dogs of any breed. That she loved to work was evidenced by her trick of barking when jumping to the heel position at the finish of an exercise.

Laura A. Dale decided to stop in at the 34th Street Armory in New York City where the American Boxer Club was holding its fourth annual specialty show and first obedience trial. There were nine entries in the obedience trial, including Alma of Skole Gate, U.D.T. Laura fell in love with the breed, but it was two years before she purchased an eight-week-old puppy, who grew up to be Mozart Sonatina, U.D. In 1950, Tina was elected "Obedience Boxer of the Year."

Laura Dale wrote, "Owners having problems training an over-exuberant and boisterous Boxer may profit from a few reminiscences. My first mistake was showing Tina when she was much too young. Although working beautifully in class at seven months of age, her wildness in the ring had to be seen to be believed. The heel free exercise provided her with an opportunity to stretch her legs at a full gallop in ever-widening circles. On the recall she would come at jet-speed and land with all four paws on my chest.

"Finally, she settled down to serious work, and, before she was two years old, she had all three obedience titles."

Alma of Skoll Gate, UD, executing the broad jump. "Bambi" was bred by Mrs. George Russel, owned and trained by Mrs. Evelyn S. Rawcliffe.

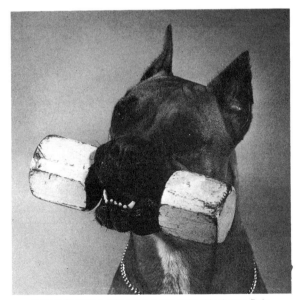

Mozart Sonatina, UD, owned and trained by Laura Dale.

Laura Dale with her Boxer—Mozart Cadenza, UDT.

Steve Krejci with, l to r: Ha-Mar Something Special, UDT; Scarborough Seeing Double, UDT; Marilyns Southern Sand, UDT; and Marilyns Summer Tan of Asgard, UDT.

What followed is history as Laura became a legend with her Boxers. To quote her again, she had "five generations of Boxers bred, owned, trained, shown, and loved by Laura Dale."

They were: Mozart Sonatina, U.D.; her daughter, Mozart Scherzo, U.D.; and Scherzo's daughter, Mozart Cadenza, U.D.T.; Cadenza's daughter, Mozart Kleine Gigue, U.D.; and Gigue's litter sisters, Mozart Fanfare, C.D.X., T.D., and Mozart Fantastia, C.D.X.

Laura A. Dale became an obedience judge in 1954 and, until her death in 1983, remained an encouragement and friend to everyone interested in Boxers and obedience.

Laura hoped that more members of our breed would find their way into the obedience ring where they would bring public attention to the outstanding temperament of the Boxer.

From an article written by Laura Dale in 1974, the writer quotes her thoughts about puppy obedience training:

> Never scold your Boxer pup for picking up and carrying an object. No matter what it is, praise him and take it gently from his mouth. Otherwise, you will run into difficulties with retrieving later on. When the pup is about three months old you can both have fun playing hide-and-seek. Hide his favorite toy, first rather obviously in the same room, then gradually at greater distances. Praise him, of course, when he finds his toy. You will be surprised to find how quickly even a young pup grasps the idea of seeking for something not in his range of vision. While he probably won't use his nose at first, the development of this concept will be helpful to him in much of the advanced obedience work, including tracking.
>
> It is often said that it is difficult to train Boxers. The problem is that Boxers, unlike many other breeds, really don't give a darn about 'pleasing' the handler. Thus, in order to get a Boxer to do an exercise happily, he must be kidded into thinking that the whole thing was his idea in the first place! Boxers have tremendous egos, a great zest for living, a sense of humor, and will do anything they find exciting. Boredom is a big problem.
>
> Anathama to our breed is constant repetition of an exercise and wishy-washy corrections. Never, never nag a Boxer. Make him understand that a swift correction inevitably follows a misdeed. He won't hold it against you. Be extravagant in your praise when he is doing well. Never be "gray." Most important of all, enjoy yourself during training sessions, and your Boxer will enjoy them, too.

The concern of the American Boxer Club with training, as exemplified by obedience competition, is said to date back to the founding of the club. In 1940 the American Boxer Club offered a sterling silver trophy to all C.D. winners. Mrs. Miriam Breed offered a sterling silver trophy to C.D.X. winners. Later the American Boxer Club offered the trophy to C.D.X. winners, and, since 1952, it has been awarded to U.D. winners only.

During World War II, American Boxer Club members Ted Kapnek

and Walter Foster trained dogs in the Armed Forces. Ch. El Wendie of Rockland participated in a special War Dog Class in conjunction with the obedience trials at the North Westchester show in 1943.

Henry H. Stoecker, noted Boxer breeder and judge, trained many Boxers and other breeds for the military at his kennel in New Jersey. He also held training classes for armed forces personnel to learn how to handle their dogs. He was a consultant on dogs to the armed forces before and during World War II.

Boxers entered in obedience at the American Boxer Club Specialty increased yearly to a record of 44 in 1958. Obedience was regrettably dropped from the American Boxer Club in 1972 because of rising costs, lack of space and lower entries. However, many enthusiasts of the sport hope it will be reinstated at some future time, as it is important to see the Boxer as a working dog.

Prominent members of the American Boxer Club who have been active and excelled in obedience are Mr. and Mrs. Judson L. Streicher, Mr. Joseph A. Galassi, Mr. and Mrs. John Archibald and Mrs. Lorraine C. Meyer. Mr. Streicher and Mrs. Meyer are both obedience judges.

Ch. Amerglo Bell Ringer, U.D., owned by Mr. and Mrs. John Ellis of California, is one of four champions to obtain the Utility Dog title and the only Sire of Merit (seven champions) to earn this title.

Current top winners are Steve and Marilyn Krejci of Orlando, Florida. They have owned Boxers since the early 1950s. When they purchased Marilyns Little Bit in 1974, they were determined that this dog would have some manners, so they started him in obedience. Little Bit completed his C.D. in 1975, his C.D.X. in 1976 and his U.D. in 1977, followed by his U.D.T.

Since then these dedicated Boxer lovers have trained Marilyns Mandy, C.D., T.D., Marilyns Tuff Decision, U.D.T., Marilyns Southern Sand, U.D.T., Scarbrough Seeing Double, U.D.T., Ha-Mar Something Special, U.D.T., and Marilyns Summer Tan of Asgard, U.D.T.

Marilyns Little Bit and Marilyns Southern Sand shared the honor of Number 1 Boxer in obedience in the Shuman rating system for the ten years 1976-1986.

Marilyn and Steve believe Boxers are intelligent and learn quickly. To circumvent bad habits and unwanted behavior, basic training should begin at four months of age. Of the seven Boxers they have trained, all had very different temperaments. The training of each required a different approach to retain the dog's willingness and enjoyment. They feel Boxers will not tolerate a heavy hand. Training should be firm, consistent and fair. The trainer needs to be an actor with body motions and verbal inflections to show pleasure or displeasure for the dog's performance.

Ruth Kayser received a Boxer puppy when she was a child and many Boxers followed, but Salgray's Bombardier, American and Canadian

Marilyns Tuff Decision, UDT, clears the boards with dumbbell in mouth. Owners: Steve and Marilyn Krejci.

Salgray's Bombardier, U.S. & Can. UD, executing a Utility exercise. Owned and trained by Ruth Kayser.

Canadian Ch. Jaegerhouse's Triple Crown, CDX, U.S. CD and TT, shown in Open work. Owner: Marie-Josee Thuot.

U.D., proved to be one of the greats. He was the Number 1 Obedience Boxer in the United States in 1968 and 1970. Bombardier won over 30 highest scoring Boxer trophies and earned the Dog World Award. He was the only Boxer to retire all three of the famous Canadian Travellers' Trophies for three consecutive years.

Salgray's Bombardier had a playmate, lovely Salgray's Keepsake, C.D.X., and Canadian C.D., who was shown in conformation as well as obedience. Since then, Mrs. Kayser has divided her interest between both rings. She is an obedience judge through Utility classes and a breed judge of Boxers and Doberman Pinschers. Over the years, Ruth has written many articles and given seminars on training dogs. Some of her helpful hints are:

If you want to teach your Boxer, first be sure you enjoy yourself. This is a frame of mind which will allow you the freedom to communicate well with your Boxer. Be ready to spend ten to 15 minutes every day working—not playing. Try to understand him before you start. Determine whether you own a "clown" or a "timid soul." After your analysis is made, remember, YOU OWN A BOXER! This means a dog with tremendous pride, who will only "follow" after you have completely earned his respect.

The rebellious Boxer is one we meet very often. He is stubborn and challenges you constantly. He must be the leader, so he thinks. Always remain calm and firm. Just one temper tantrum on your part will confirm to him that you are not greater than he. Whenever you correct him, make it firm and startling. Once you have established the Boxer's respect for you, you will find him a fine worker.

The shy, nervous animal is the one who must be turned from his cowardice to confidence. Treat this Boxer with great care. Be firm, gentle and confident of yourself. Do not push him too fast. Confidently teach him over and over again that nothing will harm him. The only way you can successfully instill confidence is to constantly bring him face to face with a problem and then reassure him. Encourage him constantly and keep corrections to a minimum. This type of Boxer can become one of the best working ones and can display the merriest of moods once he has learned there really is nothing to fear.

The aloof Boxer requires an imaginative handler. Noise is useful—clap your hands, use your voice, especially laughter, as this will excite this dog. Work this dog very fast to keep his attention. Play with him before and after training.

The boisterous and overly friendly Boxer is a very common one. Often this is a spoiled family dog. He is the perennial clown. Be very firm. Correct him swiftly and praise calmly. You will need a great deal of patience and calmness at all times.

Do not be concerned with proceeding too quickly with a Boxer. If you join a training group, choose your own pace and do not be concerned with keeping up with the group. In the training of all types of Boxers, regression is a natural way of life. Do not lose confidence in yourself. This is a necessary evil in the training of a Boxer. It is his way of testing you.

242

"Brandy"—Ch. Warsaw Siren Maly Lustig, Can. & U.S. CDX. Owner: Halina Gendek.

"Jackson" (Vagabond King of Velmead) clears the hurdle. Jackson qualified for the team at Crufts 1988 and carried the Boxer flag. Owner: Angela Chuter, England. *W. T. Bunce*

"Aran" (Velmead Viking Warrior) descending the scale. Owner: Angela Chuter.

Canadian Boxers in Obedience

The obedience fancy is very closely knit between Canada and the U.S.A. Many northern trainers like to obtain both American and Canadian titles and enjoy the challenge. In 1950, the first Boxer to obtain a C.D. in Canada was an American-bred bitch, Rafran's Gay Bar-Maid. By the late 1950s, Paul Delaney and his Boxer, Ch. Valmax Dreadnought, were obtaining good scores of 193 or higher. In October, 1957, at the Montreal Dog Obedience Training Club trial, a Boxer, Baron Rockheim, owned by O. L. and M. M. Howard, had the second highest score in trial. He competed against 12 dogs in Novice A with a score of 196.

In 1960, 14 Boxers earned their C.D. titles, three earned C.D.X. titles and three Boxers, Kay's Tar Baby, Mike's Golden Boy, and Scotts' Golden Boy, all earned U.D. titles.

Up to 1964, there was a considerable number of Boxers seen in the obedience ring, but the numbers dwindled to an average of five C.D.'s, two C.D.X.'s, and at best one U.D. title every year. Scores earned by those Boxers seem to have been either very good (193+) or very poor (175 to 180).

From 1965 onwards, the number of dogs in obedience increased, but the number of Boxers remained the same. Then in 1983, things changed and more Boxers were shown in obedience.

Marie-Josée Thuot's bitch, Canadian Ch. Jaegerhouse's Triple Crown, Canadian C.D.X. and American C.D., T.T., qualified at all three trials of the Detroit-Windsor Dog Obedience World Series in the summer of 1986. *Dogs in Canada* magazine lists the 1986 top Boxers in Obedience as O.T.C. (Obedience Trial Champion) Bingo Du Texas, Ch. Golden Haze Snow Drift, C.D.X., and Marganza Jamor Cleo, C.D.X.

Agility

If you are ready for something new, different, fun and a little wild, how about agility? In this exciting new sport, the animal's fitness and the handler's ability to train and direct the dog over and through certain obstacles are put to the test. Agility teams are composed of four dogs and owners, but the times of only the three best dogs count. Agility Tests are composed of Basic Control (Recall, Immediate Down and Heelwork), and Obstacle Training (Weaving Poles, Hurdles, Scale Jump, Tunnels, See-Saw, Long Jump, Hoop, Table and Pause, Cat Walk).

It started in England in 1978 when an agility demonstration was performed at Crufts. Since then it has become a national dog sport and a regular event at every Crufts that no one wants to miss. The dogs are very enthusiastic, and it is particularly good for Boxers, who seem to thrive on it.

While watching a demonstration of agility work by Boxers and their owners, Angela and Bill Chuter, for a group of breeders in London, a nine-year-old Boxer bitch became so excited, they had to lower the hurdles and let her take her turn around the obstacles. Her enthusiasm, aided by the cheering audience, was a joy to watch, and it was quite obvious that she was having the time of her life.

Lately agility has crossed the Atlantic and landed in Canada and the U.S. Marie-Josée Thuot writes that it is a perfect outlet for the Boxer's speed, agility and jumping ability. In the Toronto area, a Boxer team has been organized composed of Marie-Josée Thuot and her bitch, Maya; Linda Cliff and her bitch, Razmatazz; and Judy Wass and her male, Quincey.

Schutzhund

The word *Schutzhund* means "protection dog" in German. This is really a misnomer, as protection is only one phase of this multi-purpose training.

What began as a voluntary test to determine a dog's suitability for breeding soon became the foundation of the German working dog breeding programs. Offspring of a dog who has not attained a schutzhund title are today ineligible for registration with the Boxer Club of Germany. At the German National Conformation Specialty show, all dogs considered for a high show rating must have the highest schutzhund title. All other working breed clubs in Germany use schutzhund as their working aptitude test.

As the test grew more important to the breed clubs, it developed into a competitive sport and spread across Western Europe. There have been over 45,000 entries of all breeds at schutzhund trials in Germany in the last several years.

In the last ten years schutzhund has become more and more popular in the U.S.A. There are now three organizations that sponsor local training clubs and schutzhund trials. The largest of these is the United Schutzhund Clubs of America (U.S.A.), #2 Sierra Morena, Woodside, CA 94062. There are now more than 125 clubs spread across the United States.

The schutzhund test has three levels: Sch.H I, Sch.H II, and Sch.H III, each becoming progressively more difficult. Each level has three phases, tracking, obedience and protection. A dog can score a maximum of 300 points over-all and a maximum of 100 points in each phase. A passing score of at least 70 in tracking, 70 in obedience and 80 in protection is required on the same day to earn the title. If a dog fails to obtain the required number of points in any phase, he is eliminated regardless of how well he does in the other two phases. Tracking tests the dog's olfactory abilities, concentration, control, endurance, and motivation. A dog must follow precisely the exact path a person has walked in a field and indicate objects the person has dropped. The difficulty varies from a 20-minute-old, 400-pace track with two right angle turns and two objects in Sch.H I, to a 60-minute-old, 800-pace track with four corners and three objects in Sch.H III.

Jeanie Crosby with Aja's Egyptian Goddess, CD, and right: Aja's Time Loves a Hero, CD, Sch.H.I.

Aja's Samari Warrior training for escape for Sch.H.I Protection phase with decoy Mike Fernandez. Owner: Peggy York.

A dog has to have trainability, speed, agility, and a positive attitude to take direction from his handler. All these abilities are tested in the obedience phase. In Sch.H I and Sch.H II, the dog must perform on and off leash heeling, sit stay, down stay, recalls, retrieves, jumping and a send away. In Sch.H III, the dog performs everything off leash, retrieves a four-pound dumbbell and performs stand and stay exercises from walking and running. In all levels dogs are tested for gun shyness and control in a milling crowd. The routines are quite long and take up a trial area the size of a soccer field.

To protect the owner takes courage, toughness, fighting drive, and strong obedience. The protection portion of the schutzhund trial tests all these. The dog must find a suspect and hold him in place by barking. Then he must defend himself and his handler against attacks, stop a fleeing suspect, and attack a man who tries to chase him away.

As the levels progress, the protection work becomes more complicated and demanding. It is essential that the dog bite hard, fight confidently, and show good obedience by releasing the bite on command and by watching without biting when the man is standing still.

Throughout the trial, the judge is watching to be sure the dog displays proper courage, stability, and soundness.

This is an athletic event for the dogs, most of whom are the family pets of their handlers. Because of the physical demands of running, jumping, tracking, and fighting, only the dogs in the best physical condition with good structure can excel. In this way, the schutzhund sport of today fulfills its original purpose as a fit-for-breeding test. These exceptional working dogs are also valuable for their strong character and ideal temperaments, which will be passed on to their offspring.

Jeanie Crosby from Plainville, Massachusetts, has the honor of being the first American to have an American bred Boxer receive his Schutzhund I title. Her homebred male, Aja's Time Loves a Hero, C.D., Sch.H I, earned his Schutzhund I title from the United Schutzhund Clubs of America on November 13, 1982, under Chief Teaching Judge, Mr. Willi Ortner.

Properly supervised schutzhund training does not harm the handler or the dog. The handler needs the necessary open mind, and the Boxer must possess the vital ingredients which prove his heritage. There are Boxers in the United States who can be not only excellent conformation specimens but excellent working dogs as well. The Boxer can be among the finest of all working dogs, but this working aspect for the most part has been generally ignored. The working aspect of the breed must be developed.

American Boxer Club 1952 Parade of Champions. From left: Ch. Warlord of Mazelaine (10 years) owned by Mr. and Mrs. Richard Kettles, handled by Ernst Hamburger; Ch. Mazelaine's Zazarac Brandy (6 years) owned by Mr. and Mrs. John P. Wagner, handled by Phil Marsh; Ch. Bang Away of Sirrah Crest (3 years) owned by Dr. and Mrs. R. C. Harris, handled by Nate Levine.

12

The American Boxer Club, Inc.

THE FIRST recorded meeting of the group of fanciers who organized the American Boxer Club was held at the original site of Luchow's Restaurant in New York City on February 16, 1935. Later a brass plaque was placed in the restaurant commemorating the event. The secretary, Mrs. Rudolph Gaertner, made formal application for membership in the American Kennel Club on March 21 of that year. The president was Mr. Harold Palmedo, and Alexander A. Nitt was treasurer. The entire membership totalled 17 people. The American Boxer Club was elected to membership in the A.K.C. by vote of the delegates on May 14, 1935. Also in that year, the Boxer was moved from the Non-Sporting Group to the Working Group. The following year, the membership grew to 55 persons.

The first Specialty was held on June 6, 1936, and 35 Boxers competed. It was held in conjunction with the Greenwich Kennel Club show in Connecticut. The following year the American Boxer Club held its Specialty with the North Westchester club and continued to do so through 1943.

In 1938, the membership reached 106 persons. Dr. S. Potter Bartley assumed the presidency. Frederick I. Hamm became vice-president, and Mr. John P. Wagner was named honorary secretary. At the same time, Mrs. Lillian Palmedo replaced her mother, Mrs. Gaertner, as secretary and Marcia Fennessy assumed the office of treasurer.

The club arranged for Philip Stockmann, Breed Warden for the German Boxer Club, to judge the 1938 Westminster K.C. show. At the same time Philip Stockmann helped the American Boxer Club revise its breed standard.

In 1939, the American Boxer Club underwent a major change when it was incorporated under the laws of New York State. Richard C. Kettles was elected as delegate to the American Kennel Club. Mid-West and Eastern member clubs were established. Mrs. Walter Lippert chaired a Training Committee, and the A.B.C. became interested in obedience. John Wagner became lifetime honorary vice-president in 1940.

By 1943, membership had expanded to 150. Mr. Kettles became bench show chairman, and the next January the first separate A.B.C. Specialty show was held at the Hotel McAlpin in New York City. The entry of over 100 Boxers was judged by Anton Rost. Warlord of Mazelaine went Best of Breed from the Open Class and followed that triumph by going Best American-Bred Dog in Show at Westminster the next month. Boxers were very much in the public's eye.

1945 marked the introduction of the A.B.C. Futurity Stakes. Henry W. Lark assumed the presidency in 1946, and Minnie Thorne, in the newly created post of corresponding secretary, became editor of the *Boxer Club News,* which was published for the first time in January of that year.

In 1949 Alice and Carl Wood became editors of the *Boxer Club News,* and revived the publication. However, the club could not afford any more than six successive issues. Mrs. Dwight E. (Berdie) Tuttle became columnist for *Pure-Bred Dogs—American Kennel Gazette,* taking over from Albert W. Seaman.

Participation of 331 dogs for a total of 431 entries made the 1952 American Boxer Club Specialty notable. The Futurity Stakes were judged by Mrs. Mazie Wagner. For the first time there was a Parade of Champions, which was simultaneously televised. There were 71 Boxers in the parade including the three Westminster Best in Show winners, Ch. Warlord of Mazelaine, Ch. Mazelaine's Zazarac Brandy and Ch. Bang Away of Sirrah Crest. This parade was recorded on film, and it has been shown all over the world. Videos of this event and many others can be purchased from the American Boxer Club.

At the 1952 American Boxer Club dinner, a testimonial scroll was presented to Mazie and John Wagner in appreciation of their accomplishments. John Wagner was named "Foremost Boxer Breeder in the World."

1953 was the first of three years in which the Annual Futurity Stakes under the chairmanship of Robert Salomon were not held with the Specialty Show. In 1953 and 1955 they were held in Convent, New Jersey and in 1954 in Westbury, Long Island. In 1954 the only complete set of original German stud books in this country were acquired by the A.B.C. In later years, these priceless books were donated to the American Kennel Club.

In 1955, Judson L. Streicher accepted the post of treasurer and held this office through 1961. Alice Wood became vice-president and also took over the duties of the secretary. The Hon. Jouett Shouse was elected delegate to the American Kennel Club. Stuart S. Sliney became the bench show chairman.

The by-laws of the American Boxer Club were revised under the chairmanship of the Hon. Jouett Shouse. At the same time the country was divided into five geographical zones with one member club in each region. Each sent one regional director to serve a one-year term on the board of the American Boxer Club. Also, the board of directors was increased from nine to ten so that the board was composed of 15 members.

In 1957, Charles Spannaus became the second lifetime honorary vice-president. That same year the A.B.C. began issuing a certificate to every Boxer champion of record. A plaque in recognition of winning a U.D. (Utility Dog) title had been awarded for some time. The board also decided to offer an official American Boxer Club plaque to any champion who attained an obedience title. An official plaque is also offered annually to every Boxer awarded best of winners at a member club specialty show.

1960 saw the American Kennel Club approve a revision to the 1938 Boxer Standard, as proposed by the Standard Committee chaired by John P. Wagner. Carl A. Wood became a member of the Standard committee and has remained on it, becoming chairman in 1977.

In 1963 there was another Parade of Champions with an entry of 61, with four more champions in the Veterans Class and 19 in Best of Breed, making a total of 84 Boxer champions. The first membership meeting held outside of New York was held at the 1964 Regional Specialty in Phoenix, Arizona.

In 1966, Dr. Lloyd C. Flint headed up the Standard Committee. Dr. Flint and his committee clarified the existing Standard. The revisions were approved by the American Kennel Club later that year. Dr. Flint remained chairman of the Standard committee for ten years. He also prepared the attractive and educational Boxer breed leaflet available from the secretary of the American Boxer Club. The Hon. Jouett Shouse became a lifetime honorary vice-president. The constitution permits a maximum of three honorary vice-presidents.

In 1968 the American Boxer Club celebrated its 25th anniversary at the 71st Regiment Armory in New York City. Total entry was 441 dogs, including 27 Boxers in obedience. The obedience judge was Mrs. Laura A. Dale. A Parade of Champions was held in conjunction with the Specialty and recorded on sound film. The film and catalog are a treasury of information.

In 1971, the American Boxer Club began awarding life memberships to anyone who had paid dues to the parent club for 25 years. At that time there were 25 members who qualified. Every year more members become

American Boxer Club 1982 Best of Breed Ch. Quebo's Miss Saturday Night, owned by breeders Martha Vidana and Lucille Jackson. From left: Dr. Donald W. Edwards, judge Eve Whitmore, handler Chris Baum and Margaret Archibald.

American Boxer Club 1974 Best of Breed Ch. Merrilane's Love Life of Jofra shown with breeder/handler Eleanor Linderholm, and owned by Dorothy Crosier. Left to right: John Archibald, Judge Virginia Salomon and Joseph A. Galassi.

252

eligible, and the list of life members continues to grow. Also in 1971, the specialty show was moved to the Statler Hilton Hotel in New York City, where it remained until 1976. It was the first time the specialty was not a benched show. However, members became unhappy about having a specialty in congested New York City during the cold month of February. Prices were exorbitant, parking difficult, and travelling in elevators with dogs, crates, and show gear was a nightmare! So, in 1977, largely due to the efforts of Joseph A. Galassi, the specialty was moved to the Woodbridge Armory, in Woodbridge, New Jersey, where it remained for three years. The location was not ideal, as the show was growing annually, and the facilities were too crowded. The specialty show drew an all-time record entry in 1977 and, as a result, became a two-day event the following year. In 1978, the entry reached 792 with the largest-ever futurity stakes.

In 1979, membership in the American Boxer Club reached 490 individual members and 51 member clubs.

In 1980, the specialty and futurity became a three-day show. The location was changed to the Holiday Inn North, Newark, New Jersey, where it remains today.

Also in 1980, a judges education committee was formed, headed by Beverly Sachs, and they began the first of their many educational programs. The committee worked diligently with the American Kennel Club to produce the first Boxer slide show. In 1985, this slide show was released by the A.K.C. and can be purchased outright or rented. It is shown at seminars for future judges and others interested in the breed.

The 1983 Parade of Champions had grown to 245 as against the 29 entries in 1953. Membership in the American Boxer Club totalled 582, and member clubs totalled around 51.

In 1980, Carl and Alice Wood were the first members to be presented with the Larry Downey Medallion. This memorial tribute was presented to the American Boxer Club by member Pat Harrah. Her sister-in-law, the outstanding animal sculptress June Harrah, designed the medallion. The first one struck was presented to Larry Downey's widow, Alice. The medallions are awarded on an annual basis, one a year, to the person doing the most for the American Boxer Club, with the recipient chosen by the board of directors. Since then, recipients have included Judson L. Streicher, Peter Puzio and his wife, Thelma, Joseph A. Galassi, Robert C. Salomon, Pat Harrah, Daniel M. Hamilburg, and Lorraine C. Meyer.

To coincide with the 50th anniversary of the American Boxer Club in 1984, it was decided to produce an Anniversary Album. The committee, chaired by Suzie Campbell, was faced with an overwhelming task. Historian Carl Wood and researcher Sturlene Arnold, along with many other members too numerous to mention, worked diligently to produce the large album. It is a true treasure for the collector. Suzie Campbell received an award from the Dog Writer's Association of America for this publication. It was printed in a limited edition of 1500 copies in 1985.

13

Selected Reading

Books (*out of print)

The American Boxer Club 50th Anniversary Album 1935-1985, Editor Suzie Campbell, American Boxer Club, Limited Edition, 482 pp. Available from Mrs. Ann Kell, 6793 Tanglewood Drive, Boardman, Ohio 44512.

Barbaresi, Sara M., *How to Raise and Train a Boxer,* T.F.H. Publications, 1957, 64 pp. (Paperback).

*Brearley, Joan M. and Nicholas, Anna Katherine, *The Book of the Boxer,* T.F.H. Publications (1977).

British Boxer Club Year Books, England. Each covers two years and contains photographs and pedigrees of current champions.

British Boxer Club Record Book, 1939-1975.

Boxer Breeders Handbook, Suzie Campbell and John Campbell, Boxer Heritage Foundation, 9618 Classen Blvd., Oklahoma City, OK (1978).

*Daly, MacDonald, *The British Boxer,* London (1955).

*Davis, Mrs. Paul Newhall, *Pet Boxer,* All Pet Books (1958).

Denlinger, Milo G., *The Complete Boxer,* Howell Book House, New York (1948).

*Dunkels, Joan, *The Boxer Handbook,* Nicholas & Watson, London (1962).

Fairbrother, Marian and Thomson, Peggy, *Boxer Blarney,* London (1965).

*Gordon, Dr. Dan M., *The Boxer,* Judy Publishing Co., Chicago (1940).

Gordon, John F., *All About The Boxer,* Pelham Books, England (1970).

Hamilton-Wilkes, Monty, *All About The Boxer,* Instant Books, Australia (1977).

*Hemery, Margaret E., *Boxers,* Ernest Benn, London (1957).

*Mangrum, Marion, *Who's Who in Boxers,* private printing by author, College Station, Texas (1950).

*Meyer, Enno, *Judging the Boxer,* Orange Judd, New York (1945).

Meyer, Lorraine C., *Your Boxer,* Denlingers, Middleburg, Virginia (1973).

*Miller, Madeline, *Boxers as Pets,* T.F.H. (1955).

Nicholas, Anna Katherine, *The Boxer,* T.F.H. Publications (1984).

The Pet Library Ltd., Earl Schneider, Editor, *Know Your Boxer (1964).*

Pisano, Beverly, *Boxers,* T.F.H. Publications, Inc. (1979).

Royle, Jo, *The Boxer,* K & R Books, Leicester, England (1976).

Somerfield, Elizabeth, *The Popular Boxer,* Anchor Press, England (1955).

*Stockmann, Friederun, *My Life With Boxers,* Popular Dogs Publishing Co. Ltd., London (1968).

Volpe, Stanley U., *This Is The Boxer,* T.F.H. Publications (1964).

*Wagner, John P., *The Boxer,* Orange Judd, New York (1939).

White, Kay, *The Boxer,* John Bartholomew & Son, Ltd., Edinburgh (1977).

Wiley, Constance and Wilson, *Boxers,* Foyles, London (1964).

Boxer Books of Note in Foreign Languages

Le Boxer par le Boxer-Club de France (Crepin Leblond et cie Editeurs) (1966).

Boxer-Blätter, Boxer Klub E.V., Munich Boxer Club, Munich, Germany (1953).

Der Boxer, Boxer Klub E.V., Munich, Germany, foreword by Ph. Stockmann (1926).

Boxer-Bucher 1902-1906-1926, Der deutsche Boxer Club, Berlin (German Boxer Club).

Nederlandse Boxer Club 1904 - 1984 Jubileumboek (Netherlands Boxer Club's Jubilee Book).

Boxeren I Norge—Norwegian Boxer Club, Oslo, Norway (1985).

Magazines

Boxer Blätter, published monthly in German since 1904 by Boxer-Klub E.V., Veldener Strasse 66, 8000 München 60, Germany.

Boxer Quarterly, Editor Andrew H. Brace, published quarterly by Breachurst Limited, Unit One, Bowen Industrial Estate, Aberbargoed, Bargoed, Mid Glamorgan, South Wales CF8 9ET, U.K.

The Boxer Review, Kris Dahl, Editor, published monthly since 1956 by Drucker Publications, 8760 Appian Way, Los Angeles, CA 90046.

Boxer '79, Boxer '80, etc., published yearly by South Western Boxer Club, England. S.W.B.C. Secretary: Mrs. B. Murray, The Lavender House, Kington Magna, Gillingham, Dorset, England.

Brochure: *Meet the Boxer, a Unique Breed,* published by the American Boxer Club, Inc. and available from the secretary upon request.